CANADIAN
RAIL TRAVEL
GUIDE

DARYL T. ADAIR

This edition edited by Bill Linley

A **Railfare** *Book*

Fitzhenry & Whiteside

Dedicated to Gladys Thompson who impressed upon me my own family's rail history, and nurtured my love for trains and travel at a very young age. Thanks, Grandma!

Text copyright © 2004, 2007, 2008, 2014 by Fitzhenry & Whiteside
Revised and Updated Edition Printed in 2014.
Published in Canada by Fitzhenry & Whiteside, 195 Allstate Parkway, Markham,
Ontario L3R 4T8
Published in the United States by Fitzhenry & Whiteside, 311 Washington Street,
Brighton, Massachusetts 02135

Library and Archives Canada Cataloguing in Publication
Adair, Daryl
Canadian rail travel guide / Daryl Adair.
This edition edited by Bill Linley
Includes index.
ISBN 978-1-55455-298-6
Data available on file with Library and Archives Canada

Publisher Cataloging-in-Publication Data (U.S.)
Adair, Daryl
Canadian rail travel guide / Daryl Adair.
This edition edited by Bill Linley
Includes index.
ISBN 978-1-55455-298-6
Data available on file

Fitzhenry & Whiteside acknowledges with thanks the Canada Council for the Arts, and
the Ontario Arts Council for their support of our publishing program. We acknowledge
the financial support of the Government of Canada through the Canada Book Fund (CBF) for our
publishing activities.

All photos by the author unless credited otherwise
Maps by Eric Chong
Cover and interior design by Daniel Choi
Printed and bound in Canada by Friesens

MIX
Paper from
responsible sources
FSC® C016245

Front Cover: *VIA Rail*'s Jasper-Prince Rupert train has just departed McBride BC, with the
magnificent Rocky Mountains in the background. Heading eastbound for Jasper AB, it is crossing
Eddy Creek bridge. Just beyond is the 1375 km Fraser River, seen here with more than 1000 km
left in its journey. *Matthew G. Wheeler photo*

CONTENTS

ABOUT THE AUTHOR

From his youngest days at his family's summer residence, Daryl Adair can remember watching with fascination the passenger and freight trains that passed on the opposite side of Lac Lu, Ontario.

Daryl's grandmother had told him that his great grandfather, who worked for the *Canadian Pacific Railway*, was a member of the *CPR* committee that chose Lac Lu as a destination for railway workers' families. When she took him on a trip from Vancouver to Winnipeg on *The Canadian*, he became forever hooked on rail travel.

Some years later, he explored Western Canada on his own and subsequently planned and executed a 1997–98 around-the-world journey, travelling by train in England, northern and eastern Europe, as well as on the *Trans-Siberian Express* and railways in China.

His passion for rail travel and touring Canada led him to author *The Guide to Canada's Railway Heritage Museums Excursions and Attractions*. The launch of that book was followed by an extensive period researching the mile-by-mile highlights of all the rail passenger routes in Canada, resulting in the *Canadian Rail Travel Guide*.

Daryl Adair holds a diploma in tourism. He has contributed articles to the Canadian Tourism Commission publication *Tourism*, to *CN Lines*, *Branchline*, *Canadian Rail*, as well as many other publications. He was editor of Winnipeg Railway Museum's heritage newsletter *The Milepost* for five years.

Residing in Winnipeg with his wife Theresa, Daryl owns and operates *Rail Travel Tours*, packagers of Canadian rail travel, accommodation and sightseeing activities. This enables Daryl to share his passion for "riding the rails", and his "insider knowledge" about trains and interesting side-trips, with fellow travellers. If you have noticed errors or changes required to any of the routes in the book or would like to ask questions about Canadian rail travel, Daryl can be reached through his website *www.railtraveltours.com* or at 866 704-3528.

Despite the demanding schedule, Daryl still finds time to volunteer and cheer for the Winnipeg Blue Bombers, spend time with family at the Lac Lu cottage and to continue exhibiting the same love of travel first experienced in his youth, still watching those trains go by, on the other side of the lake.

Daryl Adair with *CPR* locomotive 2816, after travelling past Lac Lu, from Kenora, ON to Winnipeg, MB in 2003. *Ken Praymak photo*

About the Editor

Bill Linley has been photographing and writing about trains for over fifty years. He was introduced to train watching by his father in his native Toronto in the early 1950s and began photographing trains on the Quebec Central in 1959 while living in Sainte-Foy, Quebec. Bill was recently selected as the 25th anniversary recipient of the Canadian Railroad Historical Association's Lifetime Achievement Award in recognition of his expertise, not only as an author, but also as one of Canada's most prolific and important railway photographers. His work has been featured in countless publications and books including two volumes of *Canadian Pacific in Colour* for Morning Sun Books. Bill lives with his wife Marilynn in the Captain John G. Charlton house in Port Lorne, Nova Scotia on the Bay of Fundy near the ghosts of the *Dominion Atlantic Railway*. He may be reached at *bill.linley@gmail.com.*

FOREWORD

To travel by train to all of Canada in a single journey, or even in a single season, is no small challenge. It takes the work of many individual efforts to make it all come together. My sincere thanks to all of the people who made the many trips that made this book possible. My sincerest apologies to anyone who may have been overlooked. I hope each of you gets the chance to dip your feet into the three oceans that surround Canada as I have.

In addition to my family—who helped foster my love of train travel—my thanks are extended to each of the very helpful people whose knowledge, enthusiasm, and support encouraged me to put this book together:

Starting in the East with, Randy Brooks and Kelly Duggan, *Nova Scotia Economic and Rural Development and Tourism*, David and Pat Othen, Steven Dickie, Marilynn Linley, Nancy Wolstenholme, Valerie Kidney and Jeannine Wilmot, *Tourism New Brunswick*. Isabel Gill and Darlene Anderson, *Tourisme Québec*, John Whittingham, Béatrice Joseph at *Le Québec Maritime*, Madame Bedards, Marie-Claude Goyette at *Tourisme Saguenay-Lac Saint-Jean*, Randa Napky, *Abitibi Region*, Kevin Robinson, *Canadian Railway Museum/Exporail*, Francois, Pam, David Gaudette and Len Thibeault for the guided tours of Rue St. Denis, Eric Clegg, Rey Stephen and Tom Boyd, *Tourism Ontario*, Deneen Perrin and Jennifer Salo, *Chateau Laurier*, David Monaghan, *Canadian Museum of Science and Technology*, Douglas N.W. Smith (for his considerable expertise and generous input), James Brown, Earl Roberts and David Stremes, *Canadian Trackside Guide*, Maureen Reynold, *Ontario Northland Railway*, James Pereira, *Station Inn*. Paul Grant, *Cochrane Railway Museum*, Brian and Ann West, Lois Coo, Peter Browne, *York Durham Heritage Railway*, Lori Bursey and Ron Keffer, David Henderson, *Railfare*, (for his guidance and support of the book), Eric

Smith, *South Simcoe Railway*, Bob and Karen Kertcher, Ted Wakeford, *Orangeville-Brampton Railway*, Ron Bouwhuis, Victor Ferraiuolo, *Tourism Niagara*, Charles and Anne Becket, Ron Broda, *Discovery House Museum*, Dale Wilson, Jim Cockburn, Bruce Lafleur, Michael Morrow and S.K. Hopkins, *Algoma Central Railway*, Collette Fontaine, *Travel Manitoba*, Tom and June Adair, Laura Finlay, Bert Swan, His Worship Michael Spence, *Churchill*, Bert Couisineau, Paul Legault, *Heritage North*, *Canadian National Railways Historical Association*, Morgan Turney for his guidance, Felix Lesiuk, Murray Hammond, Lloyd Smith, Paul Pihichyn, *Winnipeg Free Press*, Larry Updike, *CJOB*, Peter Abel, the *Winnipeg Railway Museum*, Peter Thiessen, official luggage supplier of *UN Luggage*, Gary Dy and all the staff at *VIA Rail* Winnipeg. David Freeman at *Tourism Saskatchewan*, Jan Desrosiers, *Tourism Saskatoon*, Cal Sexsmith. Maria Crump and Karen Taylor, *Travel Alberta*, Sean Robitaille, John Rushton, Jim Lanigan, David J. Walker, Mark Seland, *CP*, Edna Holme, Kathy Glenn, *Jasper Museum*, Mike McNaughton, Brenda and Bryanna Bradley. Cindy Burr, *Tourism BC*, Daryl, Kristine, Grant and Amanda Moulder, Elaine and Lloyd Comish, Kelley Glazer, Ramada Prince George, Sonja Penner, *Pacific Inn*, Sally Chiang and Robert Hart, Janice Greenwood, *Rocky Mountaineer*, Andy Cassidy, Kevin Dunk, Jim Johnston, Phil Mason, Doug Lawson, Bob Webster, Clayton Jones, Don Evans, Bill Johnston, Gordon Hall, Bill Watson, *West Coast Railway Association*, Joe Volk, Dawson Wolk of *VIA Rail* Vancouver and a special thank you to Aurelio Macaraeg for his support of the project from the very beginning.
Taking the train to visit any part of Canada is pure enjoyment. The sense of adventure that comes with each mile of steel rail travelled makes each destination, and every journey, unique.

Some of my earliest memories come from spending the summer months, with my grandmother, at our family cabin at Lac Lu, Ontario, watching passing trains on the *Canadian Pacific Railway* mainline. My grandmother told me how my great-grandfather worked for the *CPR* in Winnipeg, and chose our lake as a summer destination. Another fond memory is of travelling with my grandmother and mother by train from Vancouver to Winnipeg when *VIA Rail Canada* was in its infancy—a trip I will never forget! Who knew where it would lead?

YOUR JOURNEY BEGINS

Information and Reservations

You could spend an entire summer travelling in Canada by train, so it will help to do some preparation before you begin your journey. First, research the train timetables for each of the trips you wish to take. These schedules can be secured from the various rail passenger providers at the contacts listed in each "Route Chapter" of this book, or from Canada's national rail passenger provider at the following:

VIA Rail Canada Inc.,
3 Place Ville Marie, Suite 500,
Montreal, QC, H3B 2C9
888-842-7245 *www.viarail.ca*

Timetables commonly describe the types of services available on each route, and provide instructions on booking tickets and other travel information. Many Canadian rail passenger providers make their schedules available on their websites. We have included these within each listing. Be sure to confirm the days on which trains operate, as well as frequencies and connection times. Reservations are very important, especially during the peak spring, summer, and fall seasons when some trains may be sold out.

Baggage

Personal baggage restrictions vary by the train route you are travelling. *VIA* guidelines ask that customers limit themselves to two pieces of carry-on baggage. These should be no larger than 66 cm × 46 cm × 25 cm (26 in. × 18 in. × 9 in.) and weigh no more than 23 kg (50 lb.), or 32 kg (70 lb.) on payment of a surcharge. On trains with a baggage car, luggage not needed on the journey can be shipped/stored and picked up upon arrival at your final destination. You will be required to check-in at least one hour before departure at larger stations. Some trains allow you to bring along skis, bicycles, canoes, and, in some cases, even snowmobiles. There will be a surcharge for larger items such as these. Whatever you bring, attach a proper tag with your correct name and address.

Getting to Canada

Numerous airlines fly to Canada from international and overseas locations. Canada's largest airline is Air Canada. Its routes and flights can be researched at *www.aircanada. ca*. Rail routes connecting Canada to the United States also provide a popular way to reach the country. These include: Amtrak's *Adirondack* (Washington DC–New York–Montreal); the Toronto–Niagara Falls–New York route; *VIA's* corridor service from Windsor, located across the river from Detroit; and on the west coast, Amtrak's *Cascade* (Seattle-Vancouver). All trains are subject to customs inspections when crossing the Canada-USA border. You will require a passport to cross the border and the passport number may be entered on your reservation when booking the ticket (recommended) in advance.

Currency, Taxes and Gratuities

Canadian currency is based on 100 cents to the dollar. Coins are in denominations of 5¢, 10¢, 25¢, $1.00, and $2.00. Canadians generally refer to their one and two dollar coins as the "loonie" and "toonie" respectively. Across the country there is a five percent national Goods and Services Tax as well as provincial sales taxes that vary across the country (except in Alberta which has no provincial sales tax.) In the Atlantic Provinces and Ontario, the two sales taxes are "harmonized" into a single tax surcharge. It is quite common to leave gratuities after a meal, or for sleeping car attendants and dining car staff, especially when exceptional service has been provided.

Breaking up Your Journey

This guide lists contact information for Canada's local and regional tourism authorities along the various routes. Suggested accommodations are included at the beginning and end of many "Route Chapters." It is highly recommended that reservations be made well in advance of your planned visit.

HOW TO USE THIS GUIDE

The *Canadian Rail Travel Guide* begins with regularly scheduled passenger trains, geographically from east to west. The later portion of the book lists excursion train routes in the same east-to-west manner. The text describes highlights in various directions from the rail line. Finally, the book's clearly marked maps enhance the text and make it convenient to use for travel in either direction.

Railway Subdivisions

To determine where you are, you must first identify the railway subdivision on which you are located. These subdivisions traditionally begin at the eastern point (Mile 0) and accumulate miles travelling to the western end of the subdivision where another will begin. Historically, these divisions were about 125 miles in length, based on the distance between various water and refueling stops that a steam locomotive could travel in a shift. They were named primarily after prominent communities in the area, the region where the subdivisions are located, or even after railway financiers. Because modern diesels travel these distances much more quickly, with fewer servicing stops than a steam locomotive required, many of these have now been combined to form longer subdivisions up to and exceeding 250 miles. Engine crews typically complete their workday after about 250 miles. At some places railway subdivisions intersect with other railway subdivisions, not at mileage 0, therefore mile markers may vary. Refer to the accompanying maps to locate your train on the appropriate subdivision. In some cases, the map will indicate a mileage that differs from a reference in the text, because *stations* are sometimes located a short distance away from the river, lake or community of the same name.

Mileposts/Mileboards

Each mile of a railway subdivision is counted off by a milepost. Look for a small sign, with black lettering on a white background, attached to a steel post or former telegraph pole. Mileage markers can also be located on bridge ends, signal masts, and the reverse side of road crossing signs.

Station/Siding Names
Names are another easy way to locate where you are. You'll see them featured on the end of the stations. Names of sidings are commonly identified on a white sign with black lettering.

Scheduled Stops
Many scheduled stops provide only a few minutes for passengers to depart or join the train. In larger cities, and at some service stops, you may have a somewhat longer respite, providing the opportunity to visit the station, smoke or or stretch your legs walking alongside the train.

Onboard Staff
The structure of the staff varies by train route. The person in charge might be the Conductor, Service Manager, or Train Manager. This individual is responsible for the crew and the safety and smooth running of your journey. Many of the excursions in Canada are operated by volunteers who provide a wealth of information regarding the area's railway history and its other attractions.

Options and Services
Most *VIA* onboard staff, as well as staff in the larger stations across the country, are able to serve passengers in Canada's two official languages, English and French. The seating options depend on the particular route. *VIA's* overnight trains offer a variety of travel options: economy-class seating with large reclining seats, upper and lower sections, roomettes/single rooms, bedrooms/double rooms, and drawing rooms. In the Windsor–Quebec City corridor, you can choose from economy (coach) class or *VIA's* business class. Equipment on excursion trains varies from turn of the century wicker chairs to modern Gold Class dome cars on the *Rocky Mountaineer*. Food options also vary. A majority of trains offer take-out service from a café car or snack bar. Sometimes, meal service is provided by a dining car or a sandwich/snack and beverage cart/counter on your coach. Meal sittings in the dining cars may be very busy, so reservations for lunch and dinner (where available) are recommended.

Freight Trains

Freight trains move many of the goods and products required by consumers in many nations. It will be a common occurrence that you will pass seemingly endless freight trains, carrying everything from Canadian grain, lumber products, oil, coal and ore for export, to new vehicles, television sets, and toilet paper for consumers at home. Because of the pulling power of the modern diesel locomotives, the lengths of these trains can often be longer than many of the siding tracks that allow trains to pass each other. Hence the shorter passenger train is the one that often must wait in the siding to allow the long freight train to pass.

Photography

If your camera has adjustable settings use at least a 1/500th of a second shutter speed when taking pictures from a moving train. While using any camera, these same rules apply:

- avoid the reflection inside the car by getting the camera lens as close to the window as possible
- watch the maps and mileage markers for recommended locations
- avoid shooting into the sun

Further Reading

Following are some books to enhance your journey across Canada:

The Guide to Canada's Railway Heritage by Daryl T. Adair. Sister guide to this publication features numerous railway museums, attractions and excursions in each province. North Kildonan Publications, 2001.

Canadian National's Western Stations by Charles Bohi and Les Kozma. Lavishly illustrated, with many photos in colour. identifies over 2,100 stations in western Canada, providing in-depth information on various *CNR* stations in an historical context. Detailed maps show station locations. Railfare / Fitzhenry & Whiteside, 2002.

Narrow Gauge Railways of Canada by Omer Lavallee, edited and expanded by Ronald S. Ritchie, Railfare / Fitzhenry & Whiteside, 2005.

Canadian National Steam! by Donald R. McQueen, Railfare DC Books, 2013.

Left: The *Canadian*'s "Prestige Class", set-up for daytime use.
Middle: Same suite, now ready for a restful sleep.
Right: *VIA*'s "Business Class" cars on the line between Quebec and Windsor.
VIA Rail photos

"Prestige Class" Cars for VIA Rail Passengers

Exciting new *VIA Rail* train car equipment, unveiled since the previous edition of this book was published, will further enhance your journey by rail. This billion-dollar investment in equipment and renovations includes newly upgraded Dining, Manor, Château, Park, Skyline and Economy cars, as well as newly configured Business Class cars for the popular corridor routes between Quebec City and Windsor. Trains in which these various new cars may be deployed are described in the segments on pages 16, 33, 56, 65, 68, 74, 96 and 160.

The *Canadian*, whose segment starts on page 96, has a new "Prestige Sleeper Class" providing an exciting new level of comfort and service for travellers on one of the world's greatest train journeys. Travellers will enjoy personalized dedicated service from the Prestige Concierge. The spacious cabin is half-again larger than the current cabin for two in "Sleeper Plus class", and its huge windows – sixty percent bigger than those in the "Sleeper Plus" cabin for two – are great for sightseeing. Other amenities include a private washroom with shower, flat-screen TV with video selection, and a minibar stocked with a selection of beverages. Your "reader's journey" through *Canadian Rail Travel Guide* begins with *VIA Rail*'s Halifax-Montreal train, the *Ocean*, on the very next page. Please enjoy "Happy travelling!" aboard the train that has been the longest continuously operating named-train in North America.

THE OCEAN

Shaped by the sea, Halifax—the capital of the Province of Nova Scotia—has a profound history. Named after the second Earl of Halifax, George Montagu Dunk, the town was first developed by the British. They founded a base here in 1749 to counter the French fortress to the north in Louisbourg. Shortly thereafter, New France was captured and the base became a symbol for British dominance in the North Atlantic. Its strategic importance was enhanced when the colony of New England left British rule.

The city's unique history continued into the 18th century and was linked closely to the events of the sea. Waves of immigrants looking to start a new life had their first contact with the New World in Halifax. In 1912 the city became linked with the sinking of the *Titanic*, when 150 of those who perished were buried in Halifax cemeteries. Then, on December 6th 1917, the Norwegian vessel *Imo* collided with the French

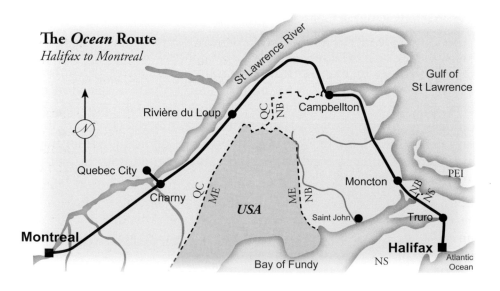

The *Ocean* Route
Halifax to Montreal

St Lawrence River

Gulf of St Lawrence

Rivière du Loup

QC / NB

Campbellton

N

Quebec City

Charny

QC / ME

USA

ME / NB

Moncton

PEI

NB / NS

Saint John

Truro

Montreal

Halifax

Atlantic Ocean

Bay of Fundy

NS

THE OCEAN

munitions ship *Mont Blanc* which caught fire and exploded, wiping out a good portion of North Halifax, and, together with the fire that followed, killed 1,700 and injured over 4,000.

Today, the city continues its close relationship with the sea. Halifax is a very busy commercial seaport, and is the base of operations for the Canadian Navy's Atlantic operations. The Halifax Regional Municipality had a population of 390,096 in 2011. The city centre is well laid out with numerous attractions located within walking distance. For your travel base in Halifax, the Lord Nelson Hotel 877 255-7136 *www.lordnelsonhotel.ca* is recommended. It is conveniently located at 1515 South Park Street across from the Halifax Public Gardens near the trendy shopping district of Spring Garden Road.

Visitors to the city will enjoy the Halifax Citadel National Historic Site where you can take a guided tour and journey back in time to see the 78th Highland Regiment in action and witness the firing of the noonday cannon. The Maritime Museum of the Atlantic, located at 1675 Lower Water Street, is a must see with numerous displays including the *Titanic* exhibit and the impressive Halifax Explosion display. The *HMCS Sackville*, the sole survivor of 123 Canadian Corvettes from World War II, is docked behind the Maritime Museum and is open in the summer for visitors. Another highlight is the Pier 21 National Historic Site, the Canadian Museum of Immigration, at 1055 Marginal Road near the railway station, where many immigrants transferred to the train to take them west. One display features a rail car that takes you on a simulated journey across Canada.

Before you go, you may wish to contact Nova Scotia Economic and Rural Development and Tourism, PO Box 456, Halifax, NS, B3J 2R5. Phone: 800 565-0000. Web: *www.novascotia.com* Email: *explore@gov.ns.ca*

The Dominion of Canada was formed when the provinces of Ontario, Quebec, New Brunswick, and Nova Scotia joined, or confederated, on July 1st 1867. At the time, there were three separate railways in the Region: the *European & North America Railway*, the *New Brunswick & Canada Railway,* and the *Nova Scotia Railway*. Each line was isolated, but played an interesting role in the early commerce of the regions it served. In fact, the *Nova Scotia Railway* was one of the first to operate an early "piggyback" service, hauling farmer's wagons and stagecoaches on flatcars. To these a fourth railway was added—the *Intercolonial*

Railway, which was needed to connect the Maritime Provinces to the rest of Canada. The first run of *The Ocean Limited* was on July 3rd 1904. In 1915, the *Intercolonial Railway* together with the *National Transcontinental Railway*, the *Prince Edward Island Railway*, and sundry other smaller lines became formally known as the *Canadian Government Railways* (CGR). With the inclusion of the *Canadian Northern*, the CGR became the *Canadian National Railways (CNR)* on December 20th, 1918. Today, operated by *VIA* with the named changed to simply the *Ocean*, it is the train that has been the longest continuously operating named-train in North America. Your journey begins next to the Westin Nova Scotian, a former *CNR* hotel at the *VIA Rail Canada* station at 1161 Hollis Street. Opened on June 19th 1930 the station's exterior features an impressive neo-Georgian style. As you pass the four columns at the entrance, the station opens up to a large concourse, well lit with numerous skylights. Your journey to Montreal will take you 840 miles (1,352 kilometres) and you will traverse the *CN*'s Bedford, Springhill, Newcastle, Mont Joli, Montmagny, Durmmondville and St. Hyacinthe Subdivisions.

Route Highlights
Halifax to Truro
Bedford Subdivision

Mileages 0–10: Whether arriving or departing Halifax, look to the east to see one or more of

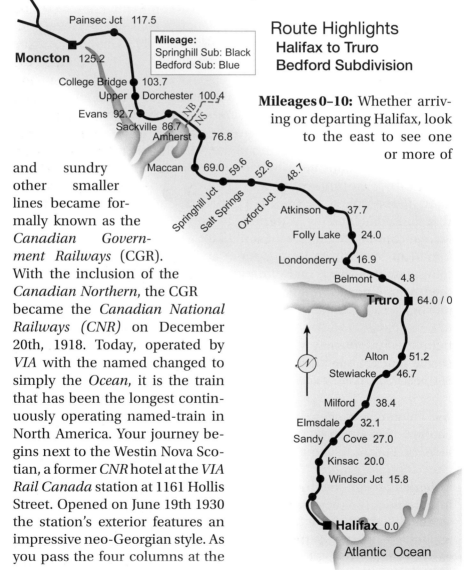

Mileage:
Springhill Sub: Black
Bedford Sub: Blue

Painsec Jct 117.5
Moncton 125.2
College Bridge 103.7
Upper Dorchester 100.4
Evans 92.7
Sackville 86.7
Amherst 76.8
Maccan 69.0
Springhill Jct 59.6
Salt Springs 52.6
Oxford Jct 48.7
Atkinson 37.7
Folly Lake 24.0
Londonderry 16.9
Belmont 4.8
Truro 64.0 / 0
Alton 51.2
Stewiacke 46.7
Milford 38.4
Elmsdale 32.1
Sandy Cove 27.0
Kinsac 20.0
Windsor Jct 15.8
Halifax 0.0
Atlantic Ocean

NB / NS

the many cruise ships that visit Halifax and the Canadian Museum of Immigration at Pier 21 where millions of immigrants entered Canada. From mileage **1** to **3** the route takes you through a unique rock cut opened in 1919 to provide direct access to the new Ocean Terminals in Halifax's South End. The original route and the city's North Street Station were severely damaged in the 1917 Halifax Explosion. At mileage **4.6**, look north to see the wooded Fairview Cemetery which has 121 graves from the Titanic tragedy, the largest location of such graves in one cemetery in the provincial capital. The Bedford Basin is visible to the east from mileages **5** to **10**. If you look to the southeast you can see the A. Murray Mackay Bridge completed in 1970 which joins Halifax to Dartmouth. Just to the east of the bridge is the Narrows, where the 1917 Halifax Explosion occurred. Edward, Duke of Kent (father of Queen Victoria), built the round building to the east at mileage **7** in the late 1790s as a music pavilion for his French mistress Julie St. Laurent. Today this unique building with its white columns and green roof is a private residence.

Mileages 17–64: As you move away from the city the scenery changes to a forested area with lakes and residences. Behind the trees to the east, from mileages **19** to **20**, sits Lake Kinsac. You cross the Nine Mile River at mileage **32.4** as you pass through the community of Elmsdale (2011 population 3,034). This is the site of the first iron railway bridge in North America, built in 1877. At mileage **47** watch for salmon fishermen as you pass over the Stewiacke River. Its name is Mi'kmaq for "place where the sands move." The railway from Halifax to Truro was originally constructed by the provincially owned *Nova Scotia Railway* and opened in December 1858. When you arrive at Truro station located in the Truro Centre Mall (mileage **64**) the tracks of the *Cape Breton & Central Nova Scotia Railway* swing away on their way to Sydney on scenic Cape Breton Island.

Route Highlights
Truro to Moncton
Springhill Subdivision

Mileages 0–24: The route of the *Ocean* ascends out of Truro (2011 population 12,059) for the next few miles towards Folly Lake. The Debert River (mileage **11.4**) is the start of what was known as the "Grecian Bend," due to the politics that shaped the route the line takes. Apparently the owner of the ironworks on the other side of the valley at Londonderry, James Livesay, had more sway than the railway engineer Sandford Fleming, who preferred a more direct route. Livesay won out and the tracks travel away from the route Fleming suggested. The term "Grecian Bend" refers to a style of women's bustle fashionable in the 1860s that accentuated the wearer's derrière. The bridge at mileage **14.5** sits 85 feet (26 metres) above the Folly River, so-named after a settler's wrong decision. After the "Bend," Folly Lake appears to the east approaching mileage **24**.

Mileages 24–79: Watch for Ski Wentworth's slopes to the east at mileage **29** as the tracks weave along high above the Wentworth Valley and the Wallace River. Just after passing through Oxford Junction you cross a 415-foot (126-metre) bridge over the River Philip at mileage **47**. Coal mining began in the area around Springhill near mileage **59.6** in the 1870s and was the mainstay of the region's economy until the late 1950s when two "bumps" or underground explosions caused the mines to be shut down. Today, you may visit the Miner's Museum and Mine Tours which pays tribute to the brave men who earned their living and to those who lost their lives underground. Anne Murray, the international singing sensation, is the subject of an interpretive centre in her hometown of Springhill. To the west of Maccan, mileage **69**, is the Joggins Fossil Centre, a UNESCO World Heritage Site that interprets remains from 300 million years ago found in the nearby seaside cliffs. At mileage **70** the scenery starts to change as the train approaches the Cumberland Basin. The large, red sandstone station in Amherst (2011 population 9,717) at mileage **76.8** was opened on August 31st 1908. Lord Jeffery Amherst was the commander-in-chief of the British army in North America in the Seven Years War following his capture of Louisbourg in 1758. He became governor-general of British North America in 1760. As you depart Amherst, the Ocean passes a red brick building to the west that once housed the Amherst Piano Ltd. (1913–1928) and enters the Trantramar Marshes. The marshes encompass a Canadian Wildlife Service sanctuary that is home to blue-wing teal, Canada geese, black ducks, and marsh hawks. A newly developed wind-farm dominates the scene to the west.

Mileages 80–124: While crossing travelling over the Missaquash River at mileage **80.1**, you also cross the provincial border between Nova Scotia and New Brunswick. This land bridge between the two provinces is known as The Isthmus of Chignecto. Watch for Fort Beausejour, a National Historic Site, on top of the hill to the east, between mileages **81** and **82**. Built by the French in 1751, the fort fell to the British

The *Ocean* at Brookfield Nova Scotia. *Bill Linley photo*

forces in 1755 after a two-week siege. The British renamed it Fort Cumberland and abandoned it in 1835. It was declared a National Historic Site in 1926. The four gravestones on the side of the hill, close to the track, indicate the location of a nineteenth-century cemetery. In 1998, modern archaeological surveys using a ground-penetrating radar unit identified over 40 burials in this area. At mileage **85.6** the train crosses the Tantramar River over a 500-foot (152-metre) long bridge, then stops at the historically designated stone station in Sackville that dates from 1907 and features locally quarried plum and olive sandstone. Sackville (2011 population 5,558) is home to Mount Allison University. Look to the south at mileage **90.7** for a glimpse of a World War I tribute, featuring a cannon carved into the boulder close to the tracks in a clearing in the forested area. A local railway worker, who switched over 30 trains a day here during the war, erected this as a memorial to all those who left the area to fight overseas. The formidable building atop the ridge to the southeast at mileage **98.2** is Dorchester Penitentiary opened in 1880 which can now house 392 medium-risk male offenders. To the west at mileage **103.7**, College Bridge, the Monument Lefebvre National Historic Site of Canada in Memramcook recognizes the history, culture and accomplishments of the Acadian people. Known as *Chiac*, the French spoken in southeastern New Brunswick is

Westbound *Ocean* nearing Folly Lake, Nova Scotia. *Bill Linley photo*

heavily mixed with English words and structure. Father Lefebvre founded Saint Joseph's College in 1864 as the first French-language, degree-granting institution in the Maritimes. Memramcook was a community that was successfully defended by the French in the face of deportation by the English. Many of the French-speaking Acadian inhabitants of Acadia in 1755 were deported and some became the Cajuns of Louisiana. At mileage **104**, look east to see how a construction company has found a new use for outdated railway boxcars— as storage buildings. At mileage **117.5**, your train passes Painsec Junction and enters a portion of the initial, 16.8-mile Shediac-Moncton route of the *European & North America Railway* that was to be a short-cut from New England to Europe when opened in August 1857. As you near the *VIA* station in Moncton, look north near mileage **123** to see the circular concrete walls that once encompassed the Sunny Brae ice skating rink which opened in December 1920. On February 15th 1928, while attending an indoor carnival in fancy dress, a young lady came too close to an open gas heater. Her outfit caught on fire; and seven days later she died of massive burns. Four days later the roof and interior was gutted by fire. The rink was never rebuilt. Moncton, the Hub City, (2011 population 69,074) is known as the heart of the French-speaking Acadian region. The Acadian Museum is located on the Moncton University campus.

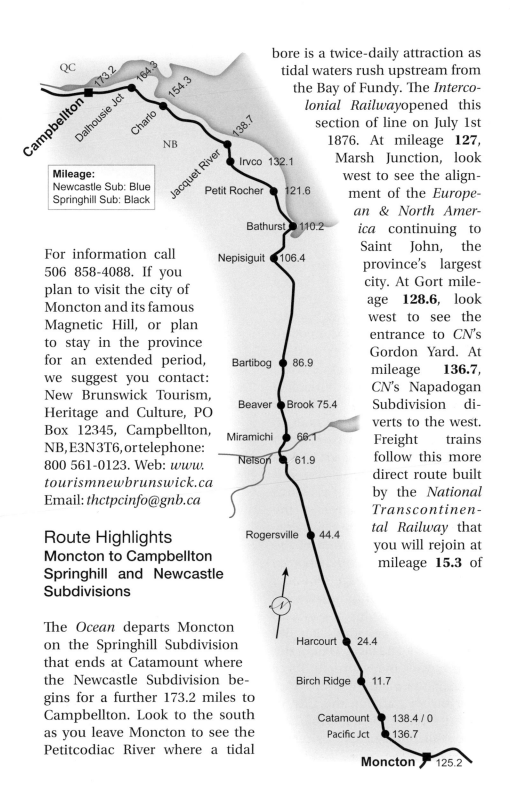

bore is a twice-daily attraction as tidal waters rush upstream from the Bay of Fundy. The *Intercolonial Railway* opened this section of line on July 1st 1876. At mileage **127**, Marsh Junction, look west to see the alignment of the *European & North America* continuing to Saint John, the province's largest city. At Gort mileage **128.6**, look west to see the entrance to *CN*'s Gordon Yard. At mileage **136.7**, *CN*'s Napadogan Subdivision diverts to the west. Freight trains follow this more direct route built by the *National Transcontinental Railway* that you will rejoin at mileage **15.3** of

QC

173.2
164.3
154.3

Campbellton

Dalhousie Jct
Charlo
NB

138.7

Jacquet River

Irvco 132.1

Mileage:
Newcastle Sub: Blue
Springhill Sub: Black

Petit Rocher 121.6

Bathurst 110.2

Nepisiguit 106.4

For information call 506 858-4088. If you plan to visit the city of Moncton and its famous Magnetic Hill, or plan to stay in the province for an extended period, we suggest you contact: New Brunswick Tourism, Heritage and Culture, PO Box 12345, Campbellton, NB, E3N 3T6, or telephone: 800 561-0123. Web: *www. tourismnewbrunswick.ca* Email: *thctpcinfo@gnb.ca*

Bartibog 86.9

Beaver Brook 75.4

Miramichi 66.1

Nelson 61.9

Route Highlights
Moncton to Campbellton
Springhill and Newcastle
Subdivisions

Rogersville 44.4

The *Ocean* departs Moncton on the Springhill Subdivision that ends at Catamount where the Newcastle Subdivision begins for a further 173.2 miles to Campbellton. Look to the south as you leave Moncton to see the Petitcodiac River where a tidal

Harcourt 24.4

Birch Ridge 11.7

Catamount 138.4 / 0
Pacific Jct 136.7

Moncton 125.2

the Montmagny Subdivision west of Rivière du Loup.

Mileages 0–110: The tracks parallel Highway 126 which becomes the main street of the proud Acadian Village of Rogersville, at mileage **44.4**. Rogersville (2011 population 1,170), dominated by the white spire of its Roman Catholic church, is also home to two Trappist monasteries. The village was named after the Most Reverend James Rogers, the bishop of nearby Chatham from 1860 to 1902. There is a Brussel Sprouts Festival on the first Monday in August. The largest river crossings of the journey occur as the *Ocean* crosses the Southwest Miramichi River on a 1,230-foot (375-metre) bridge at mileage **62.2** and on an equally long crossing of the Northwest Miramichi at mileage **63**. The Southwest Miramichi is particularly known for world-class salmon fishing. Just to the east, the two rivers join together and flow into the Gulf of St. Lawrence. The City of Miramichi (2011 population 17,811) at mileage **66.1** was formed in 1995 with the amalgamation of the towns of Newcastle, Chatham, and three smaller villages. At mileage **105.5**, the train crosses the Nepisiguit River on a 630-foot (192-metre) structure before entering the City of Bathurst (2011 population 12,275) at mileage **110.2**.

Mileage:
Mont Joli Sub: Green
Montmagny Sub: Black
Newcastle Sub: Blue

Mileages 111–173: Your train may stop at Petit-Rocher, which translates as "Little Rock"—home to one of Canada's newest railway stations. This village at mileage **121.6** had a population of 1,949 in 2006 and is home to the Acadian Society of New Brunswick. Look to the north at mileage **135**—the land on the other side of the Chaleur Bay is dominated by the Notre Dame Mountains in the Province of Quebec. Just beyond the station stop for the community of 1,200 people, the train crosses the Jacquet River at mileage **139**. Charlo, at mileage **154.3**, with a population of 1,324 in 2011, was settled in

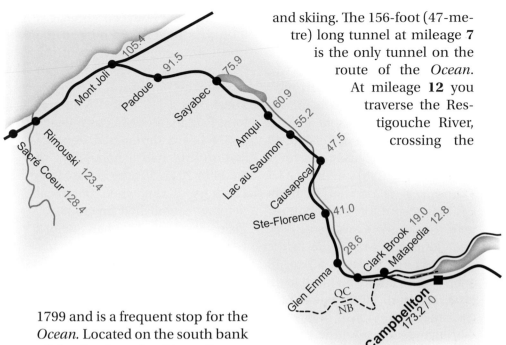

and skiing. The 156-foot (47-metre) long tunnel at mileage **7** is the only tunnel on the route of the *Ocean*. At mileage **12** you traverse the Restigouche River, crossing the

1799 and is a frequent stop for the *Ocean*. Located on the south bank of the Restigouche River, Campbellton (2011 population 7,385) mileage **173.2** is an entry point to Atlantic Canada from Quebec. The 2,641-foot (805-metre) J.C. Van Horne bridge connecting New Brunswick and Quebec by road opened on October 15th 1961 and can be seen to the north.

Route Highlights
Campbellton to Rivière du Loup
Mont Joli Subdivision

Mileages 0–12: The route you are travelling on was built between 1874 and 1876 by the *Intercolonial Railway*. As you leave Campbellton, you can see Sugar Loaf Mountain to the south. The volcanic rock mountain houses a popular provincial park featuring camping

provincial border between New Brunswick and Quebec, as well as entering the Eastern Time Zone— so adjust your travel clock and watch accordingly. Once across the river, you arrive at the town of Matapédia, and a designated heritage railway station that dates to 1903. Depending on the day of the week and the direction you are heading, you will join or part with *VIA Rail's* Montreal-Gaspé train. See page 35 for more information on this train and its route.

Mileages 13–120: The route travels through the picturesque Matapédia Valley, with the Matapédia River paralleling the route for the next 30 miles. The river has always attracted salmon fishermen, including early *CPR* president George Stephen, who fell in love with, and married, a local First Nations woman. The tracks cross the river at mileage **23** and then again at mileage **42**, and finally at Causapscal (2011 population 2,258) mileage **47.5**. Causapscal is derived from the Mi'kmaq word for "stony bottom", referring to the Causapscal River that joins the Matapedia at this point. From mileages **53** to **56**, you can see Lac au Saumon to the east. The Humqui River is crossed at mileage **60**, just before the heritage station at Amqui, mileage **60.9**. Amqui, Mi'kmaq for "place of amusement," (2011 population 6,322) was on the Kempt Road, a military road between Quebec and the Maritimes completed in 1833. It was settled in 1879 following the completion of the *Intercolonial Railway*. The Tobégote River is crossed at mileage **64**. Lake Matapédia sits to the east and north between mileages **63** and **73**. Your train may pause briefly at mileage **75.9**, Sayabec (2011 population 1,864), on the southern slope of the Chic-Choc Mountains (from the Mi'kmaq for "Rocky Mountains") that also has a heritage railway station. During the series of rock cuts at mileages **88** and **89**, look up to see an old railway flatcar now used as a footbridge above the tracks. Between mileages **95** and **99** keep watching to the north for your first views of the St. Lawrence River. The *Ocean* crosses the Mitis River at mileage **102.1** over a 418-foot (127-metre) long bridge. Mont-Joli at mileage **105.4** has a designated heritage station and had a population of 6,665 in 2011. Nearby is the Metis Gardens, a renowned botanical display established in 1928 by Elsie Stephen Meighen Reford who inherited the site from her uncle, Lord Mount Stephen. He became Canada's richest man and was the first president of the transcontinental Canadian Pacific Railway. At mileage **119** look towards the St. Lawrence near the shoreline as you may be able to catch a glimpse of the red cylinder atop the 108-foot (33-metre) lighthouse at Pointe-au-Père. This marks the watery grave of over one thousand people who died with the tragic sinking of *Canadian Pacific*'s 14,191-ton ocean-liner *Empress of Ireland*. On the foggy night of May 29th 1914, while en route to England; the liner was rammed by the Norwegian collier *Storstad* and sank in less than fifteen minutes. The lighthouse also marks the end of the St. Lawrence River and the beginning of the Gulf of St. Lawrence.

Mileages 121–188: Rimouski, mileage **123.4**, (2011 population 46,840) founded in 1696, is home to a campus of the University

The *Ocean* arrives at Matapedia Station on Quebec's Gaspé peninsula. *Bill Linley photo*

of Québec and to an important ocean science research centres. Keep your camera ready at Bic (from the French, "pic", a distant pointed peak) mileage **133.9** as the route offers a panoramic view of Bic Harbour on the St. Lawrence River. Bic Island can be seen 5 miles (8 kilometres) away; the opposite shore is approximately 20 miles (32 kilometres) away. The vast marine life that lives in these waters includes beluga, blue, and minke or fin whales, as well as gray seals. Birds also dominate the area, with over 300 varieties including the Great Blue Heron, the common eider, the northern harrier, and razorbills. Good views over the St. Lawrence continue to the north. St. Simon at mileage **153.2** is often the meeting place for the eastbound and westbound *Oceans*. In this area, the *Ocean* crosses a series of rivers, including the Grand Bic, mileage **141**, the Renouf, mileage **162**, Trois Pistoles, mileage **164.7**, and Isle Verte, mileage **174**. Trois Pistoles

(2011 population 3,456) is the site of Canada's oldest annual French immersion program operated by the University of Western Ontario since 1932. Basque Island offshore commemorates Basque whalers from the 16th century. The town's name is derived from the three French coins representing the value of a silver goblet lost in the river in the 17th century. The train crosses Rivière-du-Loup on a 372-foot (113-metre) structure when passing through the city of the same name at mileage **188.7/0.0** Rivière du Loup (2011 population 19,447) derives its name from the seals or sea wolves once found at the river's mouth and is the site of a summer home owned by Sir John A. Macdonald, Canada's first prime minister.

Route Highlights
Rivière-du-Loup to West Jct. near Charny
Montmagny Subdivision

Mileages 0–118: At mileage **15.3**,

look east to see the Pelletier Sub-division descending to St. Andre Jct. bringing the long-distance freight trains that left your route at Pacific Jct. west of Moncton. Near St. Pascal, mileage **25.4**, watch for monadnocks, small isolated hills that survived erosion around them. La Pocatière (2011 population 4,266) is reached at mileage **41.1**; look west to see the Bombardier plant that manufactures subway and railway passenger cars. Between mileages **42** and **58**, you can see the Ile-aux-Coudres across the St. Lawrence, close to the north shore. The 360-foot (110-metre) long bridge at mileage **59** crosses the Trois Saumon River. The Rivière du Sud is crossed on a 584-foot (178-metre) bridge at mileage **77.8** as you near Montmag-

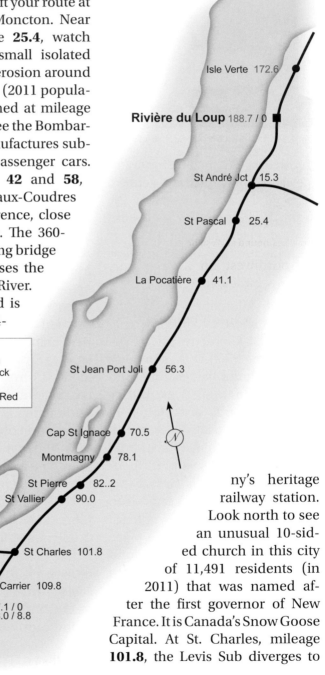

Mileage:
Mont Joli Sub: Green
Montmagny Sub: Black
Bridge Sub: Blue
Drummondville Sub: Red

Isle Verte 172.6

Rivière du Loup 188.7 / 0

St André Jct 15.3

St Pascal 25.4

La Pocatière 41.1

St Jean Port Joli 56.3

Cap St Ignace 70.5

Montmagny 78.1

St Pierre 82..2
St Vallier 90.0

St Charles 101.8

Quebec 15.9

Carrier 109.8

Charny 8.1 / 0.3 **Joffre** 117.1 / 0 **West Jct.** 118.0 / 8.8

ny's heritage railway station. Look north to see an unusual 10-sided church in this city of 11,491 residents (in 2011) that was named after the first governor of New France. It is Canada's Snow Goose Capital. At St. Charles, mileage **101.8**, the Levis Sub diverges to

Ocean eastbound at Westchester, NS. *Bill Linley photo*

the northwest on a route that formerly provided direct service to downtown Levis and via ferry to Quebec City. It now runs 15.2 miles to access the Ultramar refinery, a source of unit gas trains that run to Ontario and New Brunswick. Charny, (2006 population 10,367) is home to CN's Joffre Yard that you will see to the south at mileage **117.1**, including one of the few remaining roundhouses that formerly serviced steam locomotives. It is now a National Historic Site. At West Jct., mileage **118.0 / 8.8**, your westbound train will reverse direction while crossing the Chaudière River (Algonquin for "boiling kettle") and pass the Charny station, mileage **8.1** on the Drummondville Subdivision. The train will continue across the St. Lawrence River to Sainte-Foy station that serves the province's capital region, before returning to the south shore line. (Note: Trains from Montreal also follow this route from West Jct. to provide direct service to downtown Quebec City. See page 33 for more details about this route.)

Route Highlights
Charny to Ste Rosalie
Drummondville Sub

Mileages 8–52: The route travels away from the St. Lawrence through a region of forests that eventually gives way to large open fields. Laurier (mileage **28**) is named after Canada's first French Canadian prime minister, Sir Wilfred Laurier.

Mileages 53–124: Maddington

Falls is visible to the north as the train crosses the Bécancour River at Daveluyville, mileage **67.6**. Keep your camera ready for the high bridge above the Nicolet River, crossed at mileage **80** just west of St. Léonard d'Aston. Mileage **97.8** provides another photo opportunity while crossing the St. Francis River; look north to see the hydroelectric dam, before arriving at the brick Drummondville station at mileage **98.3**. Drummondville (2011 population 71,852) was founded in 1815 and was named after Sir Gordon Drummond, hero of the Battle of Lundy's Lane (Niagara, Ontario) in 1812. Your train then travels through an agricultural region and skirts the TransCanada Highway, Route 20, before reaching Ste. Rosalie at mileage **125.1/38.7**.

Route Highlights
Ste. Rosalie to Montreal
St. Hyacinthe Subdivision

Mileages 38.7–74.3: The route joins the double-tracked St. Hyacinthe Subdivision at mileage **125.1/38.7**. The city of St. Hyacinthe, mileage **40.9**, (2011 population 53,236) is home to world-renowned pipe organ maker, Casavant Frères, founded in 1879. One of Canada's most tragic rail accidents occurred at mileage **55** on June 29th 1864. At 1:15 am, while crossing the Richelieu River, a passenger train plummeted into the water below, killing 99 people. It was later determined that the engineer was unfamiliar with the route and did

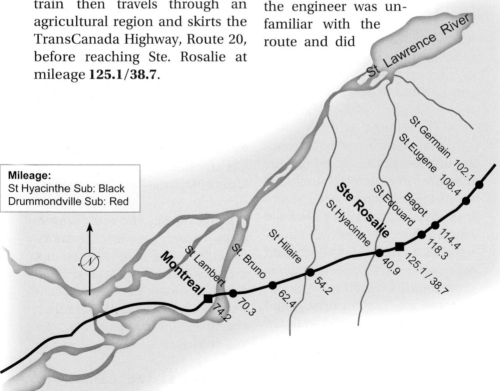

Mileage:
St Hyacinthe Sub: Black
Drummondville Sub: Red

THE OCEAN

not know about the signals intended to inform him of the open bridge ahead. The large unique mountains to the south were formed 125 million years ago as a re-

Quebec 15.9

Charny
8.1 / 0.3

Joffre 117.1 / 0
West Jct. 118.0 / 8.8

St Apolinaire

Laurier 20.0

Fortier 28.5

Villeroy 34.4

47.0

Mileage:
Bridge Sub: Blue
Montmagny Sub: Black
Drummondville Sub: Red

Lemieux 57.6

Daveluyville

Aston Jct. 67.6

St Leonard 72.4

Ste Perpetue 79.8

84.5

St. Cyrille 92.9
Drummondville
98.3

sult of volcanic eruptions on the bottom of what was then the Champlain Sea. Look to the north at mileage **62.4** to see the former St. Bruno station, now preserved as a community centre. The train stops in St. Lambert, mileage **70.3** before crossing the St. Lawrence on the historic Victoria Jubilee Bridge. Construction on the Victoria Bridge began in 1854 and was completed in 1859. At first it was a single-track enclosed bridge, with only a vent running along the top

for steam and smoke to escape. When the bridge became inadequate for the increasing traffic, work began in 1897 to rebuild it into a steel structure with two tracks and roads on each side; it was ready for service in December 1898. The road along the west side opened for carriages, cyclists, and pedestrians for a toll on December 1st 1899. These were the first users of the roadways, as Montreal only had one known motor vehicle. From 1909 to 1956, the *Montreal & Southern Counties'* interurbans and streetcars ran along the east side of the bridge. When the St. Lawrence Seaway was opened in 1959, the eastern end of the bridge was split in two, permitting trains to be diverted if there were a ship in the St. Lambert lock below. Once across the 1.7-mile (2.7-kilometre) long bridge, look to the east in the middle of the road to see the large boulder known as the Irish Stone, which was unearthed during the original construction. The stone was dedicated to the memory of immigrants who died from ship fever in 1847 and 1848. The train then travels through downtown Montreal and arrives at Central Station. For rail travellers to and from Montreal, there is nothing more convenient than the Queen Elizabeth Hotel. Located at 900 René Levesque Blvd. West, this classic railway hotel was originally built by *Canadian National Railways* and today is operated by Fairmont Hotels. Follow the signs in the station to the elevator that will take you up one floor to the lobby. For reservations call: 866 540-4483. Web: *www.fairmont.com.* Montreal (2011 population 1,649,519) was founded in 1642 and is Canada's second largest city and the largest francophone city in North America. It has numerous attractions and sights to please everyone. We recommend you start in Old Montreal with a visit to the Notre Dame Cathedral. By nightfall, you will be able to enjoy the night life along Rue St. Denis. Also plan to spend an afternoon at Exporail, the Canadian Railway Museum located on the south shore of the St. Lawrence in St. Constant, a 20-minute ride from downtown. For hours, call: 450 638-2410. Web: *www.exporail.org.* Before you visit Montreal or anywhere in Québec, you should contact Tourisme Québec, PO Box 979, Montreal, QC, H3C 2W3. Phone: 877 266-5687. Web: www.bonjourquebec.com Email: *info@bonjourquebec.com*

Dining car caters to travellers aboard The *Ocean*. David Othen photo

QUEBEC CITY TURN

T he route across the St. Lawrence into Quebec City is the northern-most destination of the Windsor-Quebec City *Corridor* trains. Trains from Montreal travel the same route as *The Ocean*, featured on page 16.

Route Highlights
Charny to Quebec City
Bridge Subdivision

Mileages 0–15.9: Charny station, on the south shore of the St. Lawrence, is located at mileage **0.3** of the Bridge Subdivision and is the start of the short remaining journey into Quebec City. As the train leaves the station, it passes through the town of Charny. To the west are the circular on and off ramps where the Robert Cliche Highway intersects with the Trans-Canada. The train crosses the Chaudiere River and then enters the impressive Quebec Bridge, opened in 1919, at mileage **1**. This crossing of the St. Lawrence River is 3,239 feet (987 metres) long and 340 feet (104 metres) high. The 1,800 foot (549 metre) cantilevered span is still the longest in the world. Keep your camera ready for great views of the river, particularly of the 1970 Pierre LaPorte Bridge to the west,

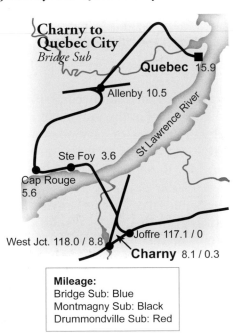

Charny to Quebec City
Bridge Sub

Quebec 15.9

Allenby 10.5

St Lawrence River

Ste Foy 3.6

Cap Rouge 5.6

West Jct. 118.0 / 8.8   Joffre 117.1 / 0

Charny 8.1 / 0.3

Mileage:
Bridge Sub: Blue
Montmagny Sub: Black
Drummondville Sub: Red

Lounge as used on Montreal-Halifax, Quebec, Ottawa and Toronto trains. *David Othen photo*

which is the longest non-tolled suspension bridge in the world, and Quebec City to the east. Once over the bridge, the tracks turn west, parallel to the river, and trains stop at Sainte-Foy station, mileage **3.6**. The train continues to travel west until Cap Rouge, mileage **5.4**, when the route turns northeast. At mileage **6** the train starts travelling east along the side of   an old glacial spillway. For the next couple of miles the train descends through an industrial area. At mileage **10** the train crosses the *Quebec-Gatineau Railway* and the Saint Charles River at mileage **11**. The train continues east and passes by Exposition Park to the south, which features a horseracing track, the Hippodrome, and the large hockey rink, Le Colisée. The route then turns to the south and heads toward the historic walled city of Quebec that dates from 1608. Finally, you once again cross the now-wider Saint Charles River before arriving at the location of stately Gare du Palais station built by the *CPR* in 1915, at mileage **15.9**. This beautiful station, with its glazed brick construction, should be thoroughly admired.

Upon leaving the station, climb the hill and enjoy the cobblestones and Old World feel of the provincial capital. Not to be missed is the large Parc des Champs-des-Batailles, also known as the Plains of Abraham. To the east of here is the Citadelle, open daily from May to September, and featuring the best views of the city atop Cape Diamond. For a memorable stay in the provincial capital, we highly recommend the classic CPR hotel first opened in 1899, Le Château Frontenac, which dominates the city skyline at 1 Rue des Carriers. Operated by Fairmont Hotels, reservations can be made at: 866-540-4460. 800-441-1414. Web: *www. fairmont.com*

MONTREAL-GASPÉ ROUTE

*V*IA's Montreal-Gaspé train between Montreal and Matapedia is covered in the route of the *Ocean*. From Matapédia the route travels east along the southern coast of the Gaspé Peninsula, a region that which has a long history of welcoming travellers. One of the earliest explorers, Jacques Cartier, named the Chaleur Bay in recognition of its warm waters. If you are laying over in Matapedia, we recommend the Motel Restigouche, located at 5 des Saumons, close to the train station and overlooking the Restigouche and Matapédia rivers. Reservations can be made by calling 877 865-2848 or visiting *www.matapedia. com*. Email: *motelrestigouche@mata-pedia.com*. Your route travels through the Gaspé Region of Quebec. Before you leave home, we suggest you contact the Gaspé Tourist Association, 357 route de la Mer, Sainte-Flavie, QC, G0J 2L0. Call: 800 463-0323.

Mileage:
Mont Joli Sub: Green
Cascapedia Sub: Black
Chandler Sub: Red

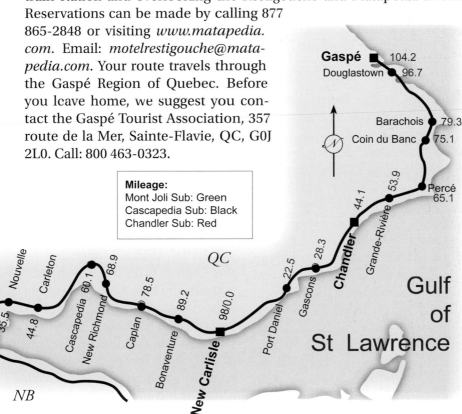

Combined *Ocean* and Gaspé trains by Matapedia River. *Bill Linley photo*

Route Highlights
Matapédia to New Carlisle
Cascapedia Subdivision

In 1893 the *Baies des Chaleurs Railway* built the route between Matapédia and Caplan. Then in 1910 the *Atlantic, Quebec & Western Railway* extended the line to New Carlisle. This line was part of the *CN* system for many years, but today it is a shortline known as the *Gaspésie Railway*.

Mileages 0–22: Depending on the direction you are travelling, at mileage **0/12.8** in Matapédia your train will detach from or join with *VIA*'s *Ocean*. Your train then travels on the north side of the Restigouche River until mileage **8**, when the river ends and the Chaleur Bay begins. Look to the south for good views of Campbellton and Sugarloaf Mountain. It was in these waters that a fierce naval battle took place where the English defeated the French in July 1760 in their last North American battle of the Seven Years' War. Timbers from the French frigate Machault and

numerous artifacts are on display at the Battle of Restigouche National Historic Site west of the town of Pointe-a-la-Croix, which can be seen to the south at mileage **12**.

Mileages 23–98: You'll continue to see fantastic views to the south, over the Bay between mileages **23** and **26**. Your train may pause for passengers at Nouvelle, mileage **35.5** named after a 17th century Jesuit missionary and having a 2011 population of 1,689. It is the world's second largest fossil site as recognized by UNESCO in 1999. Have your camera ready at mileage **42** where the train passes under Highway 132 and skirts the Bay approaching Carleton, mileage **44.8**. Carleton (2011 population 3,991) was settled by Acadians deported by the English from the Beaubassin community near Fort Beausejour, Nova Scotia in 1756. This resort community offers excellent beaches. The building on the side of Mount St. Joseph to the north is a shrine revering the Virgin Mary. The train will slowly cross the Cascapedia River at mileage **60.1** on two unusual bridges that carried automobiles on a lower level until the 1980s and then arrive at New Richmond, mileage **68.9**. New Richmond (2011 population 3,810) was settled by Scottish brothers George and John Duthie in 1755. A British Heritage Museum is found here. Your train may pause at Caplan, mileage **78.5** that had a population of 2,039 in 2011. As the route crosses a ravine over the Watt Brook at mileage **80.9**, look down to see a small secluded beach. At mileage **89.2**, you reach Bonaventure (2011 population 2,275) in an area also noted for its good beaches that was settled in 1760 by Acadians escaping the Expulsion. At mileage **90** the train crosses the Bonaventure River over a 355-foot (108-metre) bridge. Good views over the water towards New Brunswick continue before your arrival in New Carlisle at mileage **98** for an extended station stop. New Carlisle (2011 population 1,358), settled by Loyalists in 1784, is notable as the boyhood home of former Quebec premier René Lévesque (1976–1985).

Route Highlights
New Carlisle to Gaspé
Chandler Subdivision

The *Atlantic Quebec & Western Railway* built the remainder of

Nearing Carleton on the Gaspé coast. *Bill Linley photo*

the line to Gaspé, opening it for service in July 1912.

Mileages 0–48: For the first three miles, the route climbs the cliffs along the shoreline and then returns to the forest. The Shigawake ("land of the rising sun") River is crossed at mileage **13**. After descending to sea level, your train crosses the north Port Daniel River at mileage **22**, and then enters the town of Port Daniel (2011 population 2,453) where there are good views to the south. Hazel McCallion, Mississauga's, and Canada's, longest serving mayor was born here in 1921. The tracks then climb through town, entering the only tunnel on the route at mileage **23.7**. Carved out of limestone, the tunnel is 630-feet (192-metres) long. Keep your camera ready at mileage **26** as the tracks cross a trestle above a wharf; this wharf is in a protected inlet and is used by local fishing

View from the Gaspé train of a quiet harbour at mile 26 on the Cascapedia subdivision.

boats. After Gascons at mileage **28**, the train crosses the Chouinard River (mileage **29.8**). Just beyond the bridge under Route 132 look south to the waves crashing onto the shoreline as your train creeps along the cliff. After crossing the Grand Pabos River at mileage **42**, the route parallels a beach along the Gulf of St. Lawrence before reaching Chandler station at mileage **44.1**. Chandler with a population of 7,703 in 2011 was home to the first pulp and paper mill in the Gaspé Region established by Philadelphian Percy Chandler in 1912.

Mileages 48–104: It is obvious that many of the inhabitants of the area make a living from the sea. From the train you can see the lobster traps on the properties along the tracks. Your train crosses the Grand River over a 685-foot (209-metre) bridge at mileage **53** as it approaches the Grande Rivière station at mileage **53.9**. With a 2011 population of 3,456, the community is known for its crab fishery. Bonaventure Island, internationally known for its breeding colonies of gannets, puffins, cormorants and murres, comes into view at mileage **62**. Although the Percé station is at mileage **65.1**, the town itself is a couple of miles away on the coast. Percé, from the French for "pierced", had a population of 3,312 in 2011 and is a well-established tourism mecca. Cabs and hotel buses will pick up passengers at the station for this popular resort town. At mileage **65.5** a trestle crosses the L'Anse-a-Beaufils River, and then the track turns inland to avoid the coastal mountains of Mount Sainte Anne, 1,175-feet (348-metres) high, and Mount Blanc. The route descends from Summit, mileage **69.1**, emerging from the forest at sea level at mileage **74**. A causeway cuts across La Malbaie starting at Coin-du-Banc, mileage **75.1**. Coin-du-Banc was settled by the Irish in the mid-19th century. Watch to the south for St. Luke's Anglican chapel of 1893 and look for agates and jasper if you have an opportunity to visit the beach. The large saltwater marsh, or *barachois*, created by the causeway that the tracks are situated on offers good bird watching along one of the longest beaches in the area. The marsh ends at mileage **78.7** where the route crosses a bridge that releases the trapped water of the Malbaie River. Have your camera ready when the tracks return to the mainland. The route turns east as it approaches the Barachois station, the oldest on the line, at mileage **79.3**. Barachois was first recorded by the French in 1676. To the south is the area's largest attraction: the 400 million-ton Percé Rock has a 60-foot wide by 100-foot high (18-metre by 30-metre) natural-arched opening. The town of Prével was originally known as Fort Prével and featured heavy artillery aimed toward the Gulf during the Second World War. The railway track passes the community's golf course at mileage **86**. Mileage **89.8** offers a great opportunity to photograph your train on the curved, 775-foot (236.2-metre) trestle over the L'Anse-a-Brillant River. At mileage **91**, you can see excellent views over Gaspé Bay to Forillon National Park on the opposite shore. Douglastown (**96.7**) is named after its surveyor, John Douglas. The town was a project of the English government to create a model Loyalist community. Another natural causeway, with sandy beaches on both sides, is crossed at mileage **96.7**. The bridge at mileage **97.6** spans the gap that releases water from the St. Jean River. The train arrives at the end of the line opposite the Gaspé Marina, at mileage **104.2**.

It is believed that the word "Gaspé" comes from the MicMac word that translates to "land's end." The line was built in the hope that a grain elevator would be erected to load ocean-going vessels. This did not come about, however, and the end of the line is simply a "track stop" a few feet from the station. Gaspé visitors who wish to explore the area should rent a car and visit Forillon National Park or the Musée de la Gaspésie located at 80 boul. Gaspé. Here you can learn more about the people of the region, Jacques Cartier's explorations in the area, and see a replica of the cross he raised on July 24th 1534 claiming possession of Canada in the name of the French King, Francois I. This was commemorated in 1934 with a 42-ton, 32-foot (9.8-metre) granite cross placed on the hill behind the city. Gaspé had a population of 15,163 in 2011.

Travellers to Percé will enjoy numerous activities and attractions. Choices include taking a boat to Bonaventure Island, a visit to the gannet colony to view over 70,000 birds of this species, or a trip to some of the numerous shops to find that perfect souvenir. There is also the time-honoured tradition of walking to the famous Percé

A time-honoured tradition, walking at low tide to Percé Rock, is enjoyed by visitors to the resort community of Percé.

Rock at low tide. For an outstanding view and a good night's sleep, we recommend the Riôtel Percé located at No. 261 on Route 132 in Percé. For reservations, *www.riôtel.ca* or call: 800 463-4212 Email: *perce@riô-tel.com*

Note: At press time the future of *VIA*'s Montreal-Gaspé Route was in doubt and it may not be resumed. Potential travellers are encouraged to check with *VIA Rail* at 888 842-7245 or *www.viarail.ca*. You may also want to consider *L'Amiral* excursion train as described on page 181. This new *L'Amiral* service is already serving a portion of the Gaspé route (though not regularly scheduled), and there are plans to extend it even further, supplementing *VIA*'s service, or perhaps replacing it entirely.

MONTREAL-JONQUIÈRE ROUTE

Travel through northern Quebec provides views of every conceivable terrain, from fertile agricultural regions to grand valley crossings, and from countless lakes to large forests. *VIA Rail Canada*'s Montreal-Jonquière and Montreal–La Tuque–Senneterre trains share the same route from Montreal to Hervey Junction. Then the former continues north to Jonquière/Chicoutimi and the latter west to Senneterre. For travellers arriving in or departing from Montreal, we recommend staying at the Queen Elizabeth Hotel, located directly above Central Station.

The first 1.2 miles from Central Station on the Saint-Hyacinthe subdivision take us to Cape, where our journey to mileage **8.4** continues on the Montreal Subdivision. This part of your journey is described in the Montreal-Toronto "Corridor" route segment on page 56. Both the St. Laurent and the Joliette subdivisions connect with Montreal from the east, so the mile numbering starts at the opposite end of the line. This means, for the first two subdivisions, the mileages in this guide will be listed in descending order.

Route Highlights
Taschereau to Pointe-aux-Trembles
St. Laurent Subdivision

Mileages 146–127: As the train leaves the Montreal-Toronto route, it turns north through a limestone ridge and travels between Montreal's two largest railway yards: *Canadian National*'s Taschereau yard to the west and *Canadian Pacific's* St. Luc yard to the east. Once clear of the railway yards, the route continues through the city's suburbs. Mount Royal dominates the view to the east with the green dome of the St. Joseph Oratory in the foreground. The train crosses the Deux-Montagnes subdivision at mileage **141**; watch for the modern electric trains

A group awaits the arrival of the combined northern Quebec trains to Jonquière and Senneterre, at Hervey Junction, Quebec.

that carry commuters between downtown Montreal and the suburbs northwest of this island city. When the *Canadian Northern Railway* sought a route to the city centre its way was blocked by existing *CPR* and *GTR* lines so, it had to overcome a major obstacle: the 679-foot (207-metre) high Mount Royal. Construction of a tunnel through the mountain began in 1912 and was completed six years later. The box-cab electric locomotives purchased by *Canadian Northern* to haul the trains were still being used until a ceremonial last run on June 2nd 1995. Today one of these veterans with steel wheels that have wooden spokes) sits as a tribute at the Deux-Montagnes station at the northern end of the commuter line. As you

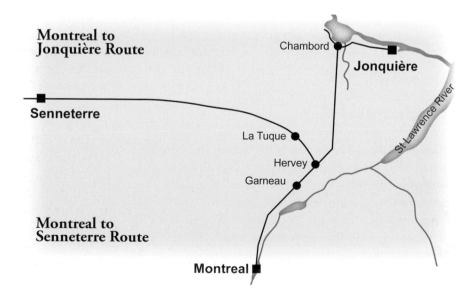

Montreal to Jonquière Route

Chambord

Jonquière

St Lawrence River

Senneterre

La Tuque

Hervey

Garneau

Montreal to Senneterre Route

Montreal

approach Pointe-aux-Trembles, mileage **127.8**, you can tell how much the locals love to swim by the number of homes with a pool in their backyards.

Route Highlights
Pointe-aux-Trembles to Garneau
Joliette Subdivision

Mileages 127–88: The train leaves the island of Montreal at mileage **125**, crossing the Rivière des Prairies over a 1,416-foot (431-metre) bridge, a small island, and then a second bridge over the same river. Once across, the community of Le Gardeur continues the urban sprawl of Montreal. At Crabtree, 2011 population 3,887, mileage **107.0** look north to see a small

hydroelectric plant as the train crosses the Ouareau River over a 490-foot (149-metre) bridge, 55 feet (17 metres) above the water. Crabtree Mills was a pioneering paper-making operation opened here in 1906 by Edwin Crabtree that became part of Domtar. At mileage **101.9**, the train stops at the manufacturing city of Joliette, formerly known as l'Industrie, which had a population of 19,621 in 2011. At mileage **101** the St. Lawrence River can be seen to the south, while at mileage **98** the Laurentian Mountains start to come into view to the north. The 250-foot (76-metre) bridge at mileage **87** crosses the Chicot River.

Mileages 88–40: Before an earthquake in the 17th century, the Maskinonge River flowed in this now dry riverbed crossed at mileage **87**. Keep your camera ready at mileage **75** for the impressive 1,071-foot (326-metre) trestle crossing the river's new route 130 feet (40 metres) below. As you cross the trestle, watch for Sainte-Ursule Falls on the opposite shore, to the south, close to the bridge. Once across the bridge, keep watching for the white water of the falls to the north. At mileage **65** the tracks cross the Rivière du Loup with miniature whirlpools seen from both sides of the train. The tracks cut right through the middle of the picturesque town

Garneau 40.1
Grand-Mère 44.0
Shawinigan 49.5

Charette 62.0
Saint-Paulin 68.0

Saint-Justin 78.1
St. Cuthbert 88.2

Mileage:
Joliette 101.9   Joliette Sub: Green
Crabtree 107.0   St. Laurent Sub: Red
Salome 109.6   Montreal Sub: Blue
                  St. Hyacinthe Sub: Black

L'Épiphanie 114.4
117.4 L'Assomption
122.3 Le Gardeur

Rivière des Prairies
Montréal-Nord
Ahuntsic 132.8
Gohier 135.6
139.6
141.2

Pointe-aux-Trembles 127.8 / 127.8

Montreal 74.2 / 0
St-Laurent 142.6
Taschereau Yard 146.2 / 8.7

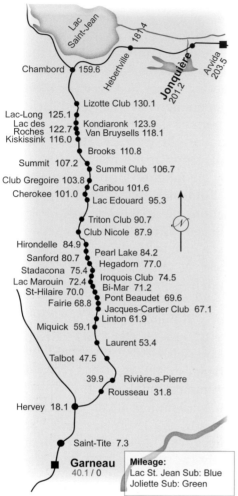

of 50,060 in 2011 and the home of Canada's 20th Prime Minister, Jean Chretien, can be clearly seen to the south. At the station one can see the wide St. Maurice River at the bottom of the hill. At mileage **43**, before and during the crossing of the St. Maurice, look to the north for good views of the Grand-Mère hydroelectric facility that powers the Laurentide Mill of Resolute Forest Products. The route swings north at mileage **42**, allowing for views of the opposite side of the dam. Finally, the train pulls into the large railway yards in Garneau at mileage **40.1**.

Route Highlights
Garneau to Jonquière
Lac St. Jean Subdivision

Mileages 0–46: As the train continues through this agricultural region, note the white grain silo with the red roof to the west at mileage **5**; this silo has been converted to a lookout. Next, the route travels through St. Tite at mileage **7.3**. Mileage **18.1** brings you to Hervey. Here, depending on the direction you are travelling, Montreal-Jonquière and the Montreal–La Tuque–Senneterre trains will be separated or joined. (See page 47 for route details of *VIA's* Senneterre route. The Montreal-Jonquière route continues north. To the west at mileage **23**, Lac-aux-Sables with its sandy beaches is very popular in the

of Charette (mileage **62**). The East Yamachiche River is located in the bog crossed at mileage **58**. At mileage **56** the Cité de l' Energie tower in Shawinigan comes into view. The Lawrence Valley is crossed next at mileage **52** before the train enters a 610-foot (186-metre) tunnel at mileage **50**. Once the train emerges from the tunnel, it crosses the Shawinigan River. Shawinigan, the electric city, with a population

The route of *VIA Rail*'s Montreal-Jonquière train winds along the shore of Lac Edouard.

summer months. You first see the Batiscan River to the east at mileage **28** and then cross it at mileage **30**. This shallow river, with its fast moving water, is the train's travelling companion for the next seventy miles. At mileage **40**, the tracks cross Rivière-à-Pierre, and at mileage **43**, the Blanche River is crossed twice.

Mileages 47–105: At mileage **47**, the train enters Portneuf Provincial Park, an area known for its trout fishing. Watch for moose, bears, and birds along the route. As you move through the park, look to the west to see the rapids on the Batiscan. The train exits the provincial park at mileage **58** where it crosses the Miquick River. Passing through Linton (mileage **61**), look to the river to see the old bridge supports of the La Tuque branch of the *Quebec & Lac St. Jean Railway* completed in 1907 to connect with the *National Transcontinental Railway*. The

connecting line was abandoned in 1949. The *Q&LSJ* built the Rivière-à-Pierre–Jonquière route between 1888 and 1893. The *Q&LSJ* passed to the *Canadian Northern* and then to Canadian National as did the *National Transcontinental*. The train crosses the Batiscan River for the last time at mileage **69**. A camp that was owned by a retired telephone company employee uses a phone booth sign to mark the trail, a sign out of place in this northern wilderness. The stop at mileage **90.7** is to service the Triton Club, which was started in 1907. Patrons leave the train and travel by boat to the lodge, located three miles down the narrow Petite Rivière Batiscan. Watch to the east at mileage **92** for the Batiscan Falls. A statue of Ava Maria on the hill to the east at mileage **95** looks over the town of Lac Edouard, formerly a railway division point.

Mileages 106–200: The aptly

named Summit (mileage **107.2**) is the highest elevation on the Jonquière line. While travelling through Kiskissink (mileage **116.0**), don't be alarmed if you see a rolled up object thrown from the cab of the locomotive; it is simply the engineer throwing out the Montreal newspaper for a friend! Watch for the wave of gratitude from someone coming down the path to receive the news. Lakes and rivers continue to come into view, such as Rivière Louis Joseph at mileage **126**. You get your first glimpse of Lac Saint-Jean to the north at mileage **157**. Your train turns to the east and descends to the station at Chambord, 2011 population 1,773. The fantastic views across this large lake continue to the north. At mileage **164**, the train crosses the Metabetchouan River. This region is known for its blueberries and for the 154-mile (256-kilometre) Veloroute des Bleuets (Blueberry Bicycle Trail) that circles Lac Saint-Jean which is seen alongside the railway tracks at mileage **165**. The route leaves the lake behind at mileage **175** and travels through a fertile valley. At Saguenay Power, mileage **183.2** you may see a *Roberval & Saguenay* freight train connecting this *CN* line to the town of Alma. Highway 170 can be seen to the north and the Rivière-aux-Sables is crossed at

mileage **200**. At mileage **201.2**, your journey ends at the modern Jonquière station.

After your long day on the rails, we recommend the Delta Saguenay Hotel located at 2675 boul. du Royaume. Reservations can be made at: 888 890-3222.

Plan to spend a few days in the area exploring Lac Saint-Jean or watching whales on the majestic Saguenay Fjord. A visit to nearby Chicoutimi should begin at La Croix de Sainte-Anne. This is located on Cap Saint-Joseph, and features an outstanding view of the city. Also, at la Pulperie de Chicoutimi, you can learn more about the history of the area. Don't miss the Petite Maison Blanche, which stands as a reminder of the devastating 1996 flood. In Jonquière, those who enjoy industrial sites should be sure to visit the Aluminum Bridge. Built in 1950, it is one-third the weight of similar iron bridges. It is truly a tribute to the community's largest employer and aluminum producer, Rio Tinto Alcan. Before you visit the region, contact Tourisme Saguenay–Lac Saint Jean, 412 Saguenay Blvd. East, Suite 100, Chicoutimi, QC, G7H 7Y8. Phone: 800 253-8387 Web: *www.tourism-saguenaylacsaintjean.qc.ca* Email: *info@tourismesaglac.net*

MONTREAL–LA TUQUE–SENNETERRE

*V*IA's Montreal–La Tuque–Senneterre route to Hervey is covered in the route of the Montreal-Jonquière route, beginning on page 41. From Hervey, the track travels west on a route built by the *National Transcontinental Railway*. This line was created in 1903 by a unique partnership between the *Grand Trunk Railway* and the federal government, under the leadership of Prime Minister Sir Wilfred Laurier. The newly formed *Grand Trunk Pacific Railway* agreed to build the portion of track west of Winnipeg, while the Government was to build the *National Transcontinental Railway* section to the east. To appease his own cabinet members, the Prime Minister decided to build the government's part of the railway from Moncton, New Brunswick, through Quebec City, then follow an almost straight line to Winnipeg. It was agreed that the *Grand Trunk Pacific* would lease the line from the government and would be responsible for running trains once the line was completed. In 1909, the first portion of the line, between Quebec City and Hervey Junction, opened for business. By 1913, passenger trains could travel Winnipeg to Quebec City over the new route. In 1915, financial difficulties on its western lines forced the *Grand Trunk* to renege on its agreement with the government. The western lines came under the control of the *Canadian Government Railways*, later renamed *Canadian National Railways*.

Route Highlights
Hervey to Fitzpatrick
La Tuque Subdivision

Mileages 71–125: Here the route to the west starts at Hervey, mileage **71.5**. Depending on the direction you are travelling, your train will join or separate from *VIA*'s Jonquière train. From Hervey, the train travels through a scenic ravine between mileages **74** and **79**. It then skirts Lake

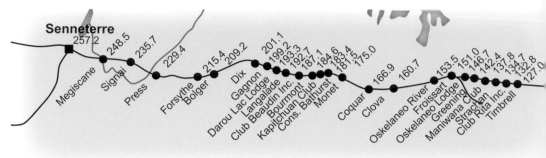

Masketsi to the west, starting at mileage **82**. The large red-roofed lodge on the opposite side of the lake, seen at mileage **84**, was a favourite destination of former Quebec premier Maurice Duplessis. The lake ends at mileage **86.5**. The Bessone River widens to form a lake, seen to the east at mileage **89**. Keep your camera ready when the train crosses the Rivière-du-Milieu at mileage **95.6**. This is the highest trestle in the province crossed by a passenger train. Good views continue to the east as the train clears a small rock cut and then continues to wind around small lakes in a forested area. La Tuque, 2011 population 11,227, (mileage **122.3**) derives its name from a First Nations word for "wool hat," an apt description of the rock in the middle of the Saint Maurice River. This rock was largely removed when a dam was built on the same site years later. A popular destination for adventure cyclists, La Tuque has a 7-mile (12-kilometre) circuit that starts at Parc des Chutes de la Petite Rivière Bostonnais and finishes at the municipal park. The town is also home to popular folk singer Felix Leclerc. The Rock-Tenn Company produces containerboard at its mill in La Tuque. As you leave La Tuque, look to the top of the hill to the east where you can see lumber cars waiting to be loaded with freshly cut forest products. The train crosses the Saint Maurice River at mileage **123** before entering Fitzpatrick.

Route Highlights
Fitzpatrick to Senneterre
St. Maurice Subdivision

When it was built, the line was made up of two subdivisions. Construction from Fitzpatrick on the Manouan Subdivision started in 1910, reached Parent in 1912, continued on the Oskelaneo Subdivision, and reached Senneterre in 1913.

Mileages 1–36: Fitzpatrick, named after former Quebec Lieutenant-Governor Charles Fitzpatrick, was a little village that became a division point with the coming

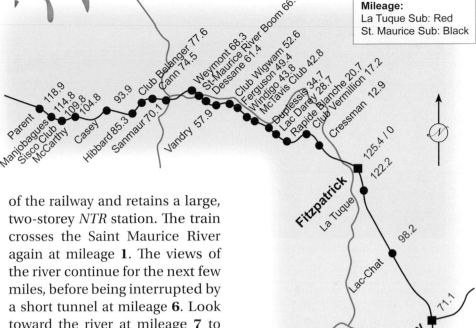

Mileage:
La Tuque Sub: Red
St. Maurice Sub: Black

Parent 118.9
Manjobagues 114.8
Sisco Club 109.8
McCarthy 104.8
Casey 93.9
Hibbard 85.3
Sanmaur 70.1
Club Belanger 77.6
Cann 74.5
Weymont 68.3
St-Maurice River Boom 66.4
Dessane 61.4
Vandry 57.9
Club Wigwam 52.6
Ferguson 49.4
Windigo 43.8
McTavis Club 42.8
Duplessis 34.7
Lac Darey 28.7
Rapide Blanche 20.7
Club Vermillion 17.2
Cressman 12.9
125.4 / 0
122.2
Fitzpatrick
La Tuque
98.2
Lac-Chat
Hervey
71.1

of the railway and retains a large, two-storey *NTR* station. The train crosses the Saint Maurice River again at mileage **1**. The views of the river continue for the next few miles, before being interrupted by a short tunnel at mileage **6**. Look toward the river at mileage **7** to see the top of Beaumont Dam. The river is crossed one more time at mileage **10** and can be seen from the north side of the train until mileage **16**. At mileage **18.4** a high trestle crosses the Vermilion River. At mileage **20.7** you'll find Rapide-Blanc. With its collection of trailers at the end of a bumpy winding road, it is a destination for only the bravest of motorists. Dercy Lake can be seen to the north between mileages **27** and **29**. Duplessis Lodge (mileage **34.7**) is a popular outfitter. The two-storey building close to the tracks is a good example of a typical sectionman's house. It was built by the *National Transcontinental Railway* from a standard plan used by the *Grand Trunk Pacific Railway*.

Mileages 37–80: McTavis (mileage **38**) features some popular fishing lodges. Note the attractive log chalet on the north side of the tracks. At mileage **39**, your train first proceeds over a trestle and then a causeway that divides the wide River Flamond. There's a photo opportunity to the north at mileage **45.8**: the Rapides-des-Coeurs (Heart Rapids) on the Saint Maurice River. The tracks parallel the river until crossing it at mileage **61**. The Saint Maurice is crossed again at mileage **69** and for the last time at mileage **70**. One mile later, the train crosses the Rivière Manouane. Soon, the lush forests change to an area

VIA's train to La Tuque and Senneterre travels high above a ravine in the Laurentian mountains.

devastated by forest fire in 1996. Good views of the new growth begin at mileage **75** when your train crosses a large trestle. Watch the numerous lakes for moose in the water or hawks circling above.

Mileages 80–190: The route now winds through the Quebec wilderness featuring small trees, marshy areas, and sandy soil. The tracks cut through another lake at mileage **100**. Letondal Lake comes into view to the south at mileage **103** and can be seen until mileage **105**. Sisco Mines has a mica loading facility here; piles of this shiny rock can be seen along the right-of-way. At mileage **117**, the train crosses the Bazin River, a popular destination for canoe-camping excursions. A local tourist attraction is the now-shut-down dam and its power station. Once across the river, you arrive in Parent, named after Simon-Napoleon Parent, a one-time mayor of Quebec City and a provincial premier from 1900 to 1905. He was chairman of the *National Transcontinental Railway* from 1906 through 1911. Look to the north for the building with the tall narrow tower. This heritage building is both the town hall and the fire hall; the tower is used for spotting fir s and drying the hoses. At mileage **118.9**, you arrive at Parent's basic white brick station. For good views of the area, visitors should climb Radar Mountain, named after a Pinetree Line radar base that served from 1954 through 1963. It is 5 miles (8 kilometres) out of town. From the lookout point on top of the mountain, you can see over 12 miles (20 kilometres) on a clear day. In the winter, Parent, 2006 population 251, is also an important part of the region's snowmobile circuit, and Kruger Inc. maintains a large FSC-certified sawmill in the community. As you leave the town, you can see a large wood-chip loading facility at mileage **120**. A microwave tower can be seen in the distance at mileage **138**. The cabin at mileage **148** looks out-of-place in the new growth; it was saved from a 1995 fire after being covered with fire retardant foam. At mileage **152.5** the train crosses Lake Oskelaneo. Look to the north, on the west side of the lake, to see the Oskelaneo Outfitters camp. The Clova station at mileage **160.7** has long been the jumping-off point for many people who travel to this remote region to try their luck at fishing its many waterways. At mileage **165** the train leaves the St. Maurice region and enters the Abitibi-Temiscamingue region. Although not readily apparent, you have reached the highest elevation of your trip. Until this point, all the rivers crossed by the train flowed south to the St. Lawrence; now, the waters flow north to Hudson Bay. The Abitibi-Temiscamingue region is rich with minerals; it is quite common to see freight trains full of copper and zinc destined for Montreal and beyond. At Monet, mileage **175.2** is another popular outfitter. To supplement facilities at the nearby Duplessis Lodge, a former *National Transcontinental Railway* crew shack is now used for accommodations, and can be

seen to the south. At mileage **186** the route cuts through the middle of Serpent Lake.

Mileages 191–257: Here the forest is thick with fir trees; watch for bears that live in this northern wilderness. At mileage **196** you get a good view over the trees while crossing a trestle. The siding at Dix is reached at mileage **201.1**. The train crosses the winding Assup River at mileage **216**; don't worry if you miss it, because you see it at again at mileage **219** and, for the last time, from a high bridge at mileage **224**. Keep your camera ready at mileage **233** for the swift-flowing Megiscane River. Because of the stunted-growth fir trees at mileage **235**, mountains can be seen to the north. These trees and marshes continue along the route, as does a Megiscane feeder river that is crossed at mileage **243**. The train crosses the Megiscane once again at mileage **253**. The train enters Senneterre, 2011 population 2,953, after crossing the Bell River at mileage **256** and then passes under Highway 113 before coming to a stop at the two-storey brick station.

This entrance to the Abitibi region is named after Lieutenant de Senneterre who fell in the last French victory of the Seven Years War in Quebec at the Battle of Sainte-Foy (Quebec City) in April 1760. The town was created with the arrival of the railway. The town was home to a Pinetree Line radar base beginning in 1954 and was home to a RCAF base until 1988 when a Search and Rescue centre was relocated. Today the main economy is based on the FSC-certified Resolute Forest Products lumber mill and the forest industry, a link that is celebrated every July with the "Festival Forestier de Senneterre".

After a long day's journey, we recommend the Motel Senabi located on 7th Avenue. Reservations can be made at: 866 737-2327. On the web at *www.motelsenabi.com* or emailing them at: *motel.senabi@sympatico.ca*

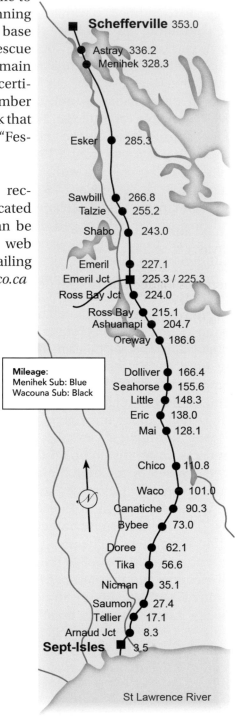

Schefferville 353.0

Astray 336.2
Menihek 328.3

Esker 285.3

Sawbill 266.8
Talzie 255.2

Shabo 243.0

Emeril 227.1
Emeril Jct 225.3 / 225.3
Ross Bay Jct 224.0

Ross Bay 215.1
Ashuanapi 204.7

Oreway 186.6

Mileage:
Menihek Sub: Blue
Wacouna Sub: Black

Dolliver 166.4
Seahorse 155.6
Little 148.3
Eric 138.0
Mai 128.1

Chico 110.8

Waco 101.0

Canatiche 90.3
Bybee 73.0

Doree 62.1
Tika 56.6

Nicman 35.1

Saumon 27.4
Tellier 17.1
Arnaud Jct 8.3
Sept-Isles 3.5

St Lawrence River

LABRADOR ROUTE

A journey over the *Quebec North Shore & Labrador Railway* and *Tshiuetin Rail* beyond Emeril Junction on board the *Tshiuetin Rail* passenger train takes travellers through a land of impressive beauty and vast mineral resources. The 359-mile (578-kilometre) railway, completed in 1954, was built to transport iron ore from the vast reserves in the north to ocean-going vessels at Sept-Isles to the south, where it is loaded onto ships and taken away for processing.

Tshiuetin Rail began operations in 2005 as the first-ever Canadian railway owned and operated by First Nations peoples. We recommend you book your tickets well in advance by contacting *Tshiuetin Rail Transportation Inc.* 1005, Boul Laure, suite 305 C, Sept-Iles QC, Canada G4R 4S6; call 866 962-0988, by Email: *billetterie@tshiuetin.ca* or visit *www.tshiuetin.net* Trains leave for the thirteen-hour journey from Sept-Isles at 8.00 am Monday and Thursday, and return from Schefferville on Tuesday and Friday. To learn more about iron ore mining in the area, visit the Iron Ore Company website at: *www.ironore.ca*

Route Highlights
Sept-Isles to Emeril Junction
Wacouna Subdivision
Mileages 3.5–69: Arrive at the Sept-Isles station early and give yourself a chance to examine the two steam locomotives, No. 48 and No. 702. Sept-Isles had a population of 25,686 in 2011 and is the site of vast iron ore transshipment facilities. At mileage **8.3**, Arnaud Junction, the railway connects with the 21-mile (33.8-kilometre) Arnaud Railway that accesses another major ore-loading facility at Pointe Noire. At mileage **10**, where a receding glacier left the rock formations found here. At mileage **11.5** the train enters a 2,197-foot (667-metre) long tunnel. Keep your camera ready—once clear of the tunnel you cross a 900-foot (275-metre) long bridge high above the Moisie River. For the next 15

Southbound train on arrival in Sept Isles. *John Whittingham photo*

miles the route offers fantastic views as it snakes along the cliffs beside the river. The junction of the Moisie and Nipisso rivers (mileage **28**) is popular with sport fishermen in the summer months. Many people leave the train here to try their luck in the region's rivers, which are full of salmon. Watch between mileages **46** and **54** for waterfalls along the route. The breathtaking scenery continues as the train climbs the region's mountains. The winding route provides many good opportunities to photograph your entire train. The train climbs high above the Wacouno River, offering the best view to the west at mileage **64**. The train enters another tunnel at mileage **65**—now would be the time for those who are squeamish about heights to close their blinds! As the train emerges from the 1,000-foot (305-metre) long tunnel, look west to see the stands of black forest spruce, the bluffs,

and a drop of over 700 feet (213 metres) to the river below. Then, at mileage **68.6**, to the west, you see the most spectacular highlight of the route, the 200-foot (61-metre) tall Tonkas Falls.

Mileages 70–224: Watch for the rapids on the Wacouno River between mileages **77** and **85**. The gravel pit passed at mileage **84** supplies the majority of ballast for the route. Soon, the terrain changes from mountains to rolling hills, and from rivers to calm lakes. At mileage **100**, the Wacouno River becomes Wacouno Lake and parallels the tracks for the next 18 miles (30 kilometres). The railway's highest point is at the Quebec/Newfoundland and Labrador border at mileage **148.8**. Prior to this point, all the water routes the train had passed flowed toward the St. Lawrence; now they flow north to the Labrador Sea. At South Ross Bay Jct., mileage **224.0**, freight connections are made to the Wabush and Carol Lake mining areas. At Emeril Junction (mileage **225.3**) the engine crew changes to one provided by the *Tshiuetin Rail* replacing the *QNS&L* crew. Passengers holding advance arrangements may make the thirty-mile highway trip into Labrador City and Wabush at the heart of the iron mining district.

Route Highlights
Emeril Junction to Schefferville
Menihek Subdivision

Mileages 225–357: The landscape of lakes and rolling hills continues, but the trees are now stunted because of the short growing season. The tracks now travel atop muskeg. This area is home to thousands of caribou. At mileage **329.5** the route crosses the impressive Menihek Dam on a 781-foot (256.2-metre) structure. Schefferville can be clearly seen on the opposite shore of Knob Lake, at mileage **354**. Schefferville, 2011 population 213, is reached at mileage **357.6**. Until the Iron Ore Company of Canada mines were closed in 1982, Schefferville had been a thriving centre and a radar station on the Mid-Canada Line.

Tshiuetin Rail passenger cars proudly bear distinctive First Nations graphics. *John Whittingham photo*

CORRIDOR ROUTE

The current rail route between Montreal and Toronto is almost the same as when the first track was laid in 1855. Previously, travellers made the journey by steamboat or stagecoach. Once able to take the trip by rail, they rode basic wooden coaches pulled by steam locomotives. Now we have comfortable coaches with at-your-seat service on trains pulled by powerful high-speed diesel locomotives. How would travellers from then compare their all-day rail journey to today's four hours and forty minutes? Passengers have changed a great deal as well. Today's travellers are busy with laptop computers or cellular phones while enjoying some of the same views as the early railway passengers.

For rail travellers arriving in Montreal, 2011 population 3,824,221, the Queen Elizabeth Hotel, connected to Central Station, is located at 900 Rene Levesque Blvd. West, and is managed by Fairmont Hotels. Reservations can be made at: 866 540-4483. Web: *www.fairmont.com*. Montreal, with its numerous attractions and sights, has something for everyone. Want to learn more about Canada's rail heritage? Visit the Exporail project at the Canadian Railway Museum, a 20-minute ride

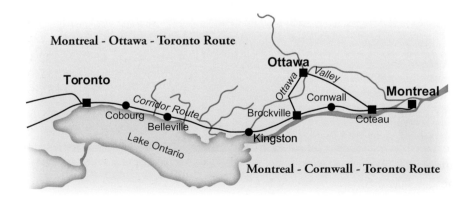

1

2

3

1: *VIA* train skirts the Lachine Canal enroute from Montreal's Central Station.
2: Now-disused overhead structure formerly carried power wires for electric locomotives that replaced steam engines for the in-town route segment into Montreal's Central Station. *Both photos Michel Lortie*
3: Ottawa to Toronto train crosses the Napanee River in Napanee, Ontario. *Don McQueen photo*

from downtown on the south shore of the St. Lawrence in Delson/St-Constant. Phone: 450 638-2410. Web: *www.exporail. org*. Before you visit Montreal or anywhere in Quebec, we suggest you contact Tourisme Québec, PO Box 979, Montreal, QC, H3C 2W3. Phone: 877 266-5687. Web: *www.bonjourquebec.com* Email: *info@bonjourquebec.com*

Route Highlights
Montreal to Dorval
Montreal Subdivision

Mileages 1.2–11.8: Central Station is located in the middle of Montreal's downtown. The 47 storey skyscraper at 1250 Rene-Levesque formerly known as the IBM-Marathon Tower when

opened in 1992 can be seen to the west of the station. Also visible is Windsor Station of the *Canadian Pacific Railway,* designed by New Yorker Bruce Price and opened in February 1889. Allow time for a visit to the station's concourse as well as to the Mary Queen of the World Cathedral directly opposite the western entrance to the station. Leaving the station, the tracks run under Place Bonaventure north-south for a short distance, paralleling the Bonaventure Highway to the east. Once the route turns to the west, look north for the historic Windsor Station, identified by its stone construction and tower. Behind it, atop the former station platforms, sits the Bell Centre, home of the Montreal Canadiens hockey team. The route then crosses the Lachine Canal for the first time. The tracks that turn east at mileage **1.2** are the route of *VIA's Ocean* (detailed on page 16). Your train travels through Pointe St. Charles, an early suburb that was once home to many railway employees who worked in the large railway shops visible to the south. The train slips past busy highways at mileage **5** and, while moving under the confusing network of freeway exits, passes through a man-made tunnel at mileage **6**. The entrance to *CN*'s Taschereau yard is passed at mileage **8.7**. This is where

can transfer to a shuttle that takes them to Montreal's busiest airport (seen to the north). Over the next 10 miles, the train parallels the *Canadian Pacific Railway*, with its numerous commuter stations and trains operated by the *Metropolitan Transportation Agency*. To the south at mileage **20** sits the Neil MacDonald Campus, McGill University's experimental farm. The tracks leave the island of Montreal at mileage **21.4**, crossing the

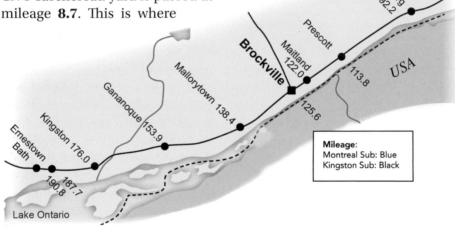

Mileage:
Montreal Sub: Blue
Kingston Sub: Black

VIA's northern Quebec trains turn north (page 41 and 47).

Route Highlights
Dorval to Toronto
Kingston Subdivision

Mileages 10.8–124: The train travels through Montreal's western suburbs, reaching Dorval at mileage **10.8**. Here, passengers

Ottawa River over a 1,370-foot (417-metre) long bridge. Many Canadian explorers, such as Samuel de Champlain, Radisson, La Verendrye, and David Thompson, are associated with the early river-route following the Ottawa River. At mileage **22** the route reaches Ile Perrot before crossing the river again at mileage **23.9**. Once across, the scenery changes to farmers' fields. Coteau, at mileage **38.0**, is where the Alexandria Subdivision, the route to Ottawa, turns to the north. Rivière Beaudette is the last town in Quebec the early 1800s. Iroquois (mileage **100.0**) also grew with people who were displaced by the Seaway.

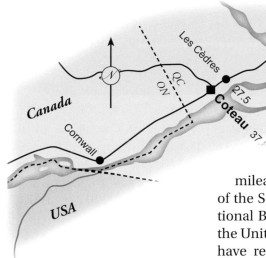

before you cross the border with Ontario at mileage **45**. Once into Ontario, the town names begin to reflect the British heritage of their earliest settlers. At mileage **65.6** the train enters a 45-mile (75-kilometre) route laid down in the 1950s as a result of the creation of the St. Lawrence Seaway. The area traversed by the original track was flooded so ocean-going vessels could reach the Great Lakes. Cornwall, an industrial city of 46,430 residents is reached at mileage **68.0**. Morrisburg (mileage **92.2**) is home to the Upper Canada Village, created by historians who relocated and preserved buildings from the area flooded by the construction of the Seaway. Today they tell the story of how the region was settled in

Look to the south at mileage **111** to catch a glimpse of the Seaway and of the International Bridge linking Canada and the United States. You can tell you have rejoined the original route at mileage **113.8**, when you pass the historic Prescott station, built in the 1850s. Look to the south at mileage **116.5** to see The Blue Church of 1845 and a cemetery, which is the final resting place of Barbara Heck, who established Methodism in North America.

Mileages 125–199: Just before reaching Brockville, 2011 population 21,870, at mileage **125.6**, the rail route to Ottawa turns north. The Brockville station mural has three panels depicting the arrival of the P.T. Barnum Circus in 1877; the 1951 visit of Princess Elizabeth and the Duke of Edinburgh; and the preserved Brockville railway tunnel. Departing the station you can look up and down Perth Street. Jon's Restaurant, seen to

Thousand Islands Railway No. 500, "The Susan Push," on display in Gananoque, Ontario.

the south, is a favourite spot of local rail enthusiasts. The decor features photos of the area's rail history as well as offering a great view of the passing trains. The rock cut at mileage **128** signals the beginning of a changing landscape; more curved rock cuts are featured at mileages **131** and **132** and then at **142** and **143**. At mileage **134** the small cemetery for Yonge's Mills can be seen on both sides of the tracks. Gananoque has long been a popular starting point for tourists to visit the Thousand Islands, a stretch of the St. Lawrence River noted for its numerous islands. Gananoque Junction Station at mileage **153.9** was part of the *Thousand Islands Railway*, completed in 1884. From here, the *CNR*'s shortest railway (4.7 miles/7.6 kilometres) followed the Gananoque River to the shores of the St. Lawrence. Station stops included a cemetery (fortunately, tickets for passengers were round-trip!) and a cheese factory, before

reaching the St. Lawrence. The last of the route was removed in 1997; today it is a nature walk. The railway is not forgotten, however. *Thousand Islands Railway* locomotive No. 500, built in 1931, and known as the "Susan Push," is proudly displayed in Sculpture Park, where the Gananoque River is crossed by Highway 2.

Your train crosses the Gananoque River at mileage **155**. Watch on both sides at mileage **169.4** for the crossing of the Rideau Canal; directly below are the Kingston Mills

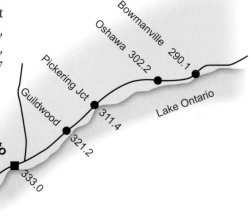

locks. In total, there are 49 locks along this 125-mile (202-kilometre) water route to Ottawa. It was built after the war of 1812 by the Royal Corps of Engineers (under the supervision of Lt. Colonel John By) as a strategic and secure way to move troops and supplies away from the American border. At mileage **172**, as you approach Kingston look south to see the Cataraqui River as well as a quarry that supplied some of the limestone that helped to build some of this city's finest buildings. You can see the limestone up close at mileage **173** as the train passes through a rock cut. Kingston's modern station (mileage **176.1**) is the fourth to serve this community of 123,363, in 2011, (the other three still survive to this day). *Grand Trunk* built both an outer and inner station, and the *Kingston & Pembroke Railway* built a station near the warerfront. Today this station is a tourist information centre, with *Canadian Pacific* steam locomotive 1095 on display

outside. This locomotive was built by Kingston's Canadian Locomotive Company, which constructed over 3,000 locomotives between 1850 and 1969. Another local historic site is Bellevue House, home of Canada's first Prime Minister, Sir John A. Macdonald. As well, Kingston houses eight correctional facilities; if you look to the south at mileage **177**, you'll see the red roof of the Collins Bay prison facility.

At mileage **179.8** the train curves along Collins Bay, with its popular marina. This is your first glimpse of Lake Ontario, with good views continuing towards Amherst Island to the south and the North Channel that separates it from the mainland. The old stone station at Ernestown sits quietly to the north of the tracks at mileage **187.7**. The route turns slightly inland, away from the lake, travelling through picturesque fields and rolling hills. Keep your camera ready and pointed to the north at mileage

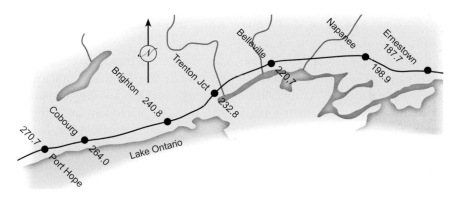

192 where there are two large barns with concrete grain silos. The Napanee River is crossed at mileage **198.5** on a stone viaduct built in 1856. Look to the west to see great views of Napanee and of a gristmill built by the government for loyalists who fled the American Revolution. Napanee features another historic station at mileage **198.9**.

Mileages 200–333: The rolling countryside continues with tree-lined fields and farms. To the north at mileage **209** you can see the bleachers for the Shannonville Motorsport Park. The train crosses the Salmon River at mileage **212.1**, and then passes under the *Canadian Pacific Railway* tracks at mileage **214**. The Belleville Community Airfield can be seen south of the old stone farmhouse at mileage **217**. Soon, at mileage **220**, the train arrives at Belleville's two-storey historic station which has recently been enhanced with a covered walkway over the main lines. The small building east of the station houses the Belleville Model Railroad Club. A popular time to visit Belleville, 2011 population 49,454, is during the annual Waterfront Festival held here each July on the shores of the Bay of Quinte. Passengers from the train get a good view of downtown Belleville at mileage **221** as the train crosses the Moira River. The community's water tower and the steeple of St. Paul's Church dominate the skyline.

Mileage 232.2 finds the train crossing the Trent River. Some trains pause at Trenton Jct. which serves the municipality of Quinte West, 2011 population 43, 086 and home to the RCAF's transport operation. The locks seen on the west side of the river are from the 240-mile (386-kilometre) Trent-Severn Canal, which connects the city of Trenton with Georgian Bay on Lake Huron. At mileage **232.8** you see a different set of tracks passing under the route of your train. This is the original route of the *Central Ontario Railway*, built in 1879. Today this small portion of track, to a grain elevator to the north, is all that remains of this line. The *Canadian Pacific Railway* tracks to the south are then paralleled starting at mileage **234**. Although the Brighton station at mileage **240.8** is no longer used by the railway, it lives on as "Memory Junction", a private museum with a few pieces of rolling stock and former *Canadian National Railways* steam locomotive 2534, built in Montreal in 1906. At mileage **260**, forests and orchards give way to good views of Lake Ontario to the south. Cobourg, 2011 population 18,519, at mileage **264.0** is home to another fine old station. The mural on the building to the south honours hometown heroine Marie Dressler, an actress in the days of silent movies. The

VIA train travelling between Montreal and Toronto at Brockville station. *Bill Linley photo*

CP Toronto-Montreal mainline passes overhead once again at mileage **265.3**. At mileage **270.3** Port Hope, was home to 16,214 people in 2011, among them renowned conservationist and author, Farley Mowat. The Ganaraska River is crossed on a curved bridge 1,232-foot (375-metres) long. After crossing the bridge, your train reaches Port Hope's restored stone station. At mileage **271** the route rises high above the lake, with great views to the south. Golfers on the course to the north have to be careful their ball does not end up in Ontario's largest water trap. Watch to the south at mileage **274.5** for a nice view of a tree-filled valley, with Lake Ontario providing the backdrop. The farms and pastures continue along the route. At mileage **288** we hope the train does not disturb the lawn bowlers to the north. The train enters Oshawa, 2011 population 149,607, at mileage **297**. The McLaughlin family earned its fortune in this city through the McLaughlin Carriage Company, established in the 1800s. They wisely foresaw the future, switching to the manufacture of motor vehi-

cles. In 1918 their enterprise became General Motors of Canada. Today GM has its Canadian head office in Oshawa. The train passes the GM plant to the south at mileage **302.2**. On the opposite side of the tracks is the Oshawa station. This is also the eastern terminal for Toronto's *GO Transit* commuter trains. At Pickering Junction, mileage **311.4**, *CN*'s York Subdivision diverges to the northwest allowing their freight trains to bypass downtown Toronto. The 3,100 MW Pickering nuclear power station, on the shore of Lake Ontario, rises in the distance at mileage **313**. The train crosses the Rouge River at mileage **316.1** and skirts the shore as it continues through an urban setting. Your train may stop at the suburban Guildwood station at mileage **321.2** near Kingston Road and Eglinton Avenue. From the GO station in Scarborough (mileage **325.2**), watch for your first glimpses of Toronto's impressive CN Tower. Evidence of this sprawling city is everywhere as you pass mileage **330** with the Gerrard Square Mall to the south and a Toronto Transit Commission subway system maintenance centre to the north. The tracks cross the Don River at mileage **331**. Look south to see GO Transit's commuter-train-staging facility before you navigate the trackage into Toronto's Union Station. Watch to the southwest for the CN Tower and Rogers Centre, formerly "Skydome". Before entering the station, you may catch a glimpse of Toronto's famous Yonge Street to the north. You reach the train-shed for Toronto's Union Station at mileage **333.8**.

For rail travellers to and from Toronto, the Fairmont Royal York is the most convenient lodging option. Located across the street from Union Station at 100 Front Street West, rail travellers can walk across Front Street or take the tunnel connecting the station to the hotel. Built by *Canadian Pacific Railway* in 1929, this classic railway hotel has hosted royalty, heads of state, celebrities, and travellers from around the world. Reservations can be made at: 800 441-1414. Web: *www.fairmont.com*

Toronto, Canada's largest city, with a metro population of 5,583,064, in 2011, has an amazing array of attractions. Close to the station, at the corner of Front and Yonge streets, sits the restored Bank of Montreal building housing the Hockey Hall of Fame. The entrance is found on the lower level of BCE Place next door. Young and old will enjoy the hockey memorabilia and the interactive events. Be sure to visit the great hall to see hockey's famous trophies including the Stanley Cup. Web: *www.hhof.com*. Further north, the Royal Ontario Museum features one of Canada's largest collection of artifacts and it is located at 100 Queens Park (Avenue Road at Bloor Street). Toronto's own castle, Casa Loma (1 Austin Terrace) was the vision of millionaire Sir Henry Pellat; it is open to all today. To learn more about the area before Toronto became Canada's largest city, visit Fort York and experience the defense of the Fort in 1812. Of course, you can see all of this from the 1,815-foot (553-metre) CN Tower. Visitors to the one of the world's tallest free-standing structures can enjoy the view from the Observation Level, and those who want to go even higher can travel another 100 metres to the Skypod Level. When you are done looking at the distant horizon, look straight down to see trains departing Toronto's Union Station.

Before you visit Toronto, or anywhere in Ontario, we suggest you contact the Ontario Travel Information Centre, Eaton Centre, Level 1, PO Box 104, 220 Yonge Street, Toronto, ON, M5B 2H1. Call: 800 668-2746. Web: *www.ontariotravel.net*

OTTAWA VALLEY

At Moose Creek Ontario on the Ottawa Valley line. *Bill Linley photo*

In 1832, settlers in the Ottawa Valley welcomed the construction of the Rideau Canal as a sign of progress. The new community was named Bytown after Lieutenant Colonel John By, who oversaw the work. Soon log booms replaced the Ottawa River's canoes as the forestry industry thrived. As the community's importance grew, its name was changed to Ottawa, after the local Outaouac First Nation. In 1857, Queen Victoria chose the settlement as the country's capital.

The route of *VIA*'s *Corridor* services from Montreal to Coteau is covered in the Montreal to Toronto route on page 56. From Coteau, the route turns northwest to travel to the nation's capital.

Route Highlights
Coteau to Ottawa
Alexandria Subdivision

Mileages 0–76: At mileage **0**, the route turns northward, away from the Kingston Subdivision. The train crosses the east-west rail route of *Canadian Pacific*'s rail line between Montreal and Toronto at De Beaujeu, mileage **6.1**. Mileage **13** marks the Quebec-Ontario border. Alexandria, at mileage **23.0**, was originally known as Priest's Mills after Father Alexander Macdonell, who built the first grist

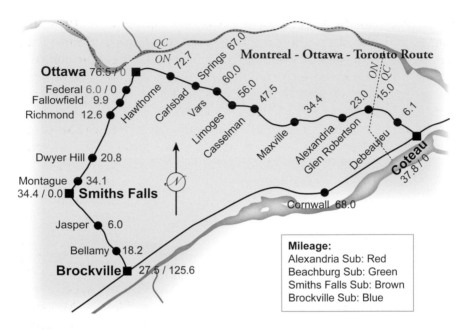

Montreal - Ottawa - Toronto Route

QC / ON

Ottawa 76.5 / 0

Federal 6.0 / 0
Fallowfield 9.9
Richmond 12.6

Hawthorne 72.7
Carlsbad 67.0
Springs 60.0
Vars 56.0
Limoges 47.5
Casselman
Maxville 34.4
Alexandria 23.0
Glen Robertson
Debeaujeu 15.0
Coteau 37.8 / 0
6.1

ON / QC

Dwyer Hill 20.8

Montague 34.1
34.4 / 0.0 Smiths Falls

Jasper 6.0

Bellamy 18.2

Brockville 27.5 / 125.6

Cornwall 68.0

Mileage:
Alexandria Sub: Red
Beachburg Sub: Green
Smiths Falls Sub: Brown
Brockville Sub: Blue

---

mill in the area and later became the first Roman Catholic bishop of Kingston, Upper Canada. The town of 3,209 people (in 2011) was incorporated in 1883, and the name was changed to honour the community's founder. South of the community's restored brick station is the Atlantic Hotel.

After Alexandria, the route travels through a forested area, then reaches Maxville, home to the Glengarry Highland Games each August, at mileage **34.4**. The terrain becomes dotted with scenic farms. Keep your camera ready at mileage **40** for a photo of the stone church located at Moose Creek. At mileage **47.5** the town of Casselman, 2011 population 3,642, can be seen as the route cuts across Main Street

and then crosses the wide South Nation River. Your train continues on *VIA*-owned rails through the Ottawa suburbs before reaching the Ottawa Station at mileage **76.5**.

Ottawa's modern station is located in the southeast corner of the city. The *OCTranspo*'s transitway has a bus stop directly in front of the station; from here you can make a connection to downtown Ottawa. Downtown, across from the former Union Station you find the stately Chateau Laurier, located at 1 Rideau Street. Built by the *Grand Trunk Railway* and operated today by Fairmont Hotels, the hotel was the vision of *Grand Trunk*'s president, Charles Melville Hays. Sadly, he perished on the ill-fated *RMS Titanic* (which also carried to the bottom of the Atlantic some furniture destined for the hotel) and never saw its official opening in June 1912. Reservations can be made at: 800 540-4410. Web: *www.fairmont.com.* There is no shortage of attractions in Ottawa/Hull. You can find everything from the Canada Science and Technology Museum to the historic Canadian parliament buildings. If you are planning a visit we suggest you contact Ottawa Tourism, Suite 1800, 130 Albert St., Ottawa, ON, K1P 5G4. Call: 800 363-4465. Web: *www.ottawatourism.ca* Email: *info@ottawatourism.ca*

Route Highlights
Ottawa to Smiths Falls East Beachburg and Smiths Falls Subdivisions

Near mileage **3** look to the north to see the Ottawa skyline. The Rideau River is crossed at mileage **5.8**. Federal and the Smiths Falls Subdivision are reached at mileage **6.0**.

Mileages 0–34: At mileage **3.5** your train will stop at Fallowfield, conveniently located in the western suburbs of Ottawa. The Jock River can be seen to the west near mileage **12** as you approach Richmond. The train then travels through an isolated area of farms, thick forests, and swamps. Thus far, the line you are travelling on was built by the *Canadian Northern Railway* in 1913. Just beyond the station at Smiths Falls, at mileage **34.4** the route connects with the *Canadian Pacific* east-west line and heads through this town of 8,978 in 2011. Nearby is the Smiths Falls Railway Museum, which includes a restored *Canadian Northern* station.

Smiths Falls to Brockville Brockville Subdivision

Mileages 0–27: Before crossing the Rideau Canal and River on *CP* rails, look to the west to see the Heritage House Museum. At mileage **6.7** the train passes through the town of Jasper. At Brockville, mileage **27.5**, (2011 population 23,354), your train will connect with the *CN's* Kingston subdivision. See page 58 to follow the route to Toronto. The *Brockville & Ottawa Railway* originally continued south to the St. Lawrence River, through Canada's first railway tunnel, which opened in 1860. Visitors to Brockville's waterfront can view the tunnel's South Portal and preserved 1954 *CPR* caboose 437464.

TORONTO-LONDON-WINDSOR ROUTE

Grand River viaduct at Paris Ontario on the Toronto-London-Windsor line. *Don McQueen photo*

Your journey through Southwestern Ontario features everything from large cities to peaceful farms. The train route visits attractive villages and towns full of charm and history, featuring some of the country's oldest and most unique railway stations.

In the 1800s, the *Great Western Railway* foresaw wealth in the region, and its supporters envisioned a railway providing endless profits. The formula was simple: build a land route for the United States, between Niagara and Windsor. This would provide a shorter, more direct route on the north side of Lake Erie for rail traffic between the American Midwest and New York state. Sod was symbolically turned on the new railway in London, Ontario, on October 23rd 1849, but construction did not begin until 1851. The route between Hamilton and London opened for traffic in the closing months of 1853, and the southern portion between Windsor and Chatham opened shortly thereafter. The last link between Chatham and London was completed in 1854. With the mainline completed, the *Hamilton & Toronto Railway* was formed by the *Great Western Railway* to connect the east-west line to Toronto. The line flourished after its

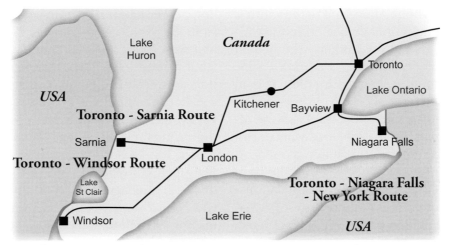

completion in 1855. The company achieved many Canadian railway firsts, including: the first railway mail car; the first Canadian-built sleeping cars; and the first Canadian-built locomotive with a steel boiler.

Competition between the *Great Western Railway* and the *Grand Trunk Railway* in the early 1880s was fierce. This came to an end in 1882 when the *Grand Trunk Railway* successfully took over the *Great Western* and amalgamated the line into its own system. The *Grand Trunk* later became a large part of the *Canadian National Railways* system. Today the train to Windsor travels the original route of the *Great Western*. Many Americans travel east from Detroit to visit Canada, spending the weekend in Toronto to shop and possibly take in a show. Canadians also travel the line to visit friends and family in southwestern Ontario, or continue on to destinations in the United States.

Route Highlights
Toronto to Bayview
Oakville Subdivision

Mileages 0–36: Departing Toronto's Union Station trainshed, you see the track-side of the Metro Toronto Convention Centre to the north. Look south and straight up to see Toronto's most distinctive attraction, the CN Tower. Your train then passes under the John Street pedestrian walkway connecting downtown Toronto with the CN Tower and Rogers Centre, a stadium that features a retractable roof. While passing under the bridge, notice the John Street tower which had to lose its roof for the walkway's construction. In this area, the tracks are below the city level while apartments and condominiums dominate the landscape between here and the harbour. Above and to the south is a memorial dedicated to the Chinese railway workers who helped to construct the *Canadian Pacific Railway*. Erected in 1989, it is in the form of bridge girders. On the north side of the tracks sit the offices of *The Globe and Mail*, one of Canada's national newspapers. At mileage **2**, to the south, the train passes by the Canadian National Exhibition grounds, site of Canada's largest fair held every August. Lake Ontario's Humber Bay can be seen to the south at mileage **3**. To the north, overlooking the lake are more of Toronto's large condominium and apartment blocks. The Humber River is crossed at mileage **5**.

The green and white bi-level *GO* commuter trains that service the Greater Toronto Area receive their maintenance at Mimico, mileage **6.7**. Established in 1967, *GO Transit*'s trains and buses now carry close to 40 mil-

lion people a year. The train crosses Etobicoke Creek at mileage **9.8** just west of the Long Branch GO station, passes the Port Credit station at mileage **12.8**, and crosses the Port Credit River at mileage **13.2**. Mileage **17** brings you past the Windsor Salt plant to the south. The Ford Canada automotive plant complex is seen to the north at mileage **19.3**. *VIA* and *GO Transit* share the modern station at Oakville, 2011 population 182,520, (mileage **21.4**). After this stop the train crosses a 490-foot (149.3-metre) long bridge high above Sixteen Mile Creek. Most *VIA* trains will stop at Aldershot, mileage **34.6**. The pedestrian bridge above the tracks at Bayview (mileage **36.9**) is a popular spot with local rail enthusiasts. Travellers get an excellent view of the Burlington Bay to the south while the

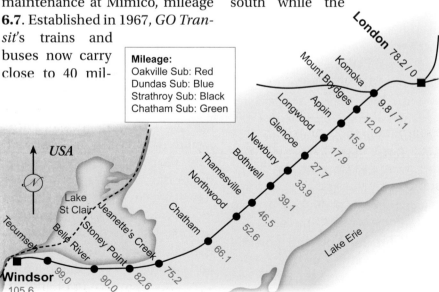

Mileage:
Oakville Sub: Red
Dundas Sub: Blue
Strathroy Sub: Black
Chatham Sub: Green

train negotiates Bayview Junction. If you are travelling to Niagara Falls, the route highlights continue on page 78.

Route Highlights
Bayview to London
Dundas Subdivision

Mileages 0–37: For the first two miles, the train continues to travel through the lush forests of

orange marks at the shoulders of their wings.

Shortly, the train enters Brantford and stops at the city's unique station (mileage **23.0**). Built by the *Grand Trunk* in 1904, it is different from other stations on the route with its four-storey tower, blue granite, and dark brick construc-

Toronto 0.0

Long Branch 9.6
Port Credit 12.8
Clarkson 16.0
Oakville 21.4
Burlington 31.0
Aldershot 35.1
Bayview 36.9 / 0

Lake Ontario

Woodstock
Ingersoll 59.0
Dorchester 69.5
49.6
Princeton 37.0
Paris 30.0
Brantford 23.0
Copetown 10.0

tion.

The red tiles on the roof each weigh seven pounds. Brantford, 2011 population 93,650, is named after renowned native leader Joseph Brant, who sided with the British during the American Revolutionary War. After the war he led the Six Nations band, displaced from what is now New York State, to settle in the area. One of the most popular attractions in this well-kept city is the Bell Homestead National Historic Site. Here visitors can learn more about Alexander Graham Bell and his famous first telephone call in 1874. Get your camera ready for

the Royal Botanical Gardens up Dundas Hill.

By mileage **3** the train has climbed to the top of the Niagara Escarpment. To the south you get a good view of Hamilton and the surrounding area. With the suburban setting left behind, the scenery changes to rolling hills and tree-lined farms. Watch for fox, deer, hawks, and redwing blackbirds. These small birds, the size of sparrows, are black with the exception of the bright reddish-

TORONTO-SARNIA ROUTE

Crossing Trout Creek near St. Marys on the Toronto-Sarnia route. *Don McQueen photo*

Affectionately referred to by some railway employees as the "Back Route," the train to Sarnia travels on a line constructed north of the first line in southwestern Ontario. It was built by the *Grand Trunk Railway* in

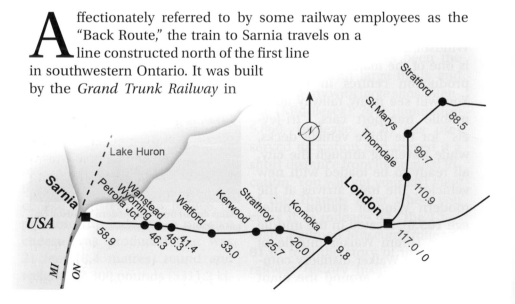

the 1850s to compete with the *Great Western Railway*. It reached London and a connection with the *Great Western* in 1858.

Route Highlights
Toronto to Halwest
Weston Subdivision

Mileages 0–17: Departing Toronto's Union Station train shed, look south and straight up to see Toronto's most distinctive attraction, and the tallest structure in the Western Hemisphere, the CN Tower that opened on June 26th 1976. Your train will then pass

er at mileage **9.6**, you can see the Weston Golf Club to the south. At mileage **13**, you can see a line of trees marking Woodbine Racetrack to the north. After this, the Lester B. Pearson International airport can be seen to the south. The route continues through suburbs and industrial areas before reaching Halwest at mileage **16.8**.

Route Highlights
Halwest to Silver
Halton Subdivision

Mileages 11–24: The Weston

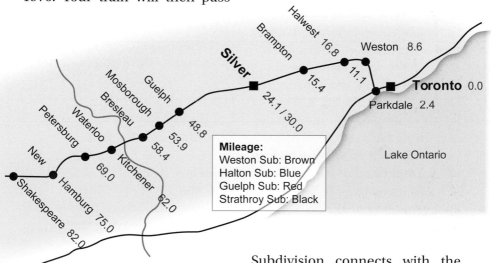

Mileage:
Weston Sub: Brown
Halton Sub: Blue
Guelph Sub: Red
Strathroy Sub: Black

under the John Street pedestrian walkway connecting downtown Toronto with the CN Tower and Rogers Centre (formerly the "SkyDome"). At mileage **6** you cross Black Creek, then pass Weston Station at mileage **8.6**. While crossing the Humber Riv-

Subdivision connects with the Halton Subdivision at mileage **11.1**. At one time, horse-drawn carriages would meet the train at Brampton station (mileage **15.4**). Both the 1857 viaduct that crosses the Credit River (mileage **22.5**) and the Georgetown station (mileage **23.5**) were built with limestone from the area. At

Silver (mileage **24.1**) the Halton Subdivision turns southward, but your passenger train continues onto the Guelph Subdivision of the Goderich-Exeter Railway.

Route Highlights
Silver to London Junction
Guelph Subdivision

Mileages 30–119: The mileage on the Goderich-Exeter begins at mileage **30**. Keep your camera ready for mileage **41** when the Credit Valley is crossed over a high bridge at Georgetown. Entering Guelph, 2011 population 121,668, (mileage **48.5**), you cross the Speed River, before arriving at the Guelph Station. Just east of the station, you can view preserved CNR steam locomotive 6167. The Halton County Radial Railway at nearby Milton offers excellent displays and rides on preserved on historic streetcars. Call 519 856-9802. The train crosses the Grand River at mileage **58**. Kitchener, 2011 population 219,153, features another historic station, on the south side of the tracks, at mileage **62**. Nearby Wateroo is the home of the *Waterloo Central Railway* that calls at the St. Jacob's Farmers' Market on its way to the picturesque village of St. Jacobs. (See page 199). The route then varies between forested areas and large fields before crossing the Nith River at mileage **75** at New Hamburg. Stratford, 2011 population 30,886,

famous for its yearly Shakespearean festival, is reached at mileage **88.5**. At mileage 98 stands a *Grand Trunk Western Railway* caboose. The same company that built stations along the Kingston Subdivision (Montreal to Toronto) built St. Marys Junction Station at mileage **98.6**. Its most famous employee, Thomas Edison, worked the night shift here in 1863. The town of St. Marys, 2011 population 6,655, has a water tower proclaiming it to be "A town worth living in." Its quaint brick station, with rounded corners, is reached at mileage **99.7**. The route continues south to connect with the Dundas Subdivision at mileage **119.9** and the mileposts change to **76.7–78.2** as you travel through London.

Route Highlights
London to Sarnia
Strathroy Subdivision

Mileages 0–58: It is only fitting that the river passing through London is called the Thames. You cross it when leaving the city, at mileage **0.4**, and again at mileage **1.4**. At mileage **9.8** the Chatham Subdivision, the route to Windsor, peels away on the south side. Komoka Station has been moved to the nearby Community Centre grounds, and makes up part of the Komoka Railway Museum. Also on display is a 1913 Shay locomotive once used in logging operations in Ontario. The station features a full wall of railway lanterns. At mileage **20,** Strathroy (2011 population 20,978), the train crosses the Sydenham River. As you depart the town, you can see large greenhouses to the north. The train passes by large fields in this rich agricultural region known as the Caradoc Sand Plains deposited from glacial Lake Whittlesey. About 4 miles (6 kilometres) south of Wyoming, mileage **45.3,** visitors can learn more about early oil exploration at the Oil Museum of Canada located in Oil Springs. Sarnia's large brick station, at mileage **59.2,** is located on the south side of the city. Freight trains continuing on to the United States will pass through the St. Clair Tunnel, built to eliminate the two hours it took for train-ferries to cross the St. Clair River. The original tunnel, constructed with cast iron tunnel shields, was completed in 1890. When the old tunnel became out-of-date for modern double-stack freight trains, *CN* built a new larger tunnel using the same technique, though this time it used curved concrete sections. The new tunnel, opened in 1994, parallels the old one. A sample of both the cast iron and concrete curved sections are on display outside the station. If you are planning a visit to Sarnia, 2011 population 72,366, we recommend a visit to the Discovery House Museum (475 Christina Street North) to learn more about the community's history and to see one of Southwestern Ontario's largest model railways. Also, the Centre by the Bay, at 120 Seaway Road, features interesting displays related to the region. It also has an interesting concrete depiction of the entire Great Lakes system, complete with flowing water. Also in nearby Centennial Park is *Canadian National Railway*'s locomotive 6069, a popular backdrop for wedding photos. For more information on visiting Sarnia, we recommend that you contact the Tourism Sarnia-Lambton 556 Christina Street North, Sarnia, ON, N7T 5W6. Call: 800 265-0316. Web: *www.tourismsarnialambton.com*

Toronto-Sarnia passengers view snow-covered fields at Middlesex Centre, Ontario.
Don McQueen photo

TORONTO–NIAGARA FALLS ROUTE

The large station in Niagara Falls greets passengers en route to the famous waterfalls from which the community gets its name.

With Lake Ontario to the North and Lake Erie to the South, the Niagara Peninsula has a very distinctive regional character. Daily rail passenger service year-round to Niagara Falls includes the joint *VIA-Amtrak* service that connects Toronto to New York. *GO Transit* also offers weekend Toronto-Niagara Falls trains during the summer months.

The trip begins at Toronto's Union Station on the Oakville Subdivision, which is detailed on page 69. After Bayview Junction, mileage **36.9** the tracks turn to the south. Look to the east for good views of Burlington Bay and the Skyway Bridge in the distance. To the west is a view of the short-lived Desjardins Canal. The Hamilton station is reached at mileage **39.3**. The Grimsby Subdivision begins in Niagara Falls, so the mileposts count down.

Route Highlights
Hamilton to Niagara Falls
Grimsby Subdivision

Mileages 43–0: With the Hamilton downtown area to the south, the train proceeds through the large ArcelorMittal Dofasco and US Steel Canada industrial works that are the source of Hamilton's nickname, "Steeltown." The city's 2011 population was 519,949. The Niagara Escarpment, a ring of dolomitic limestone atop more easily eroded shale that extends from Watertown, New York around Lake Ontario continuing north to Tobermory, can be clearly seen to the south at mileage **34**, and will be visible for the next few miles. Grimsby, 2011 population 25,325, (mileage **27.4**) once had a large brick station that was destroyed by fire. An earlier wooden station to the south still exists today as a builder's second-hand supply store and curio shop. You are now in the heart of Ontario's "Wine Country," as evidenced by the numerous vineyards passed during the next few miles. The climate is perfect for growing soft fruits—watch for cherry, apple, and peach trees in the fields alongside the track. Rock quarried from the Beamsville area (mileage **23.2**) was used in the supports of the Victoria Jubilee Bridge crossing the St. Lawrence River at Montreal, and under the cast iron shields in the original Sarnia railway tunnel beneath the St. Clair River. Keep watching to the north over Lake Ontario: on a clear day you should be able to see the CN Tower looming over the Toronto skyline. At mileage **17** you cross Twenty-Mile Creek, where you can see the supports of a previous railway bridge. Strangely, you cross Sixteen-Mile Creek at mileage **15**. A good time to visit St. Catharines, 2011 population 131,400, (mileage **11.8**) is in September for the Niagara Grape and Wine Festival. After departing the St. Catharines station, you get a good view of the city centre to the south while crossing the bridge high above the Twelve-Mile Creek. There have been four successive Welland canals provid-

ing passage for ships between Lake Ontario and Lake Erie. The train crosses the first, completed in 1829, at mileage **9.9**. On a drawbridge at mileage **8.5**, the route passes over the present canal, completed in 1932. Look to the south to see the large gates of lock number 4. The 1840s canal is passed at mileage **7.7**. At mileage **2**, you cross yet another waterway, this one carrying water diverted from the Upper Niagara River to the Queenstown Power Plant eight miles away. The train arrives at the Niagara Falls station at mileage **0**. For those passengers continuing on to the USA after departing the station, the train passes high above the Niagara River, which marks the Canada/United States border.

Whether you are visiting the area to see the magnificent falls or to enjoy the variety of activities on Clifton Hill, we recommend the Hampton Inn, north of the Falls at 4357 River Road, a short distance from the train station. Reservations can be made at: 800 465-6027.
Web: *www.niagarafallshamptoninn.com*
Email: *iagrr_hampton@hilton.com*

In 2012, Nick Wallenda walked a wire across world-famous Horseshoe Falls, seen here from Niagara Falls, ON. *Marilynn Linley photo*

THE POLAR BEAR EXPRESS

Many passengers have arrived by car to board the train in Cochrane, Ontario.

T he journey to the edge of the Arctic begins in Cochrane. Once the site of a First Nations meeting place along the overland pack trail to Moosonee, it was chosen by surveyors to be the junction of the *Temiskaming & Northern Ontario Railway* and the east-west National Transcontinental Railway. Named for Frank Cochrane, a federal minister of Railways and Canals in the Borden Government of the day, the town was incorporated in 1910. This community of 5,340 in 2011 continues to be a destination for the adventurous in all seasons. Located close to the station is the Cochrane Railway Museum display headed up by 2-8-0 steam locomotive No. 137. Today you can travel by train from Cochrane to Moosonee year-round on the Cochrane to Moose Factory train, doing a one-day roundtrip. The train features meal service cars all year. In the summer months it is known to feature a full-length dome car and sometimes a railway car specifically designed to transport canoes. As the train departs early in the morning, we suggest arriving the night before and recommend the Cochrane Station Inn. Train and bus operations together with a restaurant are on the main

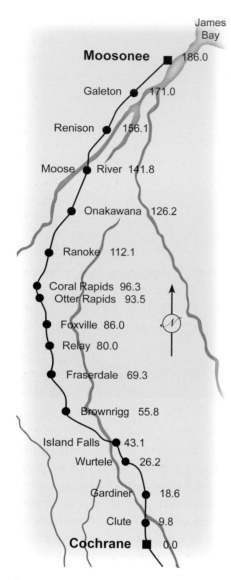

James Bay

Moosonee ■ 186.0

Galeton ● 171.0

Renison ● 156.1

Moose ● River 141.8

Onakawana 126.2

Ranoke 112.1

Coral Rapids 96.3
Otter Rapids 93.5

Foxville 86.0

Relay 80.0

Fraserdale 69.3

Brownrigg 55.8

Island Falls ● 43.1

Wurtele ● 26.2

Gardiner ● 18.6

Clute ● 9.8

Cochrane ■ 0.0

Polar Bear Habitat. This excellent attraction features both an indoor and outdoor viewing area, and provides an opportunity to swim with the bears and visit the heritage village. For more details about visiting the habitat or the community, call: 800 354-9948. Web: *www.town.cochrane.on.ca*

Route Highlights
Cochrane to Moosonee
Island Falls Subdivision

Mileages 0–186: Just beyond Cochrane, daisies crowd the areas along the track. Watch for the white signs that announce the river names along with the elevation. The first is seen at mileage **11** before you cross the Abitibi River. Gardiner Lake sits to the west at mileage **18**. River crossings continue at East Jaw Bone Creek (mileage **27**) and West Jawbone Creek (mileage **29**). The community of Island Falls is reached at mileage **43.1** where the communications tower to the east brings the outside world to Northern Ontario. Next, at mileage **44.4**, the Abitibi River is crossed again. Between mileages **56** and **67** the train travels through an area that was destroyed by forest fire in 1976. Highway 634 (crossed at mileage **69**) as you enter Fraserdale at mileage **69.3** is the last road you will see until Moosonee. The only way north now, other than the train, is by

floor. On the second floor there are 23 comfortable rooms. You can make a reservation by calling 800 265-2356, or Email: *stationinn@ontarionorthland.ca*. Although the train is named for the white bears of the North, you won't see them in Moosonee, so be sure you allow time to visit the plane, canoe, or foot! The tracks curve at mileage **73**, giving you a good view to the east over the trees. The "Keep Out" signs at Relay, mileage **80** mark where there was once a radar base on the Mid-Canada Line that operated for about ten years from the mid-1950s to provide a warning of potential Soviet air strikes. At this point you are also crossing the 50th parallel. From mileages **84** to **89** you travel through another burnt-out area. Look to the east at mileage **85** into the blackened trees for two old rusty boxcars, left from the 1975 Foxville train wreck. At mileage **93**, to the east, you get a good look at the 182 megawatt Otter Rapids power-generating station that opened in September 1961. The terrain begins to change as you enter the Hudson Bay lowlands. Coral Rapids, at mileage **96.3**, features a wye and a well- kept camp on the east side of the tracks. On the west side you can see the concrete foundations where the station and octagonal water tower once stood. The buildings of Moose River (mileage **141.8**) remain today, but the old school house has been transformed into a railway bunkhouse. The Moose River is crossed on the ONR's longest bridge an impressive, 17-span 1,800-foot (548-metre) structure completed in the Depression. Soon after passing Renison at mileage **156.1** you cross the 51st parallel at mileage **159.0**. A series of "upside-down" bridges, reversed so ice can pass underneath, are crossed. Galeton is passed at mileage **171.0**. Between mileages **174** and **180**, the train crosses three rivers, the Kwataboahegan at mileage **174**), Hancock Creek (mileage **176.5**), and Maidmans Creek (mileage **180**). Finally, after crossing Store Creek, you arrive at Moosonee Station, mileage **186.2**.

Started in 1903 when the Revillon brothers set up a trading post here, the community flourished with the coming of the railway in 1932. Visitors will enjoy visiting the displays in the railway baggage, and the numerous shops. At the town dock you can board a freighter canoe taxi (ask the price first) to cross to Moose Factory on the Arctic Tidewaters of the Moose River. This community dates back to 1673 as a Hudson's Bay Company outpost. After passing the modern hospital at the public docks, you can walk along Front Street, past the 1860 St. Thomas Anglican Church (which almost floated away during a 1912 flood—holes were drilled in the floor as a preventative measure) to the Moose Factory Centennial Museum. Here you can examine some of the island's original buildings, including the Hudson's Bay Company staff house, and a blacksmith shop built in 1740. You

Top: *Polar Bear Express* awaiting departure from Moosonee, Ontario.
Bottom: *VIA Rail*'s "Budd Car" (see opposite) is leaving Sudbury for White River, Ontario.
Marilynn Linley photo

can also visit some teepees, where First Nations women prepare bannock, and children sell fossilized rocks, before returning to Moosonee and boarding your train to travel south.

SUDBURY-WHITE RIVER ROUTE

The story of Sudbury has long been influenced by the region's minerals, most notably nickel. The popular tale of how *Canadian Pacific Railway* blacksmith Tom Flanagan discovered the nickel in the area is still told. When the *Canadian Pacific*'s transcontinental line was being built through the area, Tom Flanagan threw a hammer towards an advancing fox. He missed and the hammer struck a rock, exposing nickel and copper. Although he failed to see the value of the shiny rock, prospectors were soon staking claims and the community grew. Today Sudbury is the largest nickel-producing area in the country.

The history of *VIA Rail*'s Sudbury-White River line and its Rail Diesel Car service can be traced back to when *The Canadian* was introduced by *Canadian Pacific* in 1955 as Trains 1 and 2. *The Imperial Limited*, which made almost all scheduled stops, was then renumbered to Trains 17 and 18. This train was subsequently replaced by self-propelled Budd rail diesel cars running between Sudbury and Thunder Bay as Trains 417 and 418.

Today the Sudbury-White River trains are numbered 185 and 186 servicing isolated towns, fishing and hunting camps and residences between Sudbury and White River. The service was called *The Lake Superior* for a number of years—an interesting name, since the train operates in the Superior region of Ontario but never passes the Great Lake it after which it was named. The train is known locally simply as "the Budd Car" after the Budd Company of Red Lion, Pennsylvania that built these self-propelled rail cars in the 1950s.

Although *VIA*'s *Canadian* also operates through Sudbury, the two different trains use two different stations. The Sudbury-White River Budd Car departs and arrives from *CP* station in downtown Sudbury. A short walk up the hill from there is the Quality Inn, located at

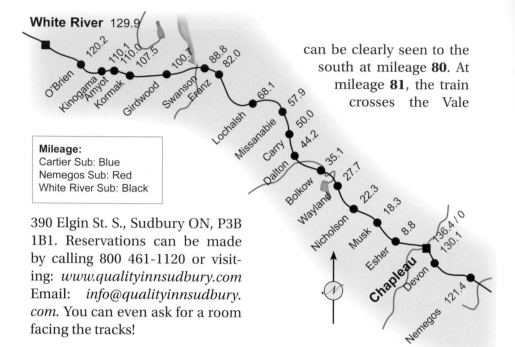

White River 129.9
O'Brien 120.2
Kinogama 110.1
Amyot 110.0
Kormak 107.5
Girdwood 100.7
Swanson 88.8
Franz 82.0
Lochalsh 68.1
Missanabie 57.9
Carry 50.0
Dalton 44.2
Bolkow 35.1
Wayland 27.7
Nicholson 22.3
Musk 18.3
Esher 8.8
Chapleau 136.4 / 0
Devon 130.1
Nemegos 121.4

Mileage:
Cartier Sub: Blue
Nemegos Sub: Red
White River Sub: Black

390 Elgin St. S., Sudbury ON, P3B 1B1. Reservations can be made by calling 800 461-1120 or visiting: *www.qualityinnsudbury.com* Email: *info@qualityinnsudbury. com.* You can even ask for a room facing the tracks!

As there is no meal service available on the train, we recommend you purchase something for lunch before leaving. Sudbury, 2011 population 160,274, is located at mileage **79** of the Cartier Subdivision, where our trip begins.

Route Highlights
Sudbury to Cartier
Cartier Subdivision

Mileages 79–113: On the station platform, before the train is boarded, you might see everything from a month's worth of groceries to a 17-foot (5.18-metre) aluminum boat and motor. As you leave the station, mileage **79**, you can see the Sudbury Arena to the north. The city's most noticeable landmark, Vale Inco's 1,250-foot (381-metre) high smokestack,

can be clearly seen to the south at mileage **80**. At mileage **81**, the train crosses the Vale Inco railway that services the mine. At mileage **86** the train begins to pass through the agricultural area of the Blezard Valley. The tracks cross the Vermillion River at mileage **97**. Then, at mileage **101** the terrain becomes more rugged—to the north you can see the white water of the Onaping Falls. To the south between mileages **103** and **105** is Windy Lake Provincial Park. Watch the sky near mileage **110** at Crab Lake for cranes and owls native to the area. The train arrives at Cartier at mileage **113**.

Route Highlights
Cartier to Chapleau
Nemegos Subdivision

Mileages 0–136: After Cartier, 2006 population 302, the train becomes a lifeline to the remote communities along the tracks. At mileage **11**, on the side of the tracks, a couple of cottages sit alongside Stralak Lake, and a resourceful cottage owner uses a windmill of barrel halves to power a pump that brings water from the lake to the house. Between mileages **13** and **30** the train travels through the scenic Spanish River Valley, crossing the river itself at mileage **23**. With the Spanish on the north side of the tracks at mileage **24.6**, look to the south to see the Little Pogamasing River. This cascading water comes from Lake Fluorite, located on the other side of the ridge. Mileage **30.5** provides your last view of the Spanish River. You can't get much more isolated than the Bon Amis cabin at mileage **32.9**. Metagama (mileage **36.6**) is a popular starting place for hunters and trappers. The lake to the north at mileage **51**, Drefal, features a cabin built by Albert Crolick, who worked this section of the railway for over forty years. The General Store at the small community of Biscotasing (mileage **54.4**) can be seen behind the small station shelter, and you can also see the southernmost tip of Biscotasi Lake. Ramsey (mileage **70**) is a loading area for the lumber industry. The A-frame building you can see was a church in the town's heyday; today it is a cottage. The Sudbury– White River train continues to traverse many water routes along the line: Bowen Creek (mileage **77**), Woman River (mileage **86**), and the Walkami River (mileage **94**). In 1956, lumbering came to an end in Sultan (mileage **96.7**), when the town's sawmill burned down. Piles of sawdust at

Sultan — 96.7
Woman River — 86.1
Ramsey — 70.7
Roberts — 60.6
Biscotasing — 54.4
Sinker — 40.0
Metagama — 36.6
Forks — 31.3
Sheahan — 22.5
Pogamasing — 20.0
Stralak — 11.5
Benny — 7.9
Cartier — 113.0 / 0
Levack — 104.0
Larchwood — 94.7
Azilda — 86.2
Sudbury — 79.0

Kormak (mileage **106**) are all that is left of this town that also once featured a large lumber mill. The train crosses the Nemegos River at mileage **121**, and passes Poulin Lake on the south at mileage **126**. The deteriorating wooden chutes at Devon (mileage **130.1**) were once used to load boxcars with wood chips that would be processed into chipboard. You arrive at Chapleau, 2011 population 2,116, at mileage **136.4**. On the north side sits the railway enginehouse with the modern station on the south side of the yards. This is a major station stop, so you will probably have time to stretch your legs behind the station at Chapleau's Centennial Park. Located here are former *CPR* steam locomotive 5433 and an historical plaque on French Canadian author Louis Hemon. The log building houses the Chapleau Museum and Tourist Information Centre featuring a taxidermy display of local animals, and railway memorabilia. If you are planning to visit the area for an extended period, we recommend you contact the Township of Chapleau, 20 Pine St. Box 129, Chapleau, ON, P0M 1K0. Call: 705 864-1330. Web: *www.chapleau.ca*

Route Highlights
Chapleau to White River
White River Subdivision

Mileages 0–129: Once you have left the Chapleau station, you proceed through the yards and cross the Chapleau River, which forms the eastern border of the Chapleau Crown Game Reserve. The line you are travelling on forms the southern border of the reserve; the western border is the *Algoma Central Railway / CN*, and the northern border is the *Canadian National* mainline. Chapleau Crown is the world's biggest reserve with 700,000 hectares (200,000 acres) of wilderness setting. Watch the forest for bears, and the low swampy areas for moose, both of which are abundant in this area. Between mileages **15** and 27 you can see the impressive Lake Windermere to the south. The lake was named by an English sportsman who was homesick; this large lake reminded him of his favorite fishing spot back home. Perhaps he also enjoyed fishing for the speckled trout in Sleith Lake to the south at mileage **46**. At mileage **55**, you first see Bay on Dog Lake; it was named before curves on the route were removed, and the line was shortened by two miles. Missanabie at mileage **57.9** is one of the oldest communities in the area—it was once the site of a rest station along the overland pack trail to James Bay. People still come here for a rest at cottages on the shores of Dog Lake, which we last see to the south at mileage **66**. Mileage **76** is a good spot to

VIA Rail's Sudbury–White River train travels past Poulin Lake on a sunny fall day.

photograph moose in the swamp; if there are none, take a picture of your train on the curve. At mileage **81** you can see miles to the south along narrow Hobon Lake; on the west shore you can see some of the few remaining buildings in Franz, mileage **81.4**, and the *Algoma Central Railway/CN*, detailed on page 91. After passing through a small rock cut, you can see the concrete foundation of the former water tower. You then cross the tracks of the *Algoma Central Railway/CN*. Look to the south at mileage **88.3** as you traverse the Magpie River to see a dam that regulates the water level on the long and narrow Esnagi Lake to the north. As you pass Summit Lake (mileage **105**), the train has reached the highest point on the route. Mileage **107** is

known as the Bermuda Triangle of the White River Subdivision for the odd occurrences here. In the 1940s westbound train personnel reported a fire at the camp belonging to engineer Jack Hargass. They presumed he had fallen asleep with a burning cigarette. The following morning an RCMP officer was dispatched from White River to make a report. He found Mr. Hargass dead with a bullet wound in his head. Shortly afterwards two men were overheard boasting about how they had gotten away with the crime. Authorities were alerted and the two men were arrested with the victim's railway watch in their possession. After being identified by the jeweller in Chapleau this evidence was used to convict them. In another eerie

Travellers board the "Budd car" at White River for points south and east. *Bill Linley photo*

episode from the 1950s, Buddy Weedon came to close up his cabin for the fall, only to disappear mysteriously with only his empty wallet to be found. You will be glad to see the shores of Negwazu Lake at mileage **110** and to be away from this troubled area. The train crosses the White River twice at mileages **122** and **127**. Rounding the curve and entering town of White River, 2011 population 607, you see a stately house on the hill that was built in 1903 for the *Canadian Pacific* superintendent. Today it houses Creations Gallery. You arrive at the large brick station at mileage **129.9**. Originally called Snow Bank, the name changed with the arrival of the railway in 1885. A popular time to visit is during Winnie's Hometown Festival. This mid-August event celebrates the famous bear cub (later named Winnie the Pooh) that was purchased by Lieutenant Harry Colebourn on the station platform while travelling with his regiment en route to England during WWI. You can learn more about the town at the White River Museum located on the corner of Elgin and Superior. After your long day on the rails, we recommend the Continental Motel, located on Highway 17. Reservations can be made at: 800 822-3616. Let them know if you are arriving by rail.

ALGOMA CENTRAL/CN

Tour train in Canyon Park.

The *Algoma Central Railway* was the vision of industrialist Francis H. Clergue, who began construction of the line in 1899 to bring iron ore from the north to the Algoma Steel Mill in Sault Ste. Marie. It was envisioned that the railway would one day terminate on the shores of Hudson Bay, but after construction reached Hearst in 1914, it went no further. Today you can ride the Agawa Canyon Tour Train from June to mid-October, and the Snow Train on weekends during February and March. Or, you can travel to Hearst on the regularly scheduled passenger train year- round. Bring your snowmobile to ride the northern trails in the winter. Regrettably, the business car *Agawa* can no longer be chartered, but the Camp Car is still available. Members of the famous Group of Seven painters once used a converted boxcar as their base from which to paint the region's incredible scenery. Now, with a few more creature comforts, you can spend a week in the Canyon View Camp Car and have the Agawa Canyon Park all to yourself

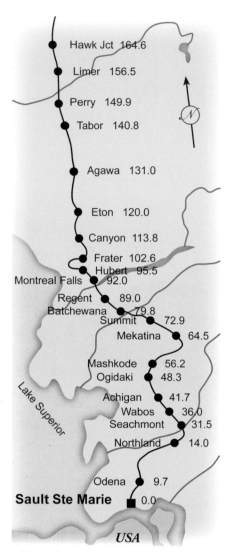

Hawk Jct 164.6

Limer 156.5

Perry 149.9

Tabor 140.8

Agawa 131.0

Eton 120.0

Canyon 113.8

Frater 102.6

Hubert 95.5

Montreal Falls 92.0

Regent 89.0

Batchewana 79.8

Summit 72.9

Mekatina 64.5

Mashkode 56.2

Ogidaki 48.3

Achigan 41.7

Wabos 36.0

Seachmont 31.5

Northland 14.0

Odena 9.7

Sault Ste Marie 0.0

USA

Lake Superior

when the sun sets. To learn more about this railway line (which is now owned by *CN*), or to make a reservation, contact *Algoma Central Railway/CN Passenger Services*, 129 Bay Street, PO Box 130, Sault Ste. Marie, ON, P6A 6Y2. Call: 800 242-9287. Web: *www. agawacanyontourtrain.com*. Arriving or departing Sault Ste. Marie, we recommend the very

convenient Quality Inn located directly across from the *Algoma Central* station at 180 Bay Street. Reservations can be made at: 800 424-6423 or by visiting: *www. choicehotels.ca*

Route Highlights
Sault Ste. Marie to Hearst
Soo Subdivision

Mileages 0–164: Departing the Soo, you pass the large St. Mary's Paper mill and cross under the international bridge that connects to Sault Ste. Marie, Michigan; the tracks then curve to the north. To the west is the Essar Steel complex and to the east are the railway shops. A turntable, used to turn locomotives, is located inside the square engine house to prevent the turntable pit from filling up with snow. At mileage **3** look to the west for the view of the city, with St. Mary's River in the background. You pass over Highway 17 first at mileage **7** and then at mileage **14**. At mileage **20** get your camera ready for the Bellevue Valley, which you cross on a 810-foot (246-metre) trestle. To the west at mileage **27** sits the forested Goulais River Valley. You see the Searchmont ski trails to the east at mileage **30** and Searchmont station at mileage **31.5**, before crossing the Goulais River at mileage **31**. Over the next several miles, you pass a number of lakes and rivers: Achigan Lake on the east at mileage **44**; Ogidaki Lake (mileage **48**); the South Branch of the Chippewa River (mileage **52**); Trout Lake (mileage **62**); with large boulders that dot the water's surface; the North Branch of the Chippewa River (mileage **69**); and Mongoose Lake at mileages **74** and **75**. The Batchewana station is passed at mileage **79.8** before the train crosses the river of the same name at mileage **80**. As the train ascends through a forest, you get a great view over the Batchewana Valley to the east at mileage **84** and Rand Lake at mileage **86**. Mileage **92** brings you to the Montreal River Bridge. Built during the summer of 1902 by the *Canadian Bridge Company*, this 1,550-foot (472-metre) curved bridge features great views to both sides. Located directly below is a concrete dam that was poured around the fifteen steel girder footings. The dam supplies power to the region, and two cylindrical surge tanks for the dam can be seen to the west. After Frater at mileage **102.6**, keep watching to the west to see the mighty Lake Superior and the twisting Trans-Canada Highway. You are now descending to the Agawa Canyon, with views continuing on the east side of the train. The Agawa River is crossed at mileage **112** on a low bridge. Watch for Bridal Falls to the east and Black Beaver Falls to the west as you approach Agawa Canyon Park at mileage **113.8**.

If you are on the tour train, you will find much to do here during your layover. Enjoy your picnic lunch, buy a reminder of your visit in the old railway passenger car souvenir shop car, hike one of the well-groomed trails, or climb the over-300 stairs to the canyon lookout for a view you will not soon forget. Railway enthusiasts will enjoy the *Algoma Central* memorabilia on display in the shelter near the track motorcars.

The canyon narrows past the park, leaving room for only the tracks and the river. Soon, the river widens and the train criss-crosses it three times: at mileages **120**, **122**, and **130**. Until mileage **138**, the railway line forms the eastern border of the Lake Superior Provincial Park. At mileage **152** the Michipicoten River is crossed. At Hawk Junction, mileage **164.6**, a subdivision once extended 26 miles to the Lake Superior ore trans-shipping town of Michipicoten. In turn, the Magpie, Helen and MacLeod mines contributed iron ore from the Wawa area to the Algoma (Essar) steel mill in the Sault via this spur line until 1998. If you have time, look inside the waiting room of the brick Hawk Junction Station, with its ornate ticket window. You can step back in time as you view the large promotional pictures of the region in its heyday.

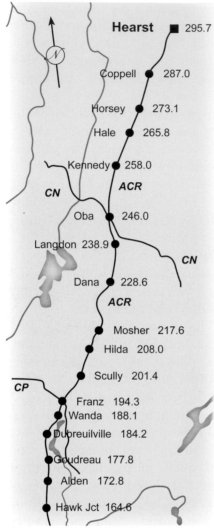

Hearst ■ 295.7

Coppell ● 287.0

Horsey ● 273.1

Hale ● 265.8

Kennedy ● 258.0

CN   *ACR*

Oba ● 246.0

Langdon 238.9 ●

CN

Dana ● 228.6

ACR

● Mosher 217.6

● Hilda 208.0

● Scully 201.4

CP

● Franz 194.3
● Wanda 188.1

● Dubreuilville 184.2

● Goudreau 177.8

● Alden 172.8

● Hawk Jct 164.6

Mileages 165–296: After leaving Hawk Junction, the train returns to the forests of the Great Lakes Region. Goudreau (mileage **177.8**) was once a gold mining town; you can still see the crumbling foundation and chimney from a smelter. Watch for Herman Lake to the east at mileage **180**. At Dubreuilville (mileage **184.2**) one of the largest lumber mill opera-

tions on the line can be seen to the west. Franz (mileage **194.3**) was named after W.J. Franz, an early superintendent of Algoma Steel. This is also where you cross the *Canadian Pacific* east-west mainline, first seen to the east on the opposite shore of Hobon Lake. In the early years of the railway, this town was a thriving community. It turned into a ghost town, however, when fewer people were needed to operate the railways, and a controlled burn even removed a number of abandoned houses in the 1980s. As you pass the *CP* line, you might catch a glimpse of *VIA Rail*'s Sudbury–White River train (see page 85). While crossing the tracks, you can see the concrete foundation still remaining from the former water tower to the east. From here to Oba, the tracks form the western border of the Chapleau Game Reserve. St. Julien Lake (mileage **198**) features a unique boulder-lined shore. Try to get your fellow passengers to spell Wabatongushi as you pass this large lake at mileage **206**. Mile **207** brings you to the Arctic watershed. All the water to the south of here flows to Lake Superior and, north of here, to Hudson Bay. Oba Lake sits to the west at mileage **209**. At mileage **211** the train crosses a low bridge known as a floating bridge because the supports are sunk deep into the bottomless muskeg forming the lake's floor. You can see the tops of the poles of the former bridge beside the modern bridge, which was installed in 1998. Another floating bridge is crossed at mileage **214**. In the distance to the west, Tatnall Lodge can be seen on an island at mileage **215.5**, before the train leaves Oba Lake at mileage **216**. The Price Lodge at mileage **221** was built with used telegraph poles from along the line. The *Canadian National* mainline is crossed at Oba at mileage **246**; this is the route of *VIA Rail*'s *Canadian*. The population of this remote railway community has dwindled, but a number of buildings still remain. If

The scenic Agawa Canyon.

you are changing trains here, make sure you bring outdoor apparel suitable for the changeable weather in Northern Ontario as there is no station or shelter here and nowhere to shop if you are setting off on a camping or canoe trip. Doreen's Handy Store is a good place to grab a snack. At mileage **247** the train crosses the Mattawitchewan River. Moose are sometimes spotted in the swamps along the route, so keep watching for these majestic animals. The terrain is quite flat as you arrive in Hearst, 2011 population 5,090, at mileage **295.7**. Hearst bears the name of William Hearst, Premier of Ontario from 1914 through 1919. After a long day's journey, we recommend the Companion Hotel (930 Front Street), only a few steps from where the train arrives and departs Hearst. Reservations can be made at 888 468-9888. Web: *www.companion-hotel-motel.ca*

VIA'S CANADIAN

If you wanted to travel to western Canada in the 1870s, you had to travel by train through the northern United States, then north by riverboat to Winnipeg. The province of British Columbia joined Confederation in 1871 based on Canada's promise that a railway would soon unite the new province to the remainder of the country. The country's first Prime Minister, John A. Macdonald, was one of many who envisioned a line of steel that would traverse the Canadian Shield in Ontario, the vast prairies, the unexplored mountains, and connect to the Pacific Ocean.

Before the country could come of age, it had the huge challenge of overcoming its own size and terrain. At the government's request, the *Canadian Pacific Railway* took on the challenge, overcame many obstacles and connected east to west by rail. After the last spike was driven home on November 7th 1885, at Craigellachie BC, untouched land began to open at a rapid pace as the railway boom had reached the west. Soon other railways wanted a piece of the action, and challenged the *CPR* monopoly by racing to the Pacific. Competition was fierce between the various railways, and the other railways did not survive. The government was eventually forced to step in and combine them into *Canadian National Railways*. Even with two major players, competition for freight and passengers continued to be strong. If one did something, the other was always quick to follow. This was never more evident than in April 1955, when the *CPR* introduced its newest transcontinental train *The Canadian*, and the *CNR* kept pace with the *Super Continental*. Fortunately, there were enough passengers to go around and ridership remained high until the 1960s. However, automobiles and airlines continued to win an ever-larger share of passenger traffic. As ridership declined, both railways wanted out of the rail passenger business.

In the late 1970s, Canada's government formed *VIA Rail Canada* to operate passenger trains on both *CP* and *CN*. As the 1980s progressed, the federal government instructed *VIA* to reorganize its transcontinental trains. In 1990, the daily *Canadian* and *Super Continental* services were rationalized. *VIA* provided a reduced frequency service connecting Toronto and Vancouver over the route of the former *Super Continental* on the *Canadian National* mainline. The name "*Canadian*" endured. *VIA* had inherited dated railway equipment, using it until the late 1980s. It then decided to rebuild the stainless steel "Budd" fleet that the Canadian Pacific originally purchased in the mid-1950s. The renovations included replacing steam heating with an electrical system, improving the air conditioning, replacing the outmoded electrical system, and adding showers. These timeless cars are being renovated once again to enhance their comfort and appeal.

When beginning or finishing your cross-Canada journey, stay at Toronto's Fairmont Royal York Hotel. This classic railway hotel is located across the street from Union Station at 100 Front Street West. Reservations can be made at: 800 441-1414. Web: *www.fairmont.com*

Before you visit Toronto or anywhere in Ontario, we suggest you

World-famous CN Tower landmark dominates the skyline en route to Toronto's Union Station. *VIA Rail photo*

contact Ontario Travel Information Centre, 20 Dundas Street West, Toronto, ON, M5G 2C2. Call: 800 668-2746. Web: *www.ontariotravel.net*

Route Highlights
Departing Toronto
Weston, Newmarket & York Subdivisions

Mileages 0–13: *VIA*'s Train 1 departs Toronto's Union Station in a westerly direction. Look to the south and straight up to see Toronto's most distinctive attraction, the CN Tower. Your train will then pass under the John Street pedestrian walkway connecting downtown Toronto with the CN Tower and Rogers Centre, formerly the "SkyDome." While passing under the bridge, notice the "switch house" or "tower" that had to lose its roof for the walkway's construction. After passing Rogers Centre, the tracks are below the city level. Above and to the south is a memorial dedicated to the Chinese railway workers who helped to construct the *Canadian Pacific Railway*. The train then turns north at Parkdale, mileage **3.0/2.6** and travels on the Newmarket Subdivision until Snider North, mileage **14.0**. Here it will change direction by backing through a wye, permitting the train to travel east for five miles on the York Subdivision to Doncaster, reaching the Bala Subdivision at mileage **16.1**. The train then turns northward once again.

Route Highlights
Arriving Toronto
Bala Subdivision

Mileages 16–0: *VIA*'s Train 2 into Toronto uses a different route from the one on which it departs. You'll arrive from the north on the eastern side of the city's core. You wind along the Don River Valley before connecting with the Kingston Subdivsion. The last two miles are spent navigating the trackage into Toronto's Union Station. Lake Ontario can be seen to the south. Before entering the station, you can look down to the north on Toronto's famous

Canadian National Railways steam locomotive 6077 today is on display in Capreol at the Northern Ontario Rail Road Museum.

Yonge Street. The restored Bank of Montreal building on the corner is the Hockey Hall of Fame, where the Stanley Cup is displayed. Then you reach the trainshed for Toronto's Union Station, located directly across from the Royal York Hotel.

Route Highlights
Toronto to Capreol
CN's Bala Subdivision and CP's Parry Sound Subdivision

Mileages 16–25: The Bala Subdivision is also used by many of Toronto's GO Transit trains, and you pass several GO commuter stations while travelling through the city's suburbs.

Mileages 26–100: Lake Simcoe can be seen to the west between mileages **60** and **66**. The Talbot River, part of the Trent-Severn Canal/Waterway, is crossed at mileage **67** just north of Beaverton. At mileage **71**, to the west, the old *CPR* Brechin Station lives on as a Wild Wing Restaurant on Highway 12. With Lake Couchiching to the west, the train arrives at Washago, mileage **88.9**. At mileages **89.8** and **100** you cross the Severn River, the most northerly river of the Trent-Severn Canal/Waterway.

Mileages 101–145: The *Canadian* travels through the scenic Muskoka "Cottage Country". Three crossings, Coulter's Narrows (mileage **112**), Jeanette's Narrows (mileage **113**), and the Wallace Cut (mileage **115**) are waterways that

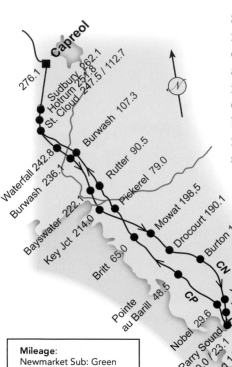

Sound had a population of 6,191 in 2011 and is home to hockey legend, Bobby Orr. It is central to the area made famous in the paintings of the Group of Seven famous Canadian artists. Both routes pass by the preserved *CPR* and *CNR* railway stations seen to the west side of the tracks. North of Parry Sound, the Canadian Shield becomes more predominant as the *Canadian* crosses many rivers flowing towards Georgian Bay. Northbound on the *CP* route at mileage **62.8**, (**183** southbound

connect Bala Bay on the west to Lake Muskoka on the east. Boyne, mileage **146.1**/Reynolds mileage **20.1** *CP* Parry Sound Subdivision: some of the busiest transcontinental rail freight traffic occurs between here and just south of Sudbury. Trains travelling north or west transfer to the *CP* mainline here, while those travelling south follow the *CN* mainline through the region. Southbound you pass through Parry Sound on a sharp curve. Alternatively, northbound on the *CP*, you cross the 1,695-foot (516-metre) long, 24 span *CP* Seguin River trestle literally above the town of Parry Sound. Parry

The train winds around the lakes and rock outcroppings of the Canadian Shield on the *Canadian*'s run through northern Ontario.

on the *CN*) the tracks cross Magnetawan River east of Byng Inlet on a long, low trestle. From the *CP* route at mileage **72** look below to see the *CN* route. If you're on the *CN* line, look up at mileage **202** to see the *CP* Mainline. Continuing north, The Pickerel River is crossed prior to the *Canadian*'s traversing the French River. The shores of the river make up the French River Provincial Park, which is over 60 miles (97 kilometres) long, connecting Georgian Bay to Lake Nipissing. At mileage **112.7/247.5**, the *CN* and *CP* lines connect at St. Cloud. North of the junction, Elbow Creek flows into the Wanapitei River. This river is crossed again at mileage **254**. The train is now travelling through the mineral- rich Sudbury region. To the west, you see a now closed

nickel smelter at Romford, to the west at mileage **256.8**. Emissions from the nickel smelting process created the scarred landscape, which was used by NASA to train its astronauts for moonwalks. A reforestation program has begun to ameliorate the damage.

Mileages 257–276: The 1,250 foot (380 metre) high stack of the Vale Inco smelter built in 1972 can be seen before reaching Sudbury, 2011 population 160,274, (mileage **262.1**). Sudbury Junction station is where passengers may detrain to ride *VIA*'s Sudbury–White River train (see page 85). This service departs from a different station in Sudbury's downtown area. After Sudbury, at mileage **275** as you arrive in Capreol, 2011 population 3,276, you pass the Northern

Ontario Railroad Museum and Heritage Centre, which is housed in the former *CN* Superintendent's house behind Prescott Park. Here, you can see locomotive No. 6077 and other railway equipment and learn about the area's rail heritage. Web: *www.normhc.ca*. The tracks then curve to the west and you arrive at the Capreol station (mileage **276.1**).

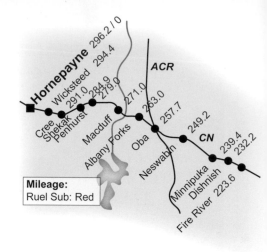

Mileage:
Ruel Sub: Red

Route Highlights
Capreol to Hornepayne
Ruel Subdivision

Mileages 0–2: There was a time when the Toronto and Montreal sections of the *Super Continental* were divided at Capreol to carry on east to each city, or were consolidated into a single train travelling westbound. (A similar operation was performed in Sudbury to the south on the *CPR's Canadian*.) When originally built, the railway was directly south of Capreol. You can see the original route's bridge supports in the Vermillion River. Shortly after the line was built, however, Capreol was chosen as the site where the tracks from Montreal (now removed) would connect with the line to the west. At mileage **1** you return to the original route on a tight curve. The river then widens to become Bass Lake.

Mileages 2–18: You can see first-hand the rugged terrain of the Canadian Shield, with its massive outcroppings of rocks and countless lakes that challenged the railway builders. Fraser Lake can be seen to the north of Milne at mileage **8.9**. The rails continue to follow the Vermillion River, crossing it at again at mileage **9.4** and **16.3**.

Mileage 19: In 1926 the Ontario Department of Education, the *Ontario Northland Railway*, the *CPR*, and *CNR* formed a unique partnership, creating six school cars. The cars featured a small living area for a teacher, family, and a classroom complete with chalkboard and a small library. The cars would be pulled behind a freight train and left in isolated communities for a week, to assist in teaching the children of railway and lumber workers, as well as woodsmen and First Nations children. Before leaving, the teacher would assign enough homework to keep the children busy until the car returned. The cars operated on the *ONR* from North Bay to Rib Lake; on the *CPR* from Chapleau to Cartier, and Cartier to White River; and three on the CNR from Capreol to Foleyet, Port Arthur (Thunder Bay) to Fort Francis, and Sioux Lookout to the Manitoba border. Fred Sloman, who created the idea,

worked on the Capreol to Foleyet car that featured stops at Raphoe (mileage **19.5**), as well as Laforest, Ruel, Ostrom, Bethnal, and Stackpool. Today his car is preserved at Clinton, Ontario.

Mileages 20–35: The scenic lakes continue: Graveyard Lake (mileages **27–30**); Post Lake (mileages **30–31**); and Pine Lake and Smoky Lake (mileages **32–35**).

Mileages 36–89: After crossing the Wahnipitae River at mileage

45 you pass Felix mileage **46.8** with its summer camps.

Mileages 63 to **65** take you past the shores of Kashnebawning Lake to the south at Westree, mileage **64.3**. To the north at mileage **76**, near Makwa, the lone trailer with its welcoming gate would make an interesting place to visit, but what would you do there? The Muskegogama River is crossed at mileage **78**. Before reaching Gogama, Ojibway for "jumping fish", at mileage **86.9**, the train crosses Minnisinaqua Lake. It was an early source of Axe ties, hand hewn ties whose longevity was said to be longer than sawn ties.

Mileages 90–147: On the curved causeway that crosses Wind-

Passing scenery is enjoyed from wraparound windows of the *Canadian*'s dome car.

egoguinzing Lake at mileage **90**, you get a good opportunity to photograph your train. The fishing must be good at Bethnal, mileage **95.5**, because the lodge is called "Camp Brag-A-Lot." The former two-storey section-men's house at Stackpool (mileage **105.4**) can be seen to the south a short distance from the tracks. At mileage **134** a 1,134-foot (345-metre) long bridge crosses the Groundhog River.

Mileages 148–183: The railway created towns when steam locomotives had to be re-supplied with coal, water, and sand. The large concrete coaling tower still remains in Foleyet, 2006 population 206, at mileage **148.3**. At mileage **179** the *Canadian* crosses the Nemegosenda River, and then the Kapuskasing River at mileage **183**. The train then skirts the lake of the same name to the south before reaching Elsas, where an old *CNR* caboose on the hill lives on as a camp. The Kapuskasing River is the eastern border of the Chapleau Crown Game Reserve, the world's largest reserve, with 200,000 acres (700,000 hectares) of wilderness setting. The Reserve's other three borders are also formed by railway lines: the northern border is the line you are travelling on, while the western border is the *Algoma Central Railway/CN*, and the southern border is the *Canadian Pacific Railway* mainline.

Mileages 184–255: At mileage 196.4, east of Dunrankin, the train passes four simple white crosses to the south. These mark a tragic accident that occurred on August 2nd 1967 when a freight train ran into *The Super Continental*, killing four *CN* employees. Another coaling facility stands alone at Fire River, mileage **223.6**.

Mileages 256–294: The tracks cross those of the *Algoma Central Railway/CN* at Oba, mileage **257.7**. The *ACR* passenger train that operates between Sault Ste. Marie to the south and Hearst to the north is detailed on page 67. If you are changing trains here, make sure you bring outdoor apparel suitable for the changeable weather in Northern Ontario as there is no station or shelter here and nowhere to shop if you are setting off on a camping or canoe trip. Doreen's Handy Store is a good place to grab a snack or last-minute items. The area here is known for its fox, moose, and bears. If you see one, call out so everyone can get a look. Arriving in the division point of Hornepayne, 2011 population 1,050, you pass the Hallmark Hornepayne Centre on the south side of the tracks. Completed in 1982, the 160,000-square-foot town complex included the town high school, a hotel, regional offices, library, apartments, a mall with stores and restaurants, the town swimming pool, medical centre, and rooms for railway crews to layover. It closed in 2011.

Route Highlights
Hornepayne to Armstrong
Caramat Subdivision

Mileages 0–2: Hornepayne is a modern-day refueling stop for locomotives, so you are likely to be here for a while. The railway engine house to the north was built in 1921 and features an enclosed turntable used for switching locomotives onto different shop tracks. The turntable is enclosed because the large amounts of snow that fall here would fill the pit in which the turntable operates. This and another similar building used by the *Algoma Central Railway/ CN* in Sault Ste. Marie are the last two active facilities of their kind in North America. The train then passes the unused two-storey Hornepayne brick station that was also built in 1921.

Mileages 3–44: The *Canadian* quickly returns to the northern wilderness. River crossings and lakes continue, with the Obaka-miga River at mileage **15**, the Stoney River at mileage **27**, the Little Stoney River at mileage **29**, and Flanders Lake to the south at mileage **30**. Watch the passing forest for the unique shape of the numerous spruce trees. The growth spurt on the top of these trees occurs during the short growing season each year. During the winter months, the lower portion of the tree remains dormant be-

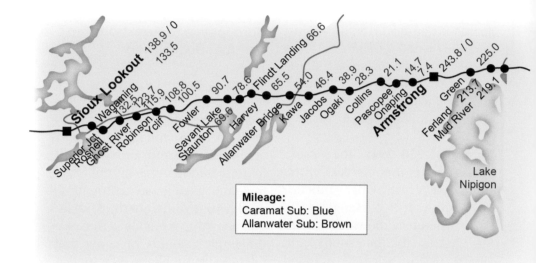

Mileage:
Caramat Sub: Blue
Allanwater Sub: Brown

cause of the extreme northern climate. This area is also the border between the Northeastern and Northwestern Ontario administrative regions. Hillsport (mileage **42.3**) is noted for its fishing lodges.

Mileages 45–98: In 1896 railway contractors William Mackenzie and Donald Mann purchased the charter to build the *Lake Manitoba Railway and Canal Company*. In 1899 it merged with the *Winnipeg & Hudson Bay Railway* to form the *Canadian Northern Railway*. From this humble beginning in the Province of Manitoba, the two men created the country's second transcontinental railway. At mileage **45.6** you cross the White Otter River where, on January 1st 1914, a cold ten-minute ceremony took place with company president William

Mackenzie driving home the last spike on the *Canadian Northern Railway* which became part of the *CNR* in 1923. The tracks cross Bowler Lake at mileage **66** and Little Charon Lake at mileage **71**. At mileage **78** Caramat Lake can be seen to the south.

Mileages 99–130: After passing through the lumber town of Longlac with its modern station, the *Canadian* crosses Long Lake between mileages **99** and **101**. This lake is 45 miles (73 kilometres) in length and 2 miles (3.2 kilometres) across. It was a major canoe route for "coureurs de bois" between Hudson Bay and Lake Superior during the fur trade heyday in the 18th century. The large white church to the west makes a nice photograph. At Longlac Junction (mileage **101.1**), the *Canadian Northern* turned south to

VIA'S CANADIAN

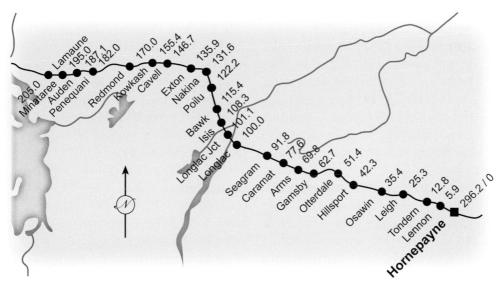

Thunder Bay before carrying on to the west. Today, the *Canadian* travels north on a stretch of track built in 1923 and 1924 to connect the former *Canadian Northern* with the former *National Transcontinental Railway* mainline. The Kenogamissis River is crossed at mileage **107** and Manitounamaig Lake can be seen to the north between mileages **111** and **114**. As the train approaches Nakina, the tracks form the eastern border of the Moraine Provincial Nature Reserve.

Mileage 131: Before the Longlac-Nakina Cutoff opened on January 24th 1924, the division point of Grant had been located 17 miles to the east. With the decision to connect the two railways, the entire town of Grant was moved to the present site, and renamed Nakina. The two-storey

Nakina Station, built around the same time, has been preserved by the community that had a population of 4,724 in 2006. The train now rides on the line built by the *National Transcontinental Railway (NTR)*. The 121 miles of track east of Nakina to Calstock was abandoned in 1986 because of a lack of freight traffic. In 1991, the portion from Calstock to Cochrane was sold to the *Ontario Northland Railway*. A section of the line in Northern Quebec, between Hervey and Senneterre, is the only other portion of the *NTR* between here and Quebec City where a passenger train is operated. Page 47 provides more detail on the evolution of the NTR and a description of the route of *VIA Rail*'s Montreal-Senneterre train.

Mileages 132–197: At mileage

134, the train passes Balkam Lake, followed by Exton Lake at mileage **139**. You see Kawashkagama Lake to the south at mileage **140**. The train crosses the Kawashkagama River (mileage **147**) on a 225-foot (68-metre) long bridge. Creek and river crossings in the wilderness continue: Trout Creek (mileage **148**), Johnson Creek (mileage **153**), Emilie Creek (mileage **176**), Spruce Creek (mileage **180**), and the Ombabika River (mileage **187**). Look to the north, at mileage **193**, to see the large hydroelectric dam on Clod Lake. Minataree Lake can be seen to the north at mileage **197**.

Mileages 197–243: One of the most impressive highlights of the Caramat Subdivision is the crossing of the 798-foot (243-metre) long Jackfish Creek Viaduct. At mileage **209.9**, the fast moving water of Jackfish Creek, 75 feet (23 metres) below, appears to cut straight through the solid rock of the Canadian Shield. Look over the trees to the south while on the bridge to see Ombabika Bay on Lake Nipigon. The most prominent building in Ferland is the yellow St. Joseph's Church at mileage **213**. The 362-foot (110-metre) high Mud River Viaduct crosses 59 feet (18 metres) above this narrow river at mileage **219**. The rustic community of the same name features a few log cabins. For the next 23 miles the tracks

form the northern border of the Windigo Bay Provincial Nature reserve, which extends to the shores of Lake Nipigon. Rapid Creek is crossed at mileage **228**. Lakes to the north of the track include Jojo Lake at mileage **235**, Flat Lake at mileage **240**, and Red Granite Lake at mileage **241**.

Communities that have been created to service the railway have long been named after the railway's financiers, employees, or even the construction foreman's children. Armstrong (mileage **243.8**) was named after the NTR's Chief Engineer, T.S. Armstrong.

Armstrong, 2011 population 220, was traditionally the dividing point for the *CNR's* eastern and western regions. In the heyday of steam locomotives, those arriving from each region would be turned and sent back, pulling the next train. Today's diesels are not returned to their home base, but crews still change here, laying over at the large *CN* bunkhouse on the north side of the tracks. It features a screened-in summer porch, where employees can await their next departure without dealing with Northwestern Ontario's mosquitoes.

Route Highlights
Armstrong to Sioux Lookout
Allanwater Subdivision

Flint Landing fishing camp, on Heathcoate Lake, is accessible only by floatplane or a pedestrian bridge connecting to the railway right-of-way.

Mileages 0–2: Since you cross the line between the Eastern and Central Time zones at Armstrong, your travel clocks and watches should be moved one hour back if travelling west, or advanced one hour if travelling east. From 1952, Armstrong had a Pine Tree Line radar station north of town originally manned by the US Air Force. It was closed by the RCAF in 1974. Leaving the town which is home to the Whitesand First Nation, you cross Highway 527, which connects Armstrong with Thunder Bay. Numerous lakes and river crossings continue along the route. The First Nations reserve at Collins can be seen to the south at mileage **21.1**.

Mileages 24–44: The *Canadian*

enters Wabakimi Provincial Park. The train travels through the southern portion of this 2,204,000-acre (892,000-hectare) park. Keep your camera ready at mileage **31** to photograph of the long narrow lake, located in a gorge that parallels the tracks. Lakes and sweeping vistas continue over the next couple of miles. At mileage **44**, a trail leads from here to a remote northern destination with the fitting name of Camp 44. The camp takes its name from the mileage on the subdivision where all the supplies are unloaded to begin the hike.

Mileages 45–75: At mileage **53** the train crosses the northern tip of Kawaweogama Lake and arrives at the community of

More than a dozen railway cars and lots of sightseeing domes make for an exciting trip aboard *The Canadian*. *F. Lesiuk photo*

Allanwater Bridge (mileage **54.1**). This community, which is only accessible by rail or by air, is a favourite destination for fishermen and canoeists. In the summer months it is quite common to see floatplanes tied up to the docks on the lake. You can also see the St. Barnabas United Church. Watch to the north at mileage **66.5**, Flindt Landing, for a unique wilderness setting, where a walking bridge (the only way across) connects the cottages on the island in Heathcote Lake to the mainland near the tracks. At mileage **67** the train departs the Wabakimi Provincial Park.

Mileages 75–76: As you cross the road at mileage **75** you can see the railway communication lines have been raised to allow the logging trucks to pass underneath. Mileage **78.6** Savant Lake, on the hill beside the tracks

to the north, was originally known as Buck Station after an *NTR* locomotive engineer. The name was changed when it was being confused with another town of the same name. In the 1940s, a local resident started construction of a building featuring concrete walls with reinforced steel. He would not tell anyone what it was to be used for when it was completed. Before he could finish it, the man died, and the structure was never completed. The train then passes the Four Winds Motel.

Mileages 78–106: Between mileages **91** and **99** the train snakes around numerous lakes and rock cuts. Listen at mileage **100.8** to hear the wheels sing. If travelling at track speed, you can hear the sound of the wheels bouncing off the rocks while in the tight curve.

Mileages 107–120: The train

crosses a bay on Marchington Lake (mileage **107**) which can be seen to the north. Although the name Ghost River at mileage **115.9** fires up one's imagination, in fact it is a quiet community with a few houses and summer residences. Look to the north at mileage **120** to see some rapids on the Sturgeon River, as well as the remains of an old mill on McDougall Bay.

Mileages 121–132: Bears and moose are numerous in the dense forest here, so watch the woods. The area at mileage **132.5** was once known as Superior Junction, because the Graham Subdivision split off the mainline towards Thunder Bay before being removed in 1995-96. The line hosted one of Canada's last mixed train services, which survived into the 1980s, and featured a combination baggage-mail-and-passenger car attached to the rear of a freight train. The coach, built in the 1920s, provided rail passenger service to the isolated communities along the route. You can see an example of this style of railway car at the Winnipeg Railway Museum.

Mileages 133–139: A 465-foot (142-metre) long bridge, with three steel spans, each 155 feet (47 metres) long, allows the *Canadian* to cross the Sturgeon River at mileage **133.3**. At mileage **137** the

train passes under the modern highway to Thunder Bay before reaching the unique British-style mock Tudor station at Sioux Lookout. The town of 5,037 people in 2011 derives its name from the Ojibway First Nation people's use of the area's highest elevations to watch to the south for invading groups from the competing Sioux First Nation. Winter temperatures have reached –46∘C and 37∘C in summer.

Route Highlights
Sioux Lookout to Winnipeg
Reddit Subdivision

Mileages 0–11: Centennial Park separates the tracks and Sioux Lookout's Front Street on the ridge to the north. The town's First Nations heritage is reflected on the sign for the park, which is written in English and Ojicree (a combination of Cree and Ojibway languages.) Leaving town, you can see Pelican Lake to the south before the train crosses it on a low 272-foot (83-metre) long bridge at mileage **1.3**. Pelican Lake then continues on the north side of the train. The tracks cross two creeks at mileage **4**: Marsh Creek at mileage **4.4**, then Vermilion Creek at mileage **4.5**.

Mileages 12–16: The train follows Lost Lake for the next five miles. The community of Hudson (mileage **12.6**) has long been a jump-

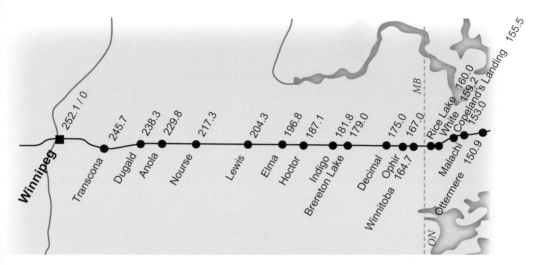

off point for float planes that travel north. A plaque commemorates the bush pilots who flew supplies to the Red Lake gold miners in the rush of 1926. Today you can rent a houseboat and spend a week or more on Lost Lake. At mileage **13**, the train passes a large lumber mill to the north.

Mileages 17–41: The train travels through a large rock cut at mileage **28**. The *Canadian* passes through a 325-foot (99-metre) long tunnel at mileage **41**.

Mileages 42–72: The northern view over Sunday Lake (mileage **45**) makes for a nice photograph. The train then winds its way through the rock cuts. Instead of realigning Niddrie siding, which begins at mileage **57**, the railway built the passing track around a railway signal light. The lake to the north here is Norse Lake; Walsh Lake is to the south. A

wide rock cut had to be created at mileage **65.5** where Morgan siding connects with the main track. Red Lake Road on Ontario Highway 105 is passed at mileage **71**. A 174-foot (53-metre) long bridge crosses 55 feet (17 metres) above the Wabigoon River at mileage **73**. While crossing the bridge, look directly below on the north side of the track to see a waterfall.

Mileages 74–81: Near the village of Quibell, the Canadian Shield disappears briefly and the landscape changes to one of fields and pastures.

Mileages 82–96: Get your camera ready as the train passes Canyon Lake, first seen on the north side of the tracks at mileage **82.5**. The train passes through two separate tunnels, at mileages **88** and **89,** each just over 500 feet (150 metres) long. There are more

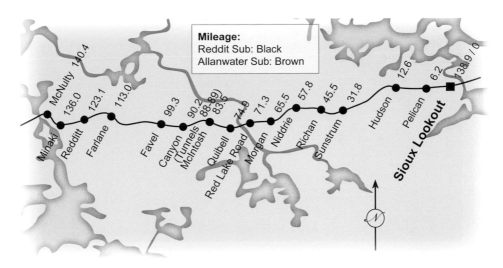

Mileage:
Reddit Sub: Black
Allanwater Sub: Brown

good views to the northwest at mileage **92**. You get your last views of Canyon Lake at mileage **95**. At mileage **96** the train passes the creek that connects the lakes along the route.

Mileages 97–114: Favel Lake is to the north between mileages **97** and **103**. Between mileages **106** and **108** the train passes Wild Lake. At mileage **113.4** the small Farlane Station sits quietly on the south side of the tracks. This was one of many stops made by the *Campers Special*, a unique train that served the area's cottagers. In operation from 1911 to 1989, the idea was originally promoted by the *CNR* to secure more passengers, thus justifying more trains. The railway encouraged employees and other Winnipeggers to build cottages along the route; of course, the only way in or out was by train. Packed with bags, pets, and all the essentials needed by

cottagers for a weekend getaway, the train would leave Winnipeg on Friday evenings, with passengers disembarking at the lakes along the way. It would remain in Sioux Lookout over the weekend and return to Winnipeg on Sunday, bringing home the weary weekenders.

Mileages 114–124: After passing through more rock cuts, keep watching to the north at mileage **116**. Years of water running down the sheer cliff on the opposite side of the lake created some interesting streaks on the rock face. Also to the north at mileage **117.5**, you can notice how the rocks on the far side of Seel Creek have given way and broken up on the shoreline. This was caused by water entering cracks in the rocks, expanding in freezing temperatures, eventually causing the rock to weaken and finally give way.

Scenic domes provide a unique vantage point to view Northwestern Ontario. *Bill Linley photo*

As you arrive in Redditt, mileage **123.1**, home to 172 persons in 2006, look to the hill to the north to see a Quonset-hut-style building housing this small town's Canadian Legion Hall, and a former *CN* steel caboose 79312 built in June 1967 by Hawker-Siddley in Trenton, Nova Scotia that contains a small museum. In its day Redditt was a large division point for the *NTR* and *CNR*. The site of the former *NTR* and *CNR* railway yard is now a grass airstrip. A small portion of the roundhouse can still be seen in front of the large and picturesque Eagle Rock.

Mileages 124–135: The train runs beside the long and narrow Corn Lake, seen to the north from mileages **124** to **126**. Then, at mileages **130.4** and **135.3** the *Canadian* travels through the last two tunnels before the Rocky Mountains.

Mileages 136–137: The train crosses the Winnipeg River at mileage **136**. Look to both sides for good views while crossing the river. To the north was once the site of the *CNR*'s grand Minaki Lodge that was built in 1927 and burned down in 2003. On the other side of the river you will arrive at the Minaki station, now home to the Blue Heron gift shop. Minaki is a First Nations word that translates into "Beautiful Country," which is quite fitting for the area.

Mileages 138–144: A public launch for putting boats into Gunn Lake can be seen to the north at mileage **138**. At mileage **139** to the north you get a good view over Pistol Lake. At mileage **140** you cross Highway 596.

Mileages 145–146: The old right-of-way viewed to the north was changed because, on the east side of the rock cut, the original road bed was located in a swampy area that was impossible to stabilize. The railway later decided to move the tracks to more stable ground.

Mileages 147–151: A cabin, known as "The Haze," is tucked into the forest on the north side of the tracks at mileage **150**. Watch for the name spelled out with white rocks on the front lawn. Then, you pass the station shelter at Ottermere, located on the south side at mileage **150.9**.

Mileages 152–154: Malachi Lake, the most popular of cottage destinations, can be seen as the tracks round the northern end of the lake. The picturesque station, with the lake in the background, still remains at mileage **153**.

Mileages 155–162: Mileage **158** brings you through a rock cut featuring jagged sides. At White (mileage **159**), a large rock quarry can be seen to the south. At Rice Lake (mileage **160**) there is another station shelter to the south. Watch for the sign at mileage **162.2**, announcing the Ontario/Manitoba border. Travelling west, you are also entering the Whiteshell Provincial Park.

Mileages 163–178: At mileage **167** the white stuccoed building on the north side of the tracks, now a summer cottage, dates to 1927 as a section foreman's house. At mileage **168** you travel high above narrow Cross Lake. When the railway was built, large amounts of fill were needed to carry the tracks over the lake's swampy bottom. Since the lake is part of the Whiteshell River system, it was necessary to blast through the rock so the water could continue to flow. It is a popular canoe route; when the water level is high canoeists climb the banks and portage over the tracks.

Mileages 179–183: After passing the stop for Brereton Lake (mileage **179**), the lake can be seen to the north at mileage **180**. This is also where the *Canadian* passes over the Rennie River, a popular snow mobile trail in the winter months. "Rail-fanning" is what railway enthusiasts call spending time waiting for trains to get that perfect photo. A favourite place in the area for the editor of *Canadian Railway Modeller* magazine to "railfan" is west of Indigo at mileage **183.3**, where the *Canadian National* tracks cross high above the *Canadian Pacific* mainline.

Mileages 184–190: As the *Canadian* exits the Whiteshell Provincial Park, the Canadian Shield starts to disappear and the terrain gradually changes to a prairie landscape.

Mileages 191–200: The Whiteshell

Provincial Forest is entered at mileage **192**. At mileage **196** the train crosses the Whitemouth River. To the north you can clearly see the dome of the Ruthenian Greek Catholic Parish of the Holy Cross. Elma is reminiscent of a prairie town of years gone by. The buildings along the highway include the old pool hall and confectionery and the Elma Hotel.

Mileages 201–237: At mileage **201**, you leave the Whiteshell Provincial Forest and enter the Agassiz Provincial Forest. The train crosses the Brokenhead River at mileage **211**. Watch for deer in the fields along the tracks. On the north side of the tracks at mileage **229.8** you get a glimpse of the pioneer village of the Anola and District Museum, featuring a pioneer home, one-room schoolhouse, and the area's first fire truck. At mileage **236** the tracks cross highway 15 diagonally.

Mileage 238.3: Note the station sign while passing Dugald. This is the site of Manitoba's worst railway accident. It occurred here on September 1st 1947, as cottagers were returning to Winnipeg on the *Campers Special* after the long weekend. The train slammed into the eastbound *Continental*, killing 31 passengers and crew, and injuring 85.

Mileages 239–244: The Winnipeg skyline to the west comes into view. At mileage **243.4**, the train crosses the 29-mile (46.7-kilometre) Winnipeg Floodway over a 903-foot (275-metre) long bridge. The city of Winnipeg is in the Red River Valley and recorded floods in the area date back to the early 1800s. After the devastating flood of 1950, officials decided to build this large diversion so excess springtime flood waters from the Red River could bypass Winnipeg, and be returned to the normal river channel north of the city. Construction began in 1962 and it was put into service in 1969. It has since saved the city from flooding numerous times.

Mileages 245–246: The train passes *CN*'s Transcona Shops. The name of this Winnipeg suburb, Transcona, is an abbreviation of "Transcontinental," derived from the name of the first railway through this area: *National Transcontinental Railway*.

Mileages 247–252: The train passes through an industrial area and, at mileage **250**, crosses high above the *CP*'s Emerson Subdivision. This was the first track on the Canadian Prairies built utilizing the locomotive *Countess of Dufferin*, which arrived in Winnipeg in 1877 on a barge pushed by the stern-wheeler *Selkirk*. At mileage **250.5** you cross the Seine River in the suburb of St. Boniface,

The beautiful vistas across Canada's prairies seem to stretch as far as the eye can see.
Steve Boyko photo

which has the largest population of French-speaking Canadians in western Canada. To the north sits Whittier Park. The park, with its replica fort, is home to the Festival du Voyageur every February. To the south you see the silver roof of the College de St. Boniface. The *Canadian* crosses the mighty Red River at mileage **251**. Once across, to the south is Shaw Park, home of the Winnipeg Goldeyes baseball team. The facade of the St. Boniface Basilica, with its round empty window, can be seen on the opposite side of the river. This is all that is left of the original Basilica, which burned in 1968. A modern church was erected behind it. To the north you can look down Portage Avenue East to see what is referred to as "the windiest corner in North America"—Portage and Main, the centre of the city's business district.

Finally, you arrive at Winnipeg's Union Station, mileage **252.1**, designed by the same architects who worked on New York's Grand Central Station. Built for the *Grand Trunk Pacific* and the *Canadian Northern Railway*, it opened in 1911. Winnipeg is derived from a Cree word that translates into "Muddy Waters," a reference to the silt from the region's fine soil that fills the Red and Assiniboine Rivers. The area was a First Nations settlement for years before the first Europeans, La Verendrye and a group of hearty explorers, initially visited the encampment. Winnipeg, 2011 population 730,018, was founded in 1738.

Before the railway came to Winnipeg, riverboats provided the major transportation link between the city and North Dakota. The railway changed all this, starting in 1878 when a rail link was built to Emerson on the Canada/ US border. Soon rival companies were building a network of rail lines across the prairie. Before long, three lines headed for the Pacific Ocean, all of which had numerous subdivisions spread across the prairies to collect the region's plentiful harvests. West of Winnipeg, the *Canadian* travels on the line built by the *Grand Trunk Pacific*, which later became part of *Canadian National Railways*. Winnipeg is the midway point for your journey. There is a lengthy scheduled stop for servicing and a change of crews. This gives you an opportunity to stretch your legs and see the opulent rotunda of the station and an opportunity for a brief tour of downtown. Be careful not

to miss your departing train! Also located in the station trainshed is the Winnipeg Railway Museum. Group tours are welcome during the layover, but tours must be pre-arranged by calling: 204 942-4632.

Winnipeg is a great place to break your journey. Attractions include The Forks National Historic Site that is directly behind Union Station, and the Exchange District, featuring the renowned Museum of Man and Nature. Also in the area is UN Luggage at 175 Mc-Dermot Avenue, if you need to repair your luggage or purchase more to carry all your souvenirs. For rail travellers to and from Winnipeg we recommend the conveniently located Fort Garry Hotel. It is a National Historic Site and one of Canada's grand railway hotels opened in 1913 by the Grand Trunk Pacific. The ho-

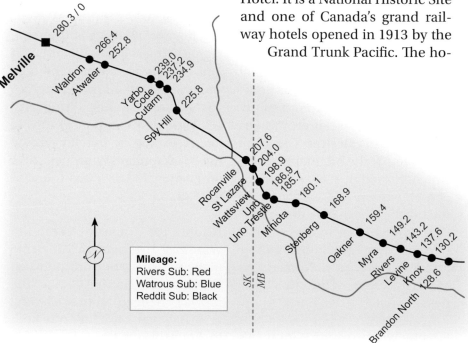

Mileage:
Rivers Sub: Red
Watrous Sub: Blue
Reddit Sub: Black

VIA'S CANADIAN

tel is directly across from the station's Main Street entrance at 222 Broadway Avenue. Reservations can be made at 855 223-7781. Web: *www.fortgarryhotel.com* Email: *ftgarry@fortgarryhotel. com*

A long standing tradition at the hotel is the Grand Sunday Brunch, which should be savoured. Weary travellers will want to experience the Fort Garry's rejuvenating TEN Spa, so-named because it occupies the tenth floor of the hotel. The spa can be reached at: 866 585-0772 or Web: *www.tenspa.ca*. For more travel information about the city of Winnipeg, contact Destination Winnipeg at 259 Portage Avenue, Winnipeg, MB, R3B 2A9. Call: 800 665-0204. Web: *www. tourism.winnipeg.mb.ca*

Winnipeg is also the starting point of *VIA*'s Churchill-The Pas-Churchill train, which travels north from Portage La Prairie, Manitoba. To request information and a detailed rail travel package about Northern Manitoba, in any

season, contact Rail Travel Tours at: 866 704-3528. Web: *www. railtraveltours.com*

If you are planning to explore Manitoba as part of your journey, we recommend that you visit the Travel Manitoba Centre in the Johnston Terminal at The Forks, or contact them at Travel Manitoba, 7th Floor, 155 Carlton Street, Winnipeg, MB, R3C 3H8. Call: 800 665-0040. Web: *www.travelmanitoba.com*

Route Highlights
Winnipeg to Melville
Rivers Subdivision

Mileages 0–10: As you depart Winnipeg, you see buildings to the south that were once used by the *Northern Pacific Railway* (later *CNR*) and now comprise the Forks Market that features fresh produce, restaurants, and numerous curio shops. To the north is the green copper roof of the Hotel Fort Garry. As you cross the Assiniboine River (mileage **0.2**), you see the junction of

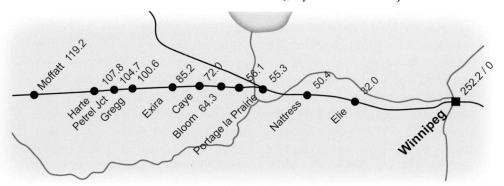

Winnipeg's skyline backdrops *VIA*'s *Canadian* as it heads eastbound. *North Kildonan Publications photo*

the Assiniboine and Red rivers below the former railway (now a pedestrian) bridge. To the north is the Main Street Bridge of the Old Forts.

The train curves to the west, high above the city's wide Main Street. Look to the north towards the downtown area, or to the south to see the Norwood Bridge. At mileage **1** look north to see the distinctive green dome of the Manitoba Legislative Building. On the roof is the five-tonne statue of the Golden Boy, holding a sheaf of wheat in one hand and a light in the other to guide the way to prosperity. The statue was sculpted and plated with gold in Paris, France. It was on its way to Manitoba when World War One intervened. The ship carrying him served as a troop carrier, and he did not arrive until 1919.

The building officially opened the following year. To the north at mileage **3.6** you can see the Pan-Am pool built when the city hosted the Pan-Am Games in 1967. It was again used when the city hosted the games in 1998. The western limits of Winnipeg are reached at mileage **10.5** when you cross under the Perimeter Highway. On the south side of the tracks is a grain elevator named after the mileage (**10.6**).

Mileages 10–27: In this area, the *Canadian* passes some of the most fertile fields in North America. The water tower to the north, between mileages **15.5** and **18**, is used by the Headingly Correctional facility. At mileage **28**, on the North side of the tracks, in past years, there were rows and rows of straw bales located here that had been used in an isoboard-manufacturing process. However, the plant is not currently in operation. It had utilized a process whereby the straw was dried, crushed and then mixed with resins and pressed into boards for use in the furniture and construction industries. The town of Elie is passed at mileage **32.0**. Look north to see the former station, now a private residence. The train parallels the Trans-Canada Highway, viewed to the north. The train again crosses the Assiniboine River on a 412-foot (125-metre) long bridge at Nattress, mileage **50.4**.

Mileages 51–58: Portage la Prairie, 2011 population 12,996, was named for the spot where the voyageurs rested before picking up their canoes and portaging over the prairie to Lake Manitoba, 14 miles (22 kilometres) to the north. At mileage **53**, to the north is the Fort La Reine Museum featuring a replica of the fur trading outpost that La Verendrye used as his base for exploring the prairies, as well as a pioneer village and a railway display. Both railways serve Portage la Prairie. The yellow-bricked former *CPR* passenger station can be clearly seen across from the former *CNR* station (mileage **55.3**) now used by *VIA*. The station also doubles as the local bus depot. Portage la Prairie enjoys more days of summer sunshine than any city in Canada.

Leaving the city, you cross the CP mainline which takes a more southerly route. The immediate track to the north leads to what was originally the *Lake Manitoba Railway & Canal Company*. From a small stretch of track north of here, between Gladstone and Lake Manitoba, railway contractors William Mackenzie and Donald Mann began building the *Canadian Northern Railway*. It is also where *VIA's* Winnipeg–The Pas–Churchill train, detailed on page 148, turns north.

Mileages 59–91: When the Assiniboine River is ready to overflow its banks in Portage la Prairie, the Portage Diversion (mileage **59**) carries water north to Lake Manitoba. The train crosses the Yellowhead highway at mileage **63**, and then passes the Bloom fertilizer complex one mile later. Squirrel Creek is crossed at mile **83**.

Mileages 92–97: Ten thousand years ago, after glaciers receded to the north, a massive lake covered the majority of southern Manitoba. Here the *Canadian* winds through a scenic area that was once a series of beach ridges forming the western shores of the glacial Lake Agasis. The train crosses a scenic valley between mileages **93.6** and **94.5**.
Mileages 98–126: Now the train returns to farm terrain, as it

moves through an area known for sunflower seeds and potatoes. Harte (mileage **107.8**) was one of many communities on the prairies created at the point where steam locomotives would require more water. These watering stops often had towers with special octagonal enclosures, designed to keep water from freezing in the winter. The old foundation of one of these can be seen here, as well as the old general store (now a private residence) with its antique gas pump.

above the Little Saskatchewan River. The river was dammed to create Lake Wahtopanah, seen to the north. Rivers was the first *Grand Trunk Pacific* division point west of Winnipeg and the community displays *CN* caboose 79528 built at *CN's* Pointe St. Charles Shops in Montreal in May 1971. Sir Charles Rivers Wilson, Chairman of the Board of the *Grand Trunk Pacific Railway* lent his name to the community in 1908. Look to the south at mileage **146** to view an airplane hangar used on the Rivers Air Base. The base was established by the British

Biggar 247.3/0 240.5 Neola Leney 227.6 Juniata 217.5 Hawoods 207.3 Farley 195.2 Saskatoon 191.0 Riverview 189.4 Clavet 174.3 Bradwell 167.2 Allan 158.8 Zelma 151.6 Young 143.0 Xena 135.5 Watrous 129.0

Mileages 127–140: Brandon, Manitoba's second largest city, 2011 population 52,368, and home to Brandon University can be seen to the south while your train is stopped at Brandon North, mileage **128.6**. Closer by, to the south-west of the highway, is the modern Agpro "through-put" elevator, noteworthy for its ability to handle vast amounts of grain.

Mileages 141–180: The trestle at Rivers, Manitoba (mileage **143.2**), carries the train 90 feet (27 metres)

Commonwealth Air Training Plan during World War Two. The train crosses the Oak River at mileage **148**.

Mileages 181–213: For all those who think the prairies are flat, the train winds through a cut in the terrain, and at mileage **182** the scenic Assiniboine Val-

No less than three dome cars enable sightseeing travellers to enjoy the views rounding Grant's Cut, near Rivers, Manitoba, aboard *VIA*'s *Canadian*. *F. Lesiuk photo.*

ley appears on the west side of the tracks. The lazy Assiniboine River meanders along the valley floor creating oxbows—curved lanes made when the river silt cuts off previous curves in the river. At mileage **185.7**, keep your camera ready for the 1,533-foot (467-metre) long Uno Trestle, 115 feet (35 metres) above Minnewasta Creek. The houses on the cliff at mileage **189** are part of the Birdtail Creek First Nation. The valley widens and the train reaches its lowest point at St. Lazare (mileage **204**), where it crosses the Assiniboine River once again. At mileage **213** the train crosses the Manitoba/Saskatchewan border.

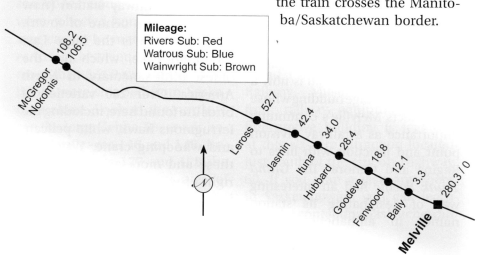

Mileage:
Rivers Sub: Red
Watrous Sub: Blue
Wainwright Sub: Brown

McGregor 108.2
Nokomis 106.5
Leross 52.7
Jasmin 42.4
Ituna 34.0
Hubbard 28.4
Goodeve 18.8
Fenwood 12.1
Baily 3.3
Melville 280.3 / 0

Tourism, 189–1621 Albert Street, Regina, SK, S4P 2S5 Call: 877 237-2273. Web: *www.sasktourism. com*. For information on the city, we recommend you contact Tour-

ism Saskatoon, 101–202 Fourth Avenue North, Saskatoon, SK, S7L 0Z1. Call: 800 567-2444. Web: *www.toursaskatoon.com*

Mileages 192–246: Carrying on past Saskatoon, the GTP system of naming towns in alphabetical order continues. Biggar, named after GTP official William H. Biggar, is reached at mileage **247.3**. It was incorporated as a village in 1909. Around the same time, a local story tells of a group of surveyors pulling a prank one night by putting up a sign saying, "New York is big, but this is Biggar." The phrase stuck, and what was once a prank is today featured in the town's emblem.

Route Highlights
Biggar to Edmonton
Wainwright Subdivision

Mileages 0–60: As you depart Biggar, look to the south to see a large roundhouse where steam locomotives were once serviced. Another style of railway buildings that have disappeared is interlocking towers that con-

trolled train movements.

These towers deployed a man who used a series of levers to control the railway switches. After Centralized Traffic Control (CTC) was introduced, hundreds of these towers were torn down. The one that controlled the crossing of the *CPR* and *CNR* near Oban (mileage **8.6**) has been restored at the Saskatchewan Railway Museum in Saskatoon. The Killsquaw Lakes are passed on both sides of the tracks between mileages **54** and **56**, before Unity is reached at mileage **57.9**. Unity is home to Compass Mineral's world class underground salt mine. At mileage **59**, to the north, a grain elevator towers above a grove of trees. The *Canadian* then crosses under the tracks of the *CP* mainline from Winnipeg to Edmonton.

Mileages 61–100: The terrain here begins to change to rolling hills and small clumps of trees. The farm country changes from fields of wheat to large cattle ranches and grazing pastures. Look to the north between miles 89 and 90 to see Manitou Lake—unusual because it features a large island

setting. The *Canadian* crosses the Saskatchewan/Alberta border at mileage **101**.

Mileages 102–138: Oil was first discovered in this part of Alberta in the early 1920s; the area is still producing the black gold. Along the route for the next few miles, you will see numerous oil pumpjacks removing the crude from the ground. Burning off the methane gas helps new wells to start producing or to increase oil production. Chauvin (mileage **106.9**) is a pretty town settled in the midst of rolling hills. While passing through Edgerton (mileage **121**), notice the town historical society's heritage village. It features the Edgerton station and *CN* caboose 79123, along with a school, the first United Church, and a display building

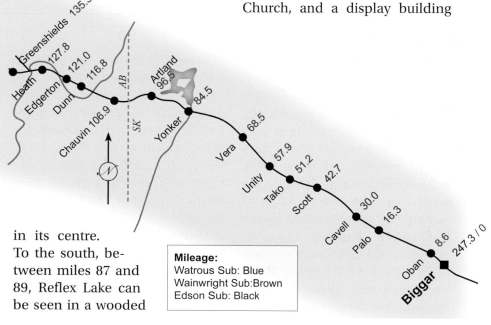

in its centre. To the south, between miles 87 and 89, Reflex Lake can be seen in a wooded

Mileage:
Watrous Sub: Blue
Wainwright Sub:Brown
Edson Sub: Black

Many photo opportunities are available as the train passes through the mountain ranges of the Canadian Rockies near Jasper, Alberta.

for agriculture machinery. The town of Greenshields, mileage **135.3**, lives up to its name, as all the houses here are surrounded by fir trees.

Mileages 139–145: Approaching Wainwright, the Buffalo Capital of Canada, 2011 population 5,925, watch for peregrine falcons in the sky as a breeding centre is nearby. Wainright marks the change from Central to Mountain time so adjust your watches accordingly. The large rodeo grounds are busy every June with the annual fair. To the south you can see the railway equipment which makes up the Wainwright Railway Preservation Society. At mileage **140** the town's large *GTP* station houses the Battle River Historical Society and Museum. The park

behind the station reflects the community's rail heritage with *CNR* caboose 78492. Military equipment honours the major army training facility: Canadian Forces Base Camp Wainwright, training facility, which is located to the south.

Mileages 146–155: At mileage **146**, the Battle River Valley can first be seen to the north, on the other side of Fabyan, mileage **146.6.** Get your camera ready for the crossing of the Battle River Valley on a 2,910-foot (886-metre) long, 195-foot (59.4-metre) high trestle at mileage **149.4.** Excellent views are available from either side of the train. Once across the bridge, the train follows Grattan Creek to the south of the tracks until mileage **154.**

Mileages 155–199: Highway 14, which is also known as the Poundmaker Trail, after a Cree chief, can be seen to the north. The *Canadian* will parallel this highway for the rest of the way to Edmonton. Viking, at mileage **184.5**, owes its name to the Scandinavian settlers who founded the town in 1903. The station has been preserved by the Canadian Northern Society, which has conserved numerous stations in central Alberta. The park next to the station features a small replica of a Norse boat. You can look down the main street of Bruce, to the north, at mileage **196.7**.

Mileages 200–250: While passing through Holden (mileage **205.9**), look across the pond to see the elaborate silver dome of the Holy Ghost Ukrainian Catholic Church. Between mileages **225** and **227** Beaverhill Lake can be seen to the north, only interrupted by Tofield at mileage **226.2**. The train travels through a forested area and at mileage **240.5** passes Cooking Lake on the south. A former station from along the line lives on as the Junction Café on Highway 14, seen to the south at Uncas, mileage **243.8**.

Mileages 251–265: After a few miles of rolling hills, starting at mileage **257**, the train passes Edmonton's numerous oil refineries and petroleum-related industries. Then, the train crosses high above the North Saskatchewan River on the Clover Bar Bridge (mileage **260**). The large Edmonton Stockyards are on the north side of the tracks at mileage **262**. Edmonton, 2011 population 1,159,859, was one of the cities in Canada to see the benefits of transforming its commuter system by reintroducing a light rail transit system. The Belvedere Station, with its bright green roof, can be seen to the north at mileage **263** before you cross over the transit line. After this, the train skirts *CN*'s large Walker rail yards and the end of the sub-division. The train continues on the Edson Subdivision and crosses 97th Street. Look to the south over the Municipal Airport for a good view of Edmonton's business district. Arriving at the Edmonton station, the train backs off the mainline on a wye and crosses the Yellowhead Trail. Edmonton is the provincial capital and features a variety of attractions, one of which is Fort Edmonton Park where four periods in the city's development are brought to life. The modern Edmonton may best be experienced at the West Edmonton Mall with its indoor amusement park, submarine rides, and numerous shops. North of the City is the Alberta Railway Museum for those who want to learn more about the province's rail history. Located close to the

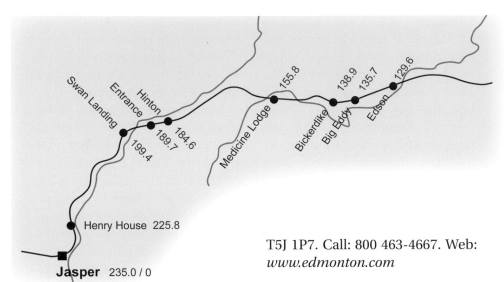

Swan Landing
Entrance 189.7
Hinton 184.6
199.4
Medicine Lodge 155.8
Bickerdike 138.9
Big Eddy 135.7
Edson 129.6

Henry House 225.8

Jasper 235.0 / 0

Edmonton station is the Ramada Hotel and Conference Centre, 11834 Kingsway. Edmonton, AB, T3G 3J5. For reservations, call: 778 473-7821. Web: *www.ramadaedmonton.com.* If you plan a visit anywhere in Alberta, you can learn more by contacting Travel Alberta, 400, 1601–9 Avenue SE, Calgary, AB, T2G 0H4. Call: 800 252-3782. Web: *www.travelalberta.com.* For information on the city, we recommend you contact Edmonton Tourism, 9990 Jasper Avenue NW, Edmonton, AB,

T5J 1P7. Call: 800 463-4667. Web: *www.edmonton.com*

Route Highlights
Edmonton to Jasper
Edson Subdivision

Arriving or departing the Edmonton station, the train turns on a wye and crosses above the Yellowhead Trail before arriving at the terminal or backing onto the mainline.

Mileages 4–18: The train runs through an industrial area in Edmonton's northwest corner.
Mileages 19–33: If you need a hard-to- find part for your vehicle

VIA's *Canadian* en route from Jasper to Edmonton, Alberta. *Matthew G. Wheeler photo*

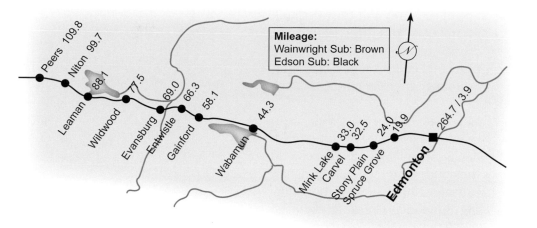

Mileage:
Wainwright Sub: Brown
Edson Sub: Black

Peers 109.8
Niton 99.7
Leaman
88.1
Wildwood
77.5
Evansburg
69.0
Entwistle
66.3
Gainford
58.1
Wabamun
44.3
Mink Lake
33.0
Carvel
32.5
Stony Plain
24.0
Spruce Grove
19.9
Edmonton
264.7 / 3.9

back home, you may want to spend some time in Spruce Grove's auto part yards near mileage **19.9**, the end of the double track out of Edmonton. Stony Plain, 2011 population 15,051, (mileage **24.0**), features sixteen large outdoor murals along its heritage Main Street. The picturesque village of Carvel (mileage **31.8**), with its general store between the large fir trees and the silver dome of the Eastern Orthodox Church, is seen on the north side of the tracks. At mileage **33** the *Canadian* curves around Mink Lake; the south side offers a fantastic opportunity to photograph your train. The train passes through the Wabamun First Nation Reserve at mileage **38** and at mileage **39** crosses Mink Creek.

Mileages 43–53: Wabamun Lake to the south is a popular weekend destination. The large Trans-Alta power plant sits on the north side

of the tracks at mileage **45**. This coal-powered plant's four units combine to burn 300 tonnes of coal per hour (equal to 72 train carloads per day) to power about 500,000 of the area's households. The Canadian Air Force once used the lake's large size to practice floatplane water landings.

Mileages 54–122: The former *GTP* Entwistle station is now a private residence; it can be seen on the north side of the tracks at mileage **66.3**. At mileage **67.6** the train crosses high above the Pembina River on a 900-foot (274-metre) long bridge. Evansburg, 2011 population 880, named after Harry Marshall Erskine Evans, former Edmonton mayor and Government of Alberta advisor, is reached at mileage **69**. Chip Lake to the north at mileage **78** can be seen intermittently behind the trees until mileage **86**. The Lobstick River is crossed at mileage **100** and Carrot Creek at mileage **105**. The train then crosses two rivers within the same mile: McLeod River at **122.1**, then Sundance Creek at mileage **122.6**.

Mileages 123–151: The train reaches Edson, 2011 population 8,475, at mileage **129.6**. Look to the south on the curved bridge at mileage **136** to see the meandering Sundance Creek. At mileage **138.9** the former Bikerdike station lives on as a farmhouse. As you reach mileage **151**, on a clear day you can get a distant view of the Miette Range of the Rocky Mountains to the south. Below is the rock-filled McLeod River.

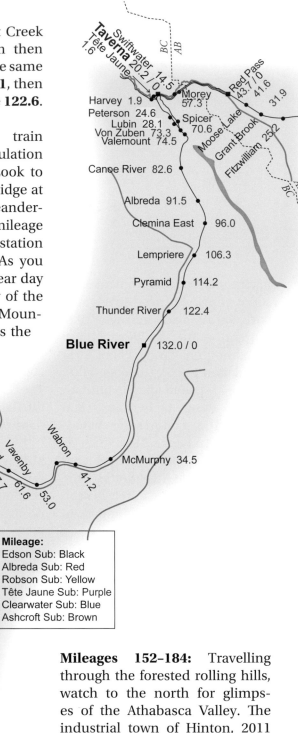

Swiftwater 14.5
Taverna
Tête Jaune 20.2 / 0
1.6
BC AB
Red Pass 43.7 / 0
41.6
Morey 57.3
31.9
Harvey 1.9
Peterson 24.6
Lubin 28.1
Von Zuben 73.3
Valemount 74.5
Spicer 70.6
Moose Lake
Grant Brook
Fitzwilliam 25.2
AB
BC
Canoe River 82.6
Albreda 91.5
Clemina East 96.0
Lempriere 106.3
Pyramid 114.2
Thunder River 122.4
Blue River 132.0 / 0

Birch Island
Clearwater
Vavenby 61.6
Wabron
Blackpool 73.8 67.7
53.0
41.2
McMurphy 34.5
Boulder 83.0
Chu Chua 90.9
Chinook Cove 98.1
Barriere 104.4
Exlou 108.2
McLure 115.8
Rayleigh 132.4
Kamloops 139.4 / 0

Mileage:
Edson Sub: Black
Albreda Sub: Red
Robson Sub: Yellow
Tête Jaune Sub: Purple
Clearwater Sub: Blue
Ashcroft Sub: Brown

Mileages 152–184: Travelling through the forested rolling hills, watch to the north for glimpses of the Athabasca Valley. The industrial town of Hinton, 2011 population 9,640, with a pre-

VIA'S CANADIAN

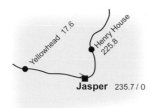

Yellowhead 17.6
Henry House 225.8
Jasper 235.7 / 0

served 1911 GTP station, is known as the "Gateway to the Rockies." While stopped here, at mileage **184.6**, you get an extended view of the valley. As you cross the Prairie Creek at mileage **187**, look to the north to see where it flows into the Athabasca River.

Mileages 193–199: The train crosses the Athabasca River (mileage **193**) on a 620-foot (189-metre) long bridge. The river's unique blue colour comes from the sunlight reflecting off the rock silt in the water. The river continues on

the south side of the tracks before it widens at mileage **196** to form Lake Brûlé. The lake was named after explorer Etienne Brûlé, who travelled this river route after fellow explorers David Thompson and Alexander Mackenzie. To the north at mileage **199.4**, the junction known as Swan Landing connects with a 233-mile (145-kilometre) *CN* line to Grand Prairie in the Peace River Country.

Mileages 200–235: At mileage **204** the train passes through a tunnel; at mileage **206** it passes the Jasper Park Gate (park border). The Snake Indian River is crossed at mileage **211**. Jasper House, a fur trading supply post built in 1813, was named after Jasper Hawes; it was located on the opposite side of Jasper Lake at mileage **215**. The causeway at mileage **217** was a

VIA's Canadian is by Moose Lake in Mount Robson Provincial Park which straddles the Alberta-BC border. *Matthew G. Wheeler photo*

popular spot to take promotional photos of *CN*'s *Super Continental.*

Mountain goats are a common sight on the steep rocks on the north side of the tracks. Snaring River is crossed at mileage **225**. Another supply station, Henry House, lies between Jasper Lake and the rails at mileage **225.8**. Watch for elk in this area. The train arrives at the picturesque Jasper station at mileage **235**. There is an extended stop here so you have a chance to stretch your legs, browse the gift shops along Connaught Drive, and photograph yourself beside *CNR* steam locomotive 6015. Take time to adjust your watch appropriately from Mountain to Pacific Time. Originally known as Fitzhugh, the town's name was changed to Jasper in 1911. Until the 1930s the only way to get to this remote park town was by horse or train. Today, situated in the middle of Jasper National Park, the growth of the town is strictly limited, but there is more than enough to see and do to keep you busy for days. If you are planning a few days here, or are transferring to *VIA*'s Jasper–Prince Rupert train (detailed on page 160), we recommend the walking tour of the town site presented by the Friends of Jasper National Park. At the Jasper-Yellowhead Museum and Archives, you can learn more about the Tent City resort that was originally set up for visitors on the shores of Lac Beauvert.

Today the same site is occupied by the Jasper Park Lodge. Built by the *Canadian National Railways,* this world-class resort, with its separate cabins, is managed today by Fairmont Hotels. Cab shuttles depart from the station to take passengers to the lodge. Reservations can be made at: 800 257-7544. Web: *www.fairmont. com.* If you wish to stay in town, a popular alternative is private home accommodation. For this we recommend the spacious two-bedroom suite of the Homestead at 23 Aspen Crescent. Contact your friendly hosts Harry and Edna Home at: 780 852-5818. Email: *hehome@shaw.ca*

Route Highlights
Jasper to Blue River
Albreda and Robson Subdivisions

Mileages 0–16: On the west side of Jasper between mileages **2** and **3**, Whistler Mountain can be clearly seen on the south side of the tracks. The small building on the mountaintop is the upper terminal of the Jasper aerial tramway 8,202 feet (2,500 metres) above sea level. At mileage **6** the train passes slide detector fences. Seen in numerous spots along the tracks, these fences warn trains if rock slides or boulders have fallen, potentially blocking the tracks. When the wires are broken, a signal is automatically sent to the train to stop. Between mileages **11** and **15** watch the small ponds and clearings for moose. At mileage **16** there is a good curve on which to photograph your train.

Mileage 17.5: The train makes two crossings here: the Alberta/British Columbia provincial border and the summit of the Yellowhead pass at the Great Divide. All rivers on the west side of the divide now flow to the Pacific. The border is also the boundary for Jasper National Park on the Alberta side and Mt. Robson Provincial Park on the British Columbia side. You also cross the line between the Mountain and Pacific Time Zones. Move your travel clocks and watches one hour back if travelling west, or one hour forward if travelling east.

Mileages 18–37: Scenic Yellowhead Lake is passed at mileages **21–22** to the south. Across the lake, Mount Fitzwilliam can be seen on the left, and Mount Rockingham to the right. On the south side of the tracks at mileage **24** is the beginning of the Fraser River. The train crosses Grant Brook at mileage **31** and Moose River at mileage **33**.

Mileages 38–73: Between the railway and the Selwyn Mountain Range sits Moose Lake at mileage **41.6**. Watch for the tall waterfalls on the opposite shore. At mileage **43.7/0.0** is Red Pass Junction; this is where the Grand Trunk Pacific (which was parallel to the Canadian Northern route) turned to the west for Prince Rupert, while the Canadian Northern continued on a southwest course for Vancouver.

To the south, eastbound trains travel along a rock cut; look up to get intermittent glimpses of the other railway tracks. Mount Robson, the highest peak in the Canadian Rockies at 12,972 feet (3,954 metres) above sea level, continues to be seen to the north for the next few miles. After a major track improvement in this area in the 1980s, the *Canadian* normally follows the Robson Subdivision to Taverna, mileage **20.2** where the Subdivision diverts towards Prince Rupert. At Taverna, you turn south and reconnect at Von Zuben, mileage **73.3**, with the Albreda Subdivision. (Turn to page 160 for details on *VIA*'s train travelling between Jasper and Prince Rupert).

As you travel south along the Robson Subdivision, the mountain range to the northwest is known as the Premier Range, since the mountain peaks are named for Canadian prime ministers.

The normal route for the eastbound train follows the original Canadian Northern route between Von Zuben, mileage **73.3** and Red Pass Jct. mileage **43.7**. Between mileages **63** and **58** watch to the north of the tracks to see Mount Robson, at a towering 12,972 feet (3,954 metres) above sea level. On the south side of the tracks is Mount Terry Fox, named for the courageous one-legged young man who set out on his 1980 Marathon of Hope to run across Canada to raise funds for cancer research. The train crosses Snowslide Creek at mileage **51.8** where the falls can be quite dramatic if the water is high; then Glacier Creek at mileage **50.5** and goes through a tunnel at mileage **48**. The Fraser River is the next river crossed. The tracks on the "high-line" are located on a ledge above the former *GTP* line before dropping down to Red Pass Junction at mileage **43.7**.

Mileages 73–113: At mileage **74.5** the train passes through Valemount, 2011, population 1,018. Main Street is located on the south side of the track, and features a hotel with the Log-n-Rail Bar (which hints at the town's two largest employers). A museum is located in the former station, beside *CN* caboose 79726, and next to the log building housing the town library. Good views of the Rocky, Monashee and Cariboo Mountains abound between mileages **76** and **80**. As the train crosses the Canoe River at mileage **80.6**, you pass a small cairn that marks the spot where soldiers en route to Korea died in a railway mishap on November 21st 1950. River crossings continue with the Clemina River at mileage **97** and Cascade Creek at mileage **102**. Look to the north side of the tracks for the white picket fence marking the grave of a railway worker who died during the line's construction. The North Thompson River, on the north side of the tracks, should be visible in this area. Serpentine Creek is crossed at mileage **110**.

Mileage 113.5: Have your camera ready, because the spectacular Pyramid Falls can be seen to the east. The water of Pyramid Creek hits a unique outcropping of rock to create a triangular effect. Below the falls, the creek passes under the tracks.

Mileages 114–132: The train crosses the North Thompson River at mileage **123.1** and Thunder River at mileage **123.4**. Then at mileage **131**, the Blue River is crossed. While on the bridge, look to the south for good views. Finally, you reach Blue River, 2011 population 260 at mileage **132.3**.

Route Highlights
Blue River to Kamloops

The tallest mountain in the Canadian Rockies, Mount Robson , seen as dawn breaks in the winter months.

Clearwater Subdivision

Mileages 0–44: The snowcapped mountains change to large rolling hills east of Blue River. At mileage **8** the train begins to travel through the narrow North Thompson River Canyon, then crosses Berry Creek three times. At mileage **12**, watch to the south for the gorge and rushing water of Little Hell's Gate Canyon. Then the train enters a tunnel. The area below Groundhog Mountain is known for its rockslides. More slide detectors are passed starting at mileage **17**. Cottonwood trees line the banks of the area's rivers. The train crosses the North Thompson River on a 352-foot (107-metre) long bridge at mileage **32**, then the

Otter Creek at mileage **33**. Look to the north at mileages **42** and **43** to see the Mad River Rapids. Good views are offered when the North Thompson is again crossed at mileage **44**. You are following the same route taken by the gold rush "Overlanders" in 1862—well before the coming of the railway—when over 200 people travelled from eastern Ontario and Quebec to Kamloops to start a new life.

Mileages 45–139: The train now travels through a region of sandy cliffs and soil. It crosses the North Thompson at mileage **59.1** and **59.5**. The community of Birch Island at mileage **61.6** can be seen both on the opposite shore and on Butchers Island in the middle of the North Thompson. At mileage **68** just beyond Clearwater, mileage **67.7**, watch for the Clearwater River flowing into the North Thompson. At mileage **103** the train again crosses Barriere River and, at mileage **107**, Lois Creek. Look to the north at mileage **114** to see Fishtrap Rapids. Y ou reach Rayleigh, a northern suburb of Kamloops, at mileage **132.4**. Look on the opposite side of the river to see the suburb of Westsyde. The Kamloops station, mileage **139.4**, is located in the northern part of this city of 98,754 that began in 1811 as a fur trading post. From the station, you can see the suburbs rising on the hills on the south side of the city. If you are planning to spend some time in the city where the North and South Thompson Rivers meet, we recommend you contact the Kamloops Visitor Info Centre, 1290 West Trans-Canada Highway, Kamloops, BC, V2C 6R3. Call: 800 662-1994. Web: *www.tourismkamloops.com*

Route Highlights
Kamloops to Boston Bar
Ashcroft Subdivision

When the *Canadian Northern Railway* construction crews reached Kamloops in 1913, the *Canadian Pacific Railway* had already chosen the easier sides

of the Thompson and Fraser River Canyons to build its line to the Pacific. So the *Canadian Northern* had no choice but to build on the opposite banks.

Mileages 0–6: Departing Kamloops the train crosses the North Thompson River. The train then travels through the suburb of Brocklehurst.

Mileages 7–25: The Thompson River widens to form Kamloops Lake. Birds are plentiful in the arid landscape, including killdeer, mallards, spotted sandpiper, and osprey, which have their large nests in the area. The lake

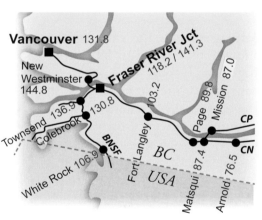

disappears from view w h e n you pass through the numerous tunnels, beginning with the Tranquile tunnel at mileage **9**, then the Battle Bluff tunnel at mileage **10**. The *CPR* had to build tunnels on the south side; at mileage **11** look to the south to see the five Cherry Creek

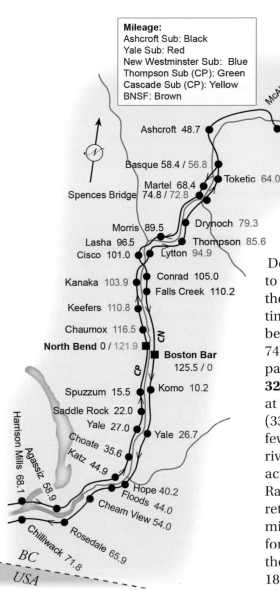

Mileage:
Ashcroft Sub: Black
Yale Sub: Red
New Westminster Sub: Blue
Thompson Sub (CP): Green
Cascade Sub (CP): Yellow
BNSF: Brown

McAbee 40.0
Walhachin 32.6
Savona 25.7
Jalesile 19.4
Frederick 13.8
Kissick 9.3
Ashcroft 48.7
Kamloops 139.4 / 0

Basque 58.4 / 56.8
Toketic 64.0
Martel 68.4
Spences Bridge 74.8 / 72.8

Morris 89.5
Drynoch 79.3
Lasha 96.5
Thompson 85.6
Cisco 101.0
Lytton 94.9

Kanaka 103.9
Conrad 105.0
Falls Creek 110.2

Keefers 110.8

Chaumox 116.5
CN
North Bend 0 / 121.9
Boston Bar 125.5 / 0
CP

Spuzzum 15.5
Komo 10.2
Saddle Rock 22.0
Yale 27.0
Yale 26.7
Choate 35.6
Katz 44.9
Harrison Mills 68.1
Agassiz 58.9
Hope 40.2
Floods 44.0
Cheam View 54.0
Chilliwack 71.8
Rosedale 65.9
BC
USA

Deadman's Valley can be seen to the north. The train crosses the Thompson River numerous times over the next few miles, beginning at mileage **28** on a 745-foot (227-metre) long bridge, passing Wallachin at mileage **32.6**, then back to the north side at mileage **34** on a 1,110-foot (335-metre) long bridge. After a few miles the train crosses the river again at mileage **45.8**. Once across, look to the north to see Rattlesnake Hill before the train returns to the north shore at mileage **47**. At mileage **47.9** look for the white post that marks the height of the water level in 1880 after a rock slide dammed the river. The town of Ashcroft (mileage **48.7**), 2011 population 1,628, is known as one of the driest places in Canada.

Mileages 50–74: At mileage **51** the train passes through a tunnel and emerges on the other side amidst the volcanic rock of Black Canyon. The curve

tunnels. At mileage **20** the train enters the Copper Creek tunnel. Savona can be seen on the opposite side of the lake, before it narrows to form the Thompson River.

Mileages 26–49: The desolate

at mileage **52** provides a good opportunity to photograph your train. The train crosses the river at mileage **55** and passes through tunnels alongside the *CP*. Some of the heaviest rail traffic in the country occurs between here at Basque and Mission to the south so the railways negotiated a one way flow of traffic on each other's lines. Trains travelling eastward from Vancouver travel on the *Canadian Pacific* line from Mission until returning to the *Canadian National* line here as Basque. At mileage **59** the *CN* line crosses back to the north side of the river. On January 23rd 1915, in a simple ceremony, the last spike on the *Canadian Northern Railway* was driven near mileage **63**. The train enters the Martel tunnels at mileages **67.5** and **67.6**.

Mileages 75–96: Master anglers visit this area of the river every year for some of the world's best steelhead fishing. The area is also known for its big horn sheep. The train enters Rainbow Canyon, named for the various colours of this gorge's steep walls. At mileage **80** you pass through three tunnels and four rock sheds. The rapids on the river here are popular with whitewater rafters. On the *CP* side, note the Indictment Hole trestle at mileage **86**. At mileage **87** you can see Nikomen Falls deep in its own gorge. There is a stone arch bridge at mileage **90**. As well, look to the river to see the Suicide Rapids, in the Jaws of Death Gorge. Note how the canyon seems to be lit up with the various colours of the rocks. The view is marred between mileages **93** and **94** when the train passes through numerous tunnels, rocksheds, and past a flume.

Mileages 97–104: Lytton can be seen on the opposite side of the river. At mileage **97.4** the train crosses the Fraser River. Look below and to the west to see the blue-green water of the Thompson mixing with the dark, silt-laden water of the Fraser. At mileage **98.3** to the east, you can see a small First Nations cemetery. At mileage **103** the railways once again trade sides in a most impressive way at Cisco, so named for a First Nations word that translates to "unpredictable." The *CN* crosses on an 810-foot (247-metre) long bridge over 200 feet (60 metres) above the swirling waters. The *CP* bridge can be seen to the south. Both bridges can be seen from the south shore at mileage **104**.

Mileages 105–125: At Conrad, mileage **105** look to the west to see the looming Pinnacle Rock. At mileage **109** the train enters a long tunnel through Jackass Mountain, named for the stubborn but sturdy mules that carried so much equipment on the Caribou Road.

The Fraser River's Hells Gate Rapids as seen from the comfort of the train.

Good views come at mileage **120** where the train crosses the Ainslie Creek, 140 feet (42 metres) below. The train crosses Stoyoma Creek on a 140-feet (232-metre) long bridge before reaching Boston Bar, mileage **125.5**, 2006 population 860. The name of this community comes from the time when many of the gold seekers ventured into this area from Boston, Massachusetts, in search of the elusive mineral. A "bar" is a gold-bearing sandbar or sandy riverbank.

Route Highlights
Boston Bar to
Fraser River Junction
Yale Subdivision

Mileages 0–6: At mileage **4** the train passes Skuzzy Creek, on the opposite shore. It is not named for its water, but for the only sternwheeler that did what was thought to be impossible. *Skuzzy*, built in 1882, was commissioned by railway contractor Andrew Onderdonk to bring supplies to assist with the building of the Dominion Government portion of the *Canadian Pacific Railway*. To get past the rapids, ringbolts were driven into the river's rock walls. Ropes attached to the boat were then passed through the rings and, with the steamship working its hardest, men pulled on the ropes. Thus, *Skuzzy* became the only sternwheeler to navigate through and beyond Hell's Gate Rapids.

Mileage 7: The rapids at Hell's Gate were altered in 1914 when the *Canadian Northern* blasted too much rock away while building its new line. This narrowed the gorge and fish ladders had to be built to assist spawning salmon. Above here are the red cars of the

Hells Gate airtram; below you, the river surges to its narrowest point—only 110 feet (35 metres) across. During every minute, 200 million gallons of water rushes past at approximately 17 mph (298 kilometres per hour). Take your photos before you enter a tunnel at mileage **7.2**.

Mileages 8–40: The train passes through a series of tunnels between mileages **8** and **9** and then at mileage **11**. At mileage **21.5** the rock formation in the middle of river is called Steamboat Island. You reach Yale at mileage **26.7**—watch the river for the large black Lady Franklin Rock. This marks the spot where the wife of noted explorer Sir John Franklin could travel no further in her desperate search for her husband. The gravel shore near mileage **28** is known as Hill's Bar; in 1875, $2 million worth of gold was discovered here. The Suka creek at mile 30 is one of many in the area that flow into the Fraser. The train passes through another tunnel at mileage **35**, then crosses the Coquihalla River (where it empties into the Fraser at mileage **39.8**). Hope, 2011 population 5,969, at mileage **40**, is surrounded by the beautiful Cascade Mountains; it was originally a Hudson Bay outpost known as Fort Hope. The community blossomed when gold was discovered in the region .
Mileages 4–59: The rugged Fraser

Canyon changes to the Fraser Valley but before the train travels through the fertile fields left by the silt deposited from the Fraser River over thousands of years, you pass some lush forests. Watch for red and orange elderberry trees and stands of BC's shaggy Maple. Cottonwood trees are visible, as are dogwoods with their twisted trunks. Once clear of the forests and into the agricultural area you pass dairy farms and fields full of produce for city markets. The area is known to some as "the food basket for Vancouver". At mileage **59**, look to the south to see the Skagit Mountain Range and 6,903-foot (2,104-metre) Cheam Peak.

Mileages 60–88: Watch for glimpses of the Fraser River to the north. Chilliwack, 2011 population 77,936, at mileage **71.8**, was originally known as Centreville. The community grew with the gold rush when passengers transferred from the riverboats to the new community on the shore of the Fraser. This milk-producing region, with its large dairy barns, is home to holstein, jersey, and guernsey cows. At mileage **77**, the train crosses the Sumas River on a 455-foot (138-metre) bridge. While passing through Matsqui, look to the north from mileages **84** to **86** to see the hill with Westminster Abbey and its high steeple. At Matsqui, your train may stop to detrain passengers for

Abbotsford, a city of 133,497 that lies to the south.

Mileage 89.8: At Page all eastbound passenger trains connect to the *Canadian Pacific Railway* mainline and cross the Fraser on the Mission bridge. The train then travels on the north side of the Fraser until it reconnects to the *CN* mainline at Basque.

Eastbound Routing
Matsqui Jct. (Page) to Basque
Mission, Cascade and
Thompson Subdivisions

Mileages 1.4–0: The Fraser River is crossed as you arrive in Mission having left the *CN* line at Page, mileage 89.8 of the Yale Subdivision. Eastbound *VIA*, *CP* and *CN* trains follow this original *CP* route along the banks of the Fraser River and later, the Thompson River.

Mileages 87.0–0.0: From Mission, 2011 population 36,426, look south to the volcanic cone of 10,788-foot (3,288-metre) Mount Baker 40 miles (64 kilometres) away in Washington State. At Harrison Mills, mileage **68.1**, an eleven-span, 962-foot (293.2-metre) bridge includes a swing span to allow boats to pass. Agassiz, 2011 population 5,664, at mileage **58.9** is the station stop for the resort community of Harrison Hot Springs. Look north to see the station built in 1893 and preserved

CPR caboose 437310 built at the railway's Angus Shops in 1947.

Your train may stop at Katz, mileage **44.9** to board passengers from Hope and vicinity. Good views of Hope Mountain and Isolilock Peak are available to the south. Yale, at mileage **27,** became a roaring gold rush town in 1858 and the starting point of the 400-mile Cariboo Trail to the goldfields at Barkerville. Ten years later it was the site of a Confederation Conference that began the process that led to British Columbia joining Canada in 1871. A chief condition of this confederation was the building of the railway on which you are riding. At mileage **14** watch for the Alexandra suspension bridge; the original structure was the first such bridge in BC when opened by its builder, Joseph Truch in 1861. North Bend is reached at mileage **0** and marks the beginning of the Thompson Subdivision at mileage **121.5.**

At Lytton, mileage **94.9**, of the Thompson Subdivision, the Thompson River joins the Fraser from the east. At mileage **79**, look across the Thompson to see the three Skoonka Tunnels on the *CN*. Spences Bridge, named after Thomas Spence who built a toll bridge across the Nicomen River in 1864, is passed at mileage **72.8**. Look west at Basque, mileage **56.8** while your train rejoins the *CN* Ashcroft Subdivision at mileage **58.4**, to see 5,905-foot (1,800-metre) White Mountain.

Westward Journey Continues

Mileages 90–117: The Fraser, now much wider and with large islands, can be seen between the trees. At mileage **101** the train passes the Fort Langley airfield. Fort Langley, 2011 population 3,400, was originally a Hudson Bay Company fort, built in 1827 to serve the area of New Caledonia and Columbia Districts (now British Columbia and northern Washington). Today the replica of this fort is a National Historic Site; it can be seen along the tracks at mileage **103.2**. Also here is the former *CN* station that now serves as home for the Langley Heritage Society, a tourist information centre, and an art gallery (in the freight shed). On the grounds are 1920 *CNR* caboose 78904, with a model railway display, and a restored 1947 *GM&O* passenger coach. At mileage **108**, you see Douglas Island in the middle of the Fraser River. Bungalow "Y" is the office for the *CN* intermodal yard serving Vancouver; cargo containers are transferred here. Between mileages **113** and **114**, to the south and above, you see where the Trans-Canada Highway crosses the Fraser on the Port Mann Bridge. The train passes through the *CN* Thornton Yards at mileage **116**.

Mileage 118.2: Your train leaves the Yale Subdivision at Fraser River Junction, mileage **118.2** and enters the BNSF's New Westminister Subdivision at mileage **142.8**. Your train runs on tracks owned by the *Burlington Northern Santa Fe* (successor to the *Great Northern Railway*) as it travels through to Vancouver.

Route Highlights
Fraser River Junction to Vancouver
New Westminster (BNSF) and Yale Subdivisions

The Fraser River Bridge is the longest crossing your train will make over the Fraser is reached at mileage **143.4**. The bridge was built in the early 1900s. It can swing open to allow large ships to pass through. Above it is the Pattullo vehicle bridge. Beyond that is a large suspension bridge for the sole use of the *Skytrain*, Vancouver's automated light-rail mass transit system.

On the north side of the river the tracks run parallel to the river; the New Westminster station and yard office can be seen to the west at mileage **144.8**, New Westminster, 2011 population 65,976, sits on the north shore, and Surrey, 2011

The end of the journey and Vancouver's Pacific Central Station.

population 468,251, sits on the south side. New Westminster was the first seaport to ship the gold being discovered along the shores of the Fraser River. As the track turns sharply northwest at mileage **145.0**, look above to see the *Skytrain*'s Braid Station.

The south side of the track forms the border of the Burnaby Lake Nature Park. The train then travels the next couple of miles through an industrial area. At Willington Junction, mileage **151.8** look north to see the portal of the 11,235-foot (3.4-kilometre) tunnel, *CN*'s longest, that provides a connection at the Second Narrows to the north shore of Burrard Inlet. After that, in a scene reminiscent of the tracks that travel through Halifax, the train travels through the Great Northern Cut, where the *Skytrain* runs parallel. The track opens into another industrial area. At *CN* Junction mileage **155.3** it rejoins the Yale Subdivision at mileage **130.6**. If you are travelling westbound, the train is "wyed" (turned around) before you back into the western terminus at Vancouver's Pacific Central Station, built by the *Canadian Northern* in 1919. In front of this grand station, at mileage **131.8**, are Thornton Park and the Main Street stop of Vancouver's *Skytrain*.

You will need more than a few days to take in this spectacular city's sights. We recommend the Fairmont Hotel Vancouver, located in the heart of the city at 900 West Georgia Street. This is another classic railway hotel, which has welcomed guests since 1887. It is actually the third hotel that bears the Hotel Vancouver name and was built on this site in 1939. You will enjoy its grand elegance, commitment to service, and comfortable rooms after a long day of sightseeing or business. Reservations: 866 540-4452 Web: *www.fairmont.com*

This area, where the mountains meet the sea, was home to the Haida First Nations people. The first European to explore this beautiful coast was Captain James Cook, who arrived in 1778. Captain George Vancouver, who had made the trip with Cook fourteen years earlier, returned in 1792 and explored the area for two years.

Vancouver traces its origins to a few entrepreneurs who started some industries on an unspoiled strip of land nearby, along the Burrard Inlet. A shantytown sprung up in the area. In 1867, a retired sailor turned bar owner named Gassy Jack Leighton opened a drinking establishment. Soon thereafter the area was known as Gassy's Town. This name did not last long; after a couple of years the name of the growing community was changed to Granville. *Canadian Pacific Railway* changed the name to Vancouver in 1884 when it chose the site as its western terminus. The new city has continued to grow ever since the first steam locomotive pulled in from Montreal in 1887.

Today this vibrant city of 2,135,201, Canada's third largest, is one of the country's favourite destinations. It is Canada's largest and busiest seaport. The *Skytrain* terminal is the former *Canadian Pacific Railway* station now known as Waterfront Station. This is also the terminal for the *West Coast Express* commuter train to Mission, and the cross-bay *Seabus* to West Vancouver. A short distance from here is Vancouver's "Gastown," with its charming old buildings featuring restaurants, boutiques, and a steam clock that has been a popular attraction since it was refurbished in 1977. Do not miss Stanley Park, where you can enjoy its 8-kilometre walking trail around the park, or the Vancouver Aquarium and Science Centre. Chinatown, with its busy streets and the tranquil Dr. Sun Yat-Sen Classical Chinese Garden, is an interesting area to visit. Across town, on the south side of False Creek, you will find the renovated warehouses of Granville Island Market featuring everything from fresh seafood to an art school. At False Creek you can jump on an Aquabus and travel to Drake Street on the opposite shore. This area was once a railway yard, and became the site of Expo 86. The glass pavilion attached to the Roundhouse Community Centre houses *CPR* locomotive 374. Here you can reflect back on your rail trip, and think about the journey experienced by those aboard the first transcontinental train that arrived in Vancouver on May 23rd 1887 behind engine number 374.

Before you visit Vancouver, we recommend you contact Tourism Vancouver at 210-200 Burrard Street, Vancouver, BC, V6C 3L6. Call: 604 682-2222. Web: *www.tourismvancouver.com.* If you plan on visiting anywhere else in the province, you can contact Super Natural British Columbia at Suite 600, 1166 Alberni Street, Vancouver, BC, V6C 3Z3. Call: 800 435-5622. Web: *www.hellobc.com*

Top: The *Canadian* westbound near Hinton Alberta May 2013, on Prairie Creek Bridge, near the Rockies. *Matthew G. Wheeler photo*
Bottom: "Daddy, this train trip has been wonderful! I can't wait to do it again!" *Matthew G. Wheeler photo*

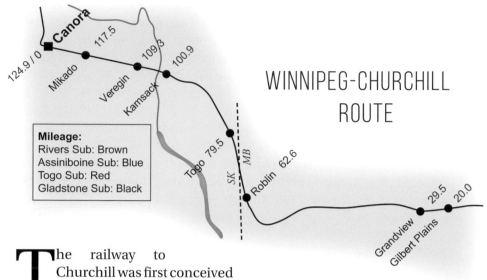

WINNIPEG-CHURCHILL ROUTE

Mileage:
Rivers Sub: Brown
Assiniboine Sub: Blue
Togo Sub: Red
Gladstone Sub: Black

T he railway to Churchill was first conceived as a way to break the monopoly that forced farmers to ship their grain via the west coast or Thunder Bay. Today, it provides travellers with an opportunity to journey northward to Hudson Bay. Here for 3,000 years, indigenous people have led a nomadic life. European visitors date back to 1619, when the Danish Munk expedition wintered here while searching for the Northwest Passage.

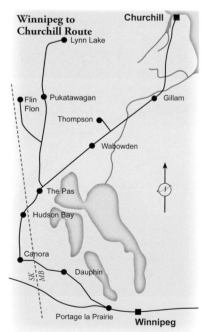

Tie-down rings can still be seen in the rocks near the mouth of the Churchill River. Also remaining today is the majestic Fort Prince of Wales, dating back to 1700. Hudson Bay Company trappers and traders started from the north, and travelled south to expand the fur trade. Travellers today on *VIA Rail*'s *Winnipeg-Churchill* route can begin in Winnipeg and travel the 1,060 miles (1,697 kilometres) in considerable comfort. The untouched scenery along the route can be full of surprises, no matter what time of year you take this journey.

The train departs Winnipeg and initially follows the route of the *Canadian*, detailed on page 119, turning north from the Rivers Subdivision at mileage **55.7** in Portage la Prairie.

Route Highlights
Portage La Prairie to Dauphin Gladstone Subdivision

Mileages 0–37: The big sky coun-try scenery of the picturesque prairies continues to be evident along the route. When the Assiniboine River (located to the south of here) is ready to overflow its banks in Portage la Prairie, water is carried north to Lake Manitoba by the Portage Diversion (crossed at mileage **3.7**). The train crosses Beaver Creek at mileage **19**, followed by Squirrel Creek (mileage **24**), and Pine Creek (mileage **29**). Dead Lake can be seen on both sides of the track at mileage **34**, before arriving in Gladstone, mileage **36.5**, 2011 population 879. Gladstone takes its name from William E. Gladstone, Britain's Prime Minister at the time of incorporation in 1882. Here the train travels surprisingly close to some of the town's buildings. The *CN* tracks parallel and then cross the *CP* Minnedosa Subdivision on their Winnipeg-Edmonton route at mileage **37** before traversing White Mud Creek. In 1895 William Mackenzie and Donald Mann purchased the *Lake Manitoba Railway & Canal Company* for its Gladstone north to Sifton railway charter. From this simple beginning, Canada's second transcontinental railway, the *Canadian Northern Railway*, began.

Mileages 37–121: The train crosses Jordan

121.7 / 0 ■ **Dauphin**

Ochre River ● 108.1

Makinak ● 100.8

Laurier ● 92.4

McCreary ● 83.9

Glencairn ● 72.5

Glenella ● 63.8

Plumas ● 50.3

36.5 ● Gladstone

N

18.6 ● Beaver

Portage la Prairie 55.3 / 0 ■

Portage La Prairie, Manitoba station serves both *VIA*'s *Canadian* and round-trip trains from Winnipeg and Churchill. It is also the local bus depot. *Rail Travel Tours photo*

River at Plumas (mileage **50.3**). Look to the west at mileage **72.5** to see the brick one-room schoolhouse in Glencairn. The landscape begins to change at mileage **75**; the forested slopes of Riding Mountain National Park can be seen to the west. The East Turtle River is crossed at mileage **77**. This area produces the largest amount of maple syrup in Western Canada. A traditional prairie station remains in McCreary at mileage **83**. The train travels northwest through fields and forests, passing through Laurier at mileage **92.4** and Makinak at mileage **100.8**. At mileage **108.1** the train crosses the Ochre River in the town of the same name. At mileage **121.7**, you arrive in the city of Dauphin, 2011 population 8,251, with its unique brick station and former station garden (now a park). The city is home to the National Ukrainian Festival and is a popular starting point for visits to Riding Mountain National Park to the south.

Route Highlights
Dauphin to Canora
Togo Subdivision

Mileages 0–77: Beside Dauphin station is preserved *CN* caboose 79727 built in Montreal in October 1974. On the south side of the tracks at mileage **1**, the former roundhouse lives on as the City of Dauphin's Public Works garage. Continuing due west, the train passes large farms, with Riding Mountain in the distance to the south. The former station in Gilbert Plains at mileage **20** has been moved slightly north to the corner of Main and Gordon, where it lives on as a seniors' centre. When you see the incredible view to the south of Grandview (mileage **29.5**); you will understand how this prairie town got its name. Watch to the north side of the tracks to see heritage buildings and the large grey sheds that house the antique cars and farm implements of the

Canora Station Museum

Watson Crossley Community Museum. The train continues to wind around the Parkland Region west of Lake Winnipeg and east of the Saskatchewan border, reaching Roblin station at mileage **62.6**. Built in 1900, the former station has been transformed into a venue that provides homemade crafts and tourist information, and is now called The Station Café.

Mileages 79–124: The Manitoba-Saskatchewan border is crossed just east of Togo, mileage **79.5**. Instead of a trestle bridge the train crosses a large earth fill at mileage **92** and winds through an area of rolling hills before arriving at Kamsack, Saskatchewan, 2006 population 1,713, (mileage **100.9**). Kamsack comes from a similarly-named Russian city and a word meaning something "vast and large." The Assiniboine River is crossed at mileage **101**, before the tracks curve away from town. Veregin (mileage **109.3**) was formed by a group of Doukhobours who left Russia and followed Peter Veregin to settle here in 1899. The National Doukhobour Heritage Village sits behind the grain elevators on the west side of the tracks. The Canora (from: CAnadian NOrthern RAilway) station at mileage **124.9** in this town of 2,400 is now a museum that features a *CN* 76659, a rare transfer caboose built in 1979. Look into the station's bay window—it appears that the telegrapher has just the telegrapher has just stepped away for a moment.

Route Highlights
Canora to Hudson Bay
Assiniboine and Tisdale Subdivisions

Mileages 0–92: Arriving in Sturgis, 2011 population 620, at mileage **21.2**, the train will cross the Assiniboine River. On the hill where the town is, you can catch a glimpse of the former railway station, now a museum, and a small terrace at the end of the main street over- looking the track and river. The train passes Hinchcliffe at mileage **32.5**, Endeavour at mileage **39.7**, and Usherville at mileage **44.7**. You will know how Tall Pines at mileage **53.4** received its name when you see the towering trees here. The Atomani River is

The Pas 88.1 / 0

Whithorn 60.5

SK | MB

Mileage:
Wekusko Sub: Brown
Turnberry Sub: Black
Assiniboine Sub : Blue
Togo Sub: Red

Relitz 1.8

Muchler 92.2 — Hudson Bay 0.0

Clemenceau 78.1

Bertwell 72.1

Reserve 63.1

Tall Pines 53.4

Usherville 44.7

Endeavour 39.0

Hinchcliffe 32.5

Lady Lake 29.5

Sturgis 21.2

Canora
124.9 / 0

crossed in Bertwell (mileage **72.1**). Watch for the white huts with black identifying designs in the fields. These are to protect the hives for cutter bees that pollinate the crops. At mileage **92** the tracks connect with the east-west Tisdale Subdivision at Mutchler mileage **92.2** and you travel east for 1.5 miles before arriving at Hudson Bay, Saskatchewan. Named for the frigid bay to the north and site of a fur trading post in 1757, this community of 1,504 people is the start of the route to the Bay and the tracks here curve north. Look south east to see the 1905 Desrochers Hotel, with its attractive dormer windows on the third floor.

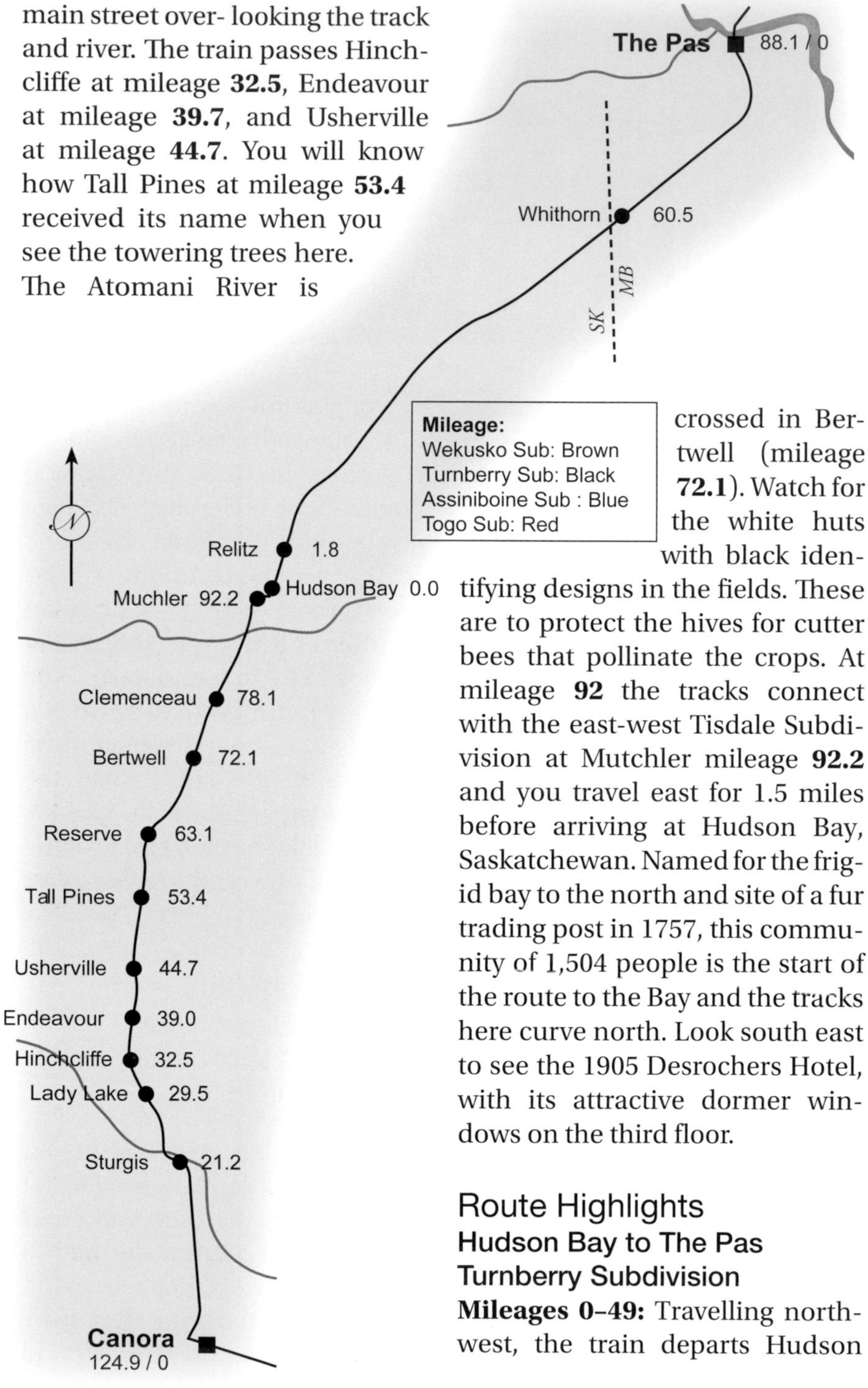

Route Highlights
Hudson Bay to The Pas
Turnberry Subdivision
Mileages 0–49: Travelling northwest, the train departs Hudson

Overlooking the "Gateway to the North," The Pas, Manitoba.

Bay. Between mileages **7** and **8**, on the west side of the tracks, the train passes Ruby Lake and Ruby Beach Provincial Park. Then you travel through a thickly forested area. The Saskatchewan/Manitoba border is crossed at mileage **49**.

Mileages 50–88: The train crosses the Pasquia River at mileage **50**. West of Whithorn, mileage **60.5**, you re-enter Manitoba. Then at mileage **68** it crosses Highway No. 10, and begins to parallel the highway at mileage **71**. Getting closer to The Pas, you pass through the most northerly agricultural area in the province, the Carrot River Valley. At mileage **87** the train curves into the town's railway yard. Looking to the east you see the white, 5-stall railway roundhouse (if it is not obscured by freight cars) before arriving at The Pas station. Known as the "Gateway to the North" there has been evidence of people residing here as far back as 5,000 years. The Pas can trace its first European visitor back to July 5th 1691, when Hudson Bay explorer Henry Kelsey passed through. When Sir John Franklin went missing in the arctic while searching for the North West Passage, the Richardson search party spent the winter here in 1847 and 1848. Some of the members of that party were carpenters who carved the pews still used in the local Anglican church today. In 1908 the *Canadian Northern Railway* arrived. The former Community Building and Court House added to the growing community when completed in 1917; it was the first brick building in northern Manitoba. Today, the building houses the Sam Waller Museum with over 70,000 very diverse items. The city is home to a Trapper's Festival dating from 1916, Manitoba's oldest festival. If you are planning to spend some time here, possibly to take the "Puckatawagan Wayfreight" (a mixed freight and passenger train), a 156.3-mile (251.5-kilometre) trip to Pukatawagan on the Lynn Lake line of the *Keewatin Railway (www.krcrail.ca)* for a wilderness paddling trip, you might see the cars used for this train outside the 1928-era station. We recommend the convenient Wescana Inn, a short distance from the station at

For tourism information, call: 866 965-3386. Web: *www. visitnorthernmanitoba.ca*

Route Highlights
The Pas to Wabowden
Wekusko Subdivision

Mileages 0–136: History repeats itself through the railway's name. Originally known as the *Hudson*

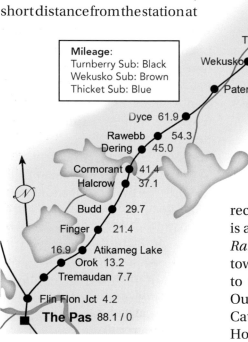

Mileage:
Turnberry Sub: Black
Wekusko Sub: Brown
Thicket Sub: Blue

Wabowden ■ 136.4
Pipun ● 129.4
Dunlop ● 121.8
Button ● 114.2
Ponton ● 107.1
Turnbull ● 93.2
Wekusko ● 81.2
Paterson 70.0
Dyce 61.9 ●
Rawebb ● 54.3
Dering ● 45.0
Cormorant ● 41.4
Halcrow ● 37.1
Budd ● 29.7
Finger ● 21.4
16.9 ● Atikameg Lake
Orok 13.2 ●
Tremaudan 7.7 ●
Flin Flon Jct 4.2 ●
The Pas 88.1 / 0 ■

Bay Railway, it later became part of *Canadian National Railways*, owned by the federal government. In 1997 it was sold to OmniTrax who reclaimed the original name, and it is again known as the *Hudson Bay Railway*. The tracks curve through town as they depart The Pas. Look to the west to see the steeple of Our Lady of the Sacred Heart Cathedral opposite St. Anthony's Hospital. You also pass Devon Park with preserved *CN* Hawker-Siddley caboose 79304, and the *Skippy L*, which was built in 1936

439 Fischer Avenue. Reservations can be made at: 800 665-9468.

by The Pas Canoe Company, then worked the Saskatchewan River and its tributaries for over 40 years. At mileage **0.6** you cross this impressive river on an 850-foot (259-metre) long bridge. On the north side of the river, to the east, you pass the Opaskwayak First Nation Reserve, the Otineka Mall and the Aseneskak Casino in the distance. To the east the large Tolko Industries Ltd. kraft paper complex is passed at mileage **3** Flin Flon Junction is passed at mileage **4.2** where mixed service continues north from The Pas to Pukatawagan with freight service to Flin Flon. On the north side of the tracks sits Clearwater Lake Provincial Park. Atikameg Lake can be glimpsed between the trees at mileage **16.9**. The interesting tripod telegraph poles, now no longer in service, were built because standard poles sunk in the ground would be pushed out after time by the permafrost. Keep your camera ready to photograph the beautiful Cormorant Lake (mileages **32-35**), an area known for its waterfowl, and a place where more than one fishing legend has been caught. At mileage **38.9** on the west side of the tracks, you can see a former pink marble quarry. Then you arrive in the community of Cormorant (mileage **41.4**) and cross the narrows that connect to Little Cormorant Lake on the east side.

Between mileages **85–87** look to the east to see Hargrave Lake. The landscape changes the further north you go, from limestone outcroppings to shallow muskeg, i.e. a grassy bog, to small tracts of clay. Wabowden, with its old station and row of buildings, and a population of 498 in 2006, is reached at mileage **136.4**. It was named after W. A. Bowden, a chief engineer of the federal Department of Railways and Canals.

Route Highlights
Wabowden to Gillam
Thicket Subdivision

Mileage 136–326: Mileage **143** offers a good curve to photograph your train. Thicket Portage (mileage **184.3**), 2011 population 148, was where the Franklin Expedition rested before continuing north. The unique white pipes sticking out of the ground at mileages **196** and **197** are thermal pipes. They help to prevent sinkholes by keeping the ground under the tracks frozen in the spring as long as possible. At mileage **199.8** the train takes a 30-mile diversion on the Thompson Subdivision. This was built to connect the main line to the location of a large deposit of nickel where the city of Thompson was emerging, and was completed when the premier of Manitoba, Douglas Campbell, drove home a spike of solid nickel on October 20th 1957. Thompson had a population of 12,829 in 2011. Inco chairman, John F. Thompson gave his name to the community. The Grass River is crossed at mileage **12.9**. You will see a mine head on the south side of the tracks at mileage **28.8**, before you arrive at Thompson station at mileage **30.5** River. Returning to the Thicket Subdivision and continuing north,

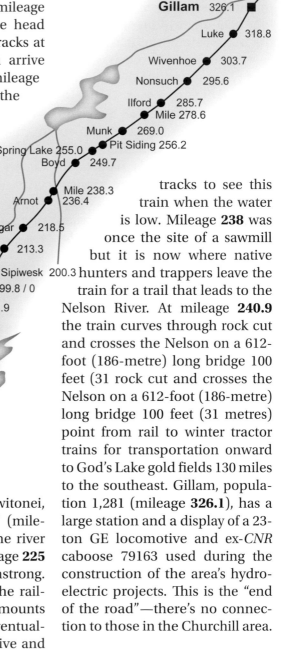

Mileage:
Thicket Sub: Blue
Thompson Sub: Red

Gillam 326.1 ■
Luke ● 318.8
Wivenhoe ● 303.7
Nonsuch ● 295.6
Ilford ● 285.7
Mile 278.6
Munk ● 269.0
Spring Lake 255.0 ● Pit Siding 256.2
Boyd ● 249.7
Mile 238.3
Arnot ● 236.4
Bridgar ● 218.5
Thompson ● 30.5
Pikwitonei ● 213.3
Grass River 12.9 ●
Sipiwesk 200.3
Thompson Jct ● 199.8 / 0
Leven ● 191.9
Thicket Portage ● 184.3
La Pérouse ● 171.1
177.6 ● Hockin
164.3 ● Earchman
158.2 ● Odhill
148.7 ● Lyddal
Wabowden ■ 136.4

some flat cars slid into the lake. Watch on the east side of the tracks to see this train when the water is low. Mileage **238** was once the site of a sawmill but it is now where native hunters and trappers leave the train for a trail that leads to the Nelson River. At mileage **240.9** the train curves through rock cut and crosses the Nelson on a 612-foot (186-metre) long bridge 100 feet (31 rock cut and crosses the Nelson on a 612-foot (186-metre) long bridge 100 feet (31 metres) point from rail to winter tractor trains for transportation onward to God's Lake gold fields 130 miles to the southeast. Gillam, population 1,281 (mileage **326.1**), has a large station and a display of a 23-ton GE locomotive and ex-*CNR* caboose 79163 used during the construction of the area's hydro-electric projects. This is the "end of the road"—there's no connection to those in the Churchill area.

the train arrives at Pikwitonei, Cree for "broken mouth" (mileage **213.3**), and crosses the river of the same name. At mileage **225** the tracks cross Lake Armstrong. When building the line, the railway dumped endless amounts of fill to cross the lake. Eventually, a small steam locomotive and

Route Highlights
Gillam to Churchill
Herchmer Subdivision

Mileages 326–509: At mileage **332** the largest bridge on the route, over 1,000 feet (300 metres), crosses the Nelson River. To the west you can clearly see the Kettle generating station. Manitoba Hydro's second largest facility in the province, built from 1966 to 1973, is 2,900 feet (885 metres) long, and contains twelve turbines. The high-voltage direct current transmission of its electricity 575 miles (925 kilometres) to Rosser, near Winnipeg is listed by the IEEE as a milestone project. The train crosses the Limestone River at mileage **349.8**. Watch to the east where the river flows into the Nelson, creating the Upper Limestone Rapids. At mileage **351** to the east is the Limestone Generating Station. Thus far, the route has actually been travelling toward Port Nelson, the site originally chosen for the line's northern terminus. In fact a 17-span, 2,460-foot (250-metre) long bridge was built to cross the Nelson River, and the line was cleared and graded for track. It was then discovered that Port Nelson would not make an adequate port because of the silt deposits from the Nelson River. The decision was made to extend the line to Churchill; hence the sharp turn at Amery, mileage **355**. Now the

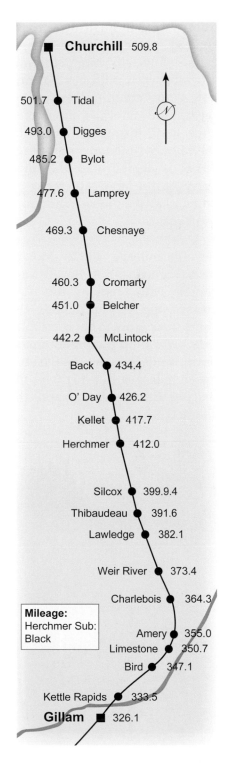

Churchill 509.8

501.7 Tidal

493.0 Digges

485.2 Bylot

477.6 Lamprey

469.3 Chesnaye

460.3 Cromarty

451.0 Belcher

442.2 McLintock

Back 434.4

O' Day 426.2

Kellet 417.7

Herchmer 412.0

Silcox 399.9.4

Thibaudeau 391.6

Lawledge 382.1

Weir River 373.4

Charlebois 364.3

Mileage:
Herchmer Sub:
Black

Amery 355.0

Limestone 350.7

Bird 347.1

Kettle Rapids 333.5

Gillam 326.1

train travels through an area of stunted spruce and tamarack trees, with still more thermal pipes between mileages **362** and **366**. The "communities" along the way are merely sidings named after local historical figures by the railway. Thibaudeau, mileage **391.6**, is named after the line's surveyor. The landscape is like no other you have passed since your trip began.

Beyond mileage **442.2**, McLintock, named for a Royal Navy captain with Franklin, the train crosses the barren lands. The short trees grow to their leeward side, away from the predominant north winds. Look to the East between mileages **450–451.5** for the Belcher Beach project and the characters here.

At Digges, mileage **493**, the red building on the east side of the tracks was once a telemetry station for the Churchill rocket range. Churchill comes into view at mileage **507**, and you arrive at *VIA*'s northernmost station at mileage **509.8**. Look to the north to see the 140,000-tonne capacity grain elevator next to the mouth of the Churchill River.

The sights you see during a visit to Churchill vary by the season. In the winter months, you can witness the dancing northern lights; in the spring, birders come to glimpse the rare ross gull and other northern birds; the beluga whales appear in the summer months; and in the fall the famous polar bears are waiting for the ice to freeze on the bay. Attractions

Thermal pipes along the train route.

Churchill, Manitoba, is *VIA Rail*'s most northern destination and the furthest north you can travel on continuous trackage in North America.

include the Eskimo Museum, Parks Canada Interpretive Centre, and the impressive town complex. While here, book a beluga whale tour by contacting Sea North Tours at: 888 348-7951. Web: *www.seanorthtours.com*

For a roundtrip rail journey from Winnipeg to Churchill for Northern lights in the spring, birding in June, beluga whales in the summer and polar bears in fall, with hotel, tours, transfers and more, contact Rail Travel Tours at 1-866-704-3528 or *www.railtraveltours.com*.

THE JASPER–PRINCE RUPERT ROUTE

Low clouds hide the majestic mountains at McBride, British Columbia.

O ne of the most picturesque rail journeys in the country, *VIA Rail*'s Jasper–Prince Rupert Route takes passengers on a journey through the heart of British Columbia. Along the way, the passing scenery includes everything from mountains, meandering and rushing rivers, or glaciers, to areas where history appears to stand still. The train runs year-round, with an overnight stop in Prince George. *Grand Trunk Pacific* president Charles Melville Hays chose the community of Prince Rupert (then known as Port Simpson) for the western terminus of Canada's third transcontinental railway, which was built between 1911 and 1914. Hays never witnessed its completion, having been a passenger on the *Titanic*. Hays's vision thrives today as *Canadian National* moves ever increasing volumes of freight over the line, while *VIA* operates the passenger train known locally as the "Rupert

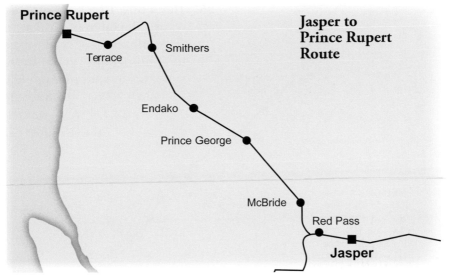

Jasper to Prince Rupert Route

Prince Rupert

Terrace

Smithers

Endako

Prince George

McBride

Red Pass

Jasper

Rocket". Information about the first few miles of the Jasper–Prince Rupert route, and also the park town of Jasper with its great attractions and accommodations, are provided in the Jasper-to-Red Pass portion of the *Canadian*, page 133.

Route Highlights
Red Pass to Taverna
Robson Subdivision

Mileages 0–20: At mileage **2.4** the train crosses the Fraser River, which is followed by tracks on the north side of the route. To the south, the train travels along a rock cut; look up to get intermittent glimpses of the other railway tracks. Mount Robson, the highest peak in the Canadian Rockies at 12,972 feet (3,954 metres) above sea level, continues to be seen to the north for the next few

miles. The train crosses numerous mountain streams before arriving at Taverna, where the tracks turn south to Vancouver or west to McBride. The normal route for the eastbound train follows the route you have just traversed. However, traffic patterns may cause it to turn south just east of Tête Jaune at Harvey, Mileage **1.9** of the Tête Jaune Subdivision and proceed south to Lubin, at mileage **28.1** of the Robson Subdivision, and then east to follow the original *Canadian Northern* route between Spicer, mileage **70.6** and Red Pass Jct. mileage **43.7** of the Albreda Subdivision.

Route Highlights
Taverna to McBride
Tête Jaune Subdivision

Mileages 0–43: The passing scenery includes everything from

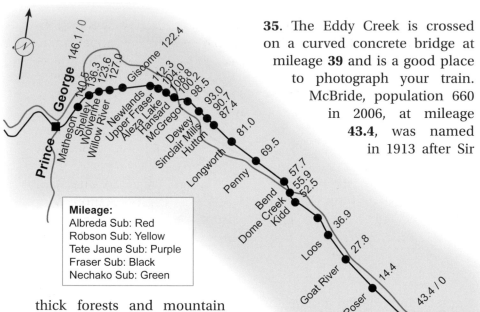

Mileage:
Albreda Sub: Red
Robson Sub: Yellow
Tete Jaune Sub: Purple
Fraser Sub: Black
Nechako Sub: Green

35. The Eddy Creek is crossed on a curved concrete bridge at mileage **39** and is a good place to photograph your train. McBride, population 660 in 2006, at mileage **43.4**, was named in 1913 after Sir Richard McBride, the then youngest (33) premier of B.C.

thick forests and mountain streams to grazing cattle. Tête Jaune (Yellowhead), 2011 population 500, at mileage **4.3** is named for the blond-headed trapper and guide, Pierre Bostonais, who led traders and explorers through the 3,718-foot (1,133-metre) pass in the Rocky Mountains in 1819. It was also the last stop for the stern-wheelers that worked along the Fraser River.

At mileage **9.5** you cross the Little Shuswap River. The station in Dunster (mileage **23.4**) is now a museum. At mileage **25** you get a good view to the north over the meandering Fraser River; watch for grizzly and black bears and moose along the shores. River crossings continue with the 507-foot (315-metre) Raush River Viaduct at mileage **32.7** and Cottonwood Creek at mileage

The Rocky Mountains lie to the south and the Cariboo Mountains to the north. You pass the refurbished McBride Hotel before arriving at the 1919 station, which today serves as the McBride Arts Centre and as a Tourism Information Centre.

Route Highlights
McBride to Prince George
Fraser Subdivision

Mileages 0–69: The Fifty Mile River is crossed three times at mileages **2.5**, **6.4**, and **6.6**. Your train travels high above Twin Creek at mileage **16.5** and at mileage **18** enters an 820-foot (250-metre) tunnel. On the west side of the tunnel, the train travels along a stretch of track known for mud slides and falling rocks. At mileage **25,** as the train skirts the Fraser River, you can see that the river has be- come much wider, as a result of the many creeks and tributaries feeding into it. A former sawmill, with its metal roof and weather-beaten walls, still stands on the south side of the tracks at mileage **33**. The train crosses the

bridge at mileage **56** was built in 1913, it halted all riverboat traffic on the Upper Fraser. The tracks now run along the north side of the river. Watch for the small Penny Post Office building in Penny, BC, at mileage **69.5** on the south side of the tracks; its proportions are comparable to the village's size. Chinook salmon are hatched here. The Penny Station was moved from this location to the Prince George Railway and Forest Museum in 1986.

Mileages 70–146: At mileage **70** the track straightens out and travels through a thickly forested area of spruce, hemlock, and cedar. The train then makes several water crossings: Read Creek at mileage **78**, Boulder Creek at mileage **83**, Pritchard Creek at mileage **91**, Cabin Creek at mileage **93.2**, and Ringland Creek at mileage **93.7**. The most interesting river crossing is at mileage **99,** where the Jasper – Prince Rupert train again traverses the Fraser. This bridge once carried both road and rail traffic, but the new vehicle bridge nearby changed this when it was opened for road traffic in November 2005. Upper Fraser, at mileage **104**, is a company town for the large lumber mill that can be seen to the north. Also to the north, between mileages **105** and **108**, you can see Hansard and Aleza lakes. Eaglet Lake can also be seen

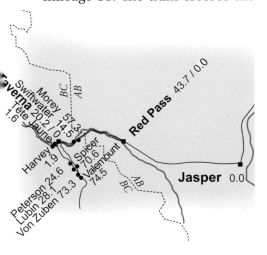

meandering Snowshoe Creek at mileage **38** and Catfish Creek at mileage **40**. Ptarmigan Creek is first crossed at mileage **46**, then again at mileage **47**; the route follows the creek before it turns toward the Fraser. When the low

on the north side of the tracks at mileages **117** and **121**. Giscome, named for an early Afro-American miner, at mileage **122.4**, features a large gravel quarry; much of the rock quarried here is used for railway ballast in western Canada. The General Store at Willow River is still operating at mileage **127**. The Fraser River comes into view again to the north. On the opposite shore at mileage **136**, Simon Fraser established the North West Company's Fort George trading post in 1807. At mileage **143**, the train ducks under the former British Columbia Railway trestle across the Fraser River The Jasper Prince Rupert train makes its own river crossing on the Grand Trunk Bridge, starting at mileage **144.7**; the Yellowhead Highway.

Known as BC's "Northern Capital," Prince George, 2011 population 76,828, at the confluence of the Fraser and Nechako Rivers, has no shortage of things to do or see. As your train lays over here for the night, you will get a chance to walk around the downtown area and visit its numerous boutiques, or enjoy the colourful nightlife. We recommend you book your hotel reservations well in advance of your visit. One hotel to consider is the Ramada, located at 444 George Street. You can make reservations at: 800 830-8833. Web: *www. ramadaprincegeorge.com* Also

highly recommended is the extensive Prince George & Region Railway and Forestry Museum, which offers a great way to learn more about the history of the railway and the forest industry in this region. Displays at the museum, located near Cottonwood Island Park and close to the *CN* rail yards, include a wooden 1903 Russell snowplow, and an 8-foot diameter band saw once used in Giscome. The museum is open daily from May until September. Groups travelling by train are encouraged to contact them in advance for group tours at: 250 563-7351. Web: *www. pgrfm.bc.ca* Email: *trains@pgrfm.bc.ca*

If you are planning a visit to Prince George, contact Tourism Prince George, 101–1300 First Avenue, Prince George, BC, V2L 2Y3. Call: 800 668-7646 or visit: *www.tourismpg.com*. If you plan to leave the train anywhere along your route, you can obtain information from the Northern British Columbia Tourism Association, 1274 5th Ave, Prince George, BC, V2L 3L2. Call: 250 561-0432. Web: *www. travelnbc.com*

Route Highlights
Prince George to Endako
Nechako Subdivision

Mileages 0–30: As you move through the *CN*'s Prince George yards, look to the north to see

Townspeople in pioneer dress greet passengers in *VIA*'s Jasper-Prince Rupert train.
Matthew G. Wheeler photo

the steep banks of the Nechako River. This is the site of the Sandblast event: every August; contestants ski and snowboard down this sandy cutbank and are judged on best style and costumes. The train moves swiftly through Prince George, and the city is soon left behind. At mileage **15** the Chilako River (which translates to "river of mud") is crossed. As mileage **30** approaches, keep watching the river for the Isle de Pierre Rapids, a considerable navigation obstacle for the riverboats that once travelled up and down the river.

Mileages 30–68: Fishermen are not the only ones who try to catch the Nechako's prize-winning trout. You might also get a glimpse of an osprey swooping toward the river to catch lunch. The sandbank on the opposite shore of the river at mileage **58** makes for an interesting photo. Between mileages **63** and **68** the tracks form the southern border of the Nechako Migratory Bird Sanctuary, which is home to various types of birds, most notably migrating Canadian Geese.

Mileages 68–92: Vanderhoof, 2011 population 4,500, named after a *Grand Trunk Pacific* advertising agent, is reached at mileage **69.4**. Look to the south to see the Vanderhoof Heritage Museum. With its restored village, you can return to a farming community of the Nechako Valley in the 1920s. The museum also has modern *CN* transfer caboose 76664. The Jasper–Prince Rupert train continues past large lumber mills and farmers' fields. Watch to the south at mileage **89** to see an early homestead built in a V-shape, possibly to take advantage of the view.

Mileage 93: The picnic table and road- side stop on the south side of the tracks overlook the spot where the last spike on the Grand Trunk Pacific was put in place on April 7th 1914. The honour of driving it home fell to the west crew construction foreman Peter Titiryn. It was declared a Heritage Site in 1998.

Mileages 94–115: At mileage 94.3 the train passes through Fort Fraser. This community dates to 1806, when Simon Fraser started a trading centre called the Fraser Lake Post; it was a large community during the heyday of railway construction. At mileage **95** your train crosses the Nechako River. Then, between mileages **100** and **108**, the picturesque Lake Fraser can be seen to the north. White Swan Park (mileage **107**) is a popular picnic spot in the summer months. At mileage **109.5** the train crosses the swift-moving Stellako River. Endako (mileage **115.4**) is very unassuming as a division point, with only a few buildings along the highway. It features a modern bunkhouse for the *CN* freight crews.

Route Highlights
Endako to Smithers
Telkwa Subdivision

Mileages 0–55: At mileage **10.9** your train crosses the Endako River for the first time. This meandering river will be crossed a total of eight times between here and mileage **21.7**. While you count the crossings, look at mileage **15** to catch a glimpse of part of an old railway boxcar in the bush; this marks the spot of the former railway town of Freeport. Passing through the marsh at mileage **19**, you might notice the log pylons along the north side of the tracks. These pylons were installed by a steam pile driver to stabilize the right of way. At Tintagel, mileage **27.1**, on the north side of the tracks next to the highway, look for a stone cairn at a roadside stop. The cairn features a stone from the Tintagel Castle in Cornwall, England (thought by some historians to be the birthplace of King Arthur, known for forming the Knights of the Round Table). At mileage **32** Burns Lake comes into view. The fill used to cross a portion of the lake comes from the "Big Cut." This is where the railway contractors had the most difficulty building the line. Deadman's Island now sits quietly in the middle of the lake; however, it received its name for a horrific construction mishap, when fifteen men near the cut and another fifteen standing on the island died in a blasting accident. The lake ends at mileage **35** at the community of Burns Lake home to 2,029 people in 2011 and site of the disastrous Babine Forest Products mill fire in 2012. This is a popular starting point for a visit to the Tweedsmuir Provincial Park, located to the south. Decker Lake can be seen to the west from mileage **38 to 48**. Situated on a watershed, Rose Lake at mileage **51.3** empties to the east towards the Fraser River and to the west towards the Skeena. The Nadina and Pimpernel mountains sit on the opposite side of the lake.

Mileages 56–125: Starting at mileage **56**, the train makes the first of 11 crossings of the Bulkley River; the last will be made at **84.3** as the train travels through the Bulkley River Valley. Houston (mileage **85.1**) is renowned for its steelhead and coho salmon fishing. They must be big here— the largest fly fishing rod 60 feet (18.3 metres) in length can be seen in Steelhead Park on the south side of the tracks, as well as a steelhead sculpture. At mileage **93** the train crosses the Morice River. Keep your camera pointed to the south at mileage **98** for a view of the Telkwa Mountains, obscured slightly by a unique 2,725-foot (830-metre) high round hill in the foreground. Mileage **103** brings you to a good curve to photograph your train. Turn your camera to the north at mileage **104** and look across the Bulkley River for your first views of the Skeena Mountain Range. Where you cross the Telkwa River, look to the north to see the town of Telkwa, 2011 population 1,350 at mileage **116**, where the river empties into the Bulkley River. An annual Jimmy Stewart Day is

held on August 30th. On the south side of the bridge you can see the pilings of a former river crossing. At mileage **125.2** you arrive at the large Smithers Station, built in 1918. Since this station was built by *Grand Trunk Pacific* as part of its Winnipeg-to-Prince Rupert line, the station sign proudly proclaims the distance in miles between these two points. The eastern portion of the line, the *National Transcontinental Railway*, was built by the federal government and stretched from Winnipeg to Moncton, New Brunswick. The plan was for it to be operated by the *GTP*, but when the line was completed the *GTP* could not make the required payments to the government. Thus it was incorporated into the government-owned *Canadian National Railways*. Smithers is named after the GTP's chairman, Sir Alfred Smithers and had a population of 5,404 in 2011, and is named after Sir Alfred Smithers. If your train is on time, you might get a chance to stretch your legs here on the platform and visit the station

Route Highlights
Smithers to Terrace
Bulkley Subdivision

Mileages 0–19: The square-looking building directly behind the station is the Smithers Courthouse. Departing Smithers, the building seen next to the tracks is not a small motel but the bunkhouse where *CN* and *VIA* engine crew employees layover.

Kathlyn Lake, to the Skeena—River of Mists at the hatchery; they tag these fish, collecting data on their life cycle when the fish return to spawn. Your train crosses the Trout Creek

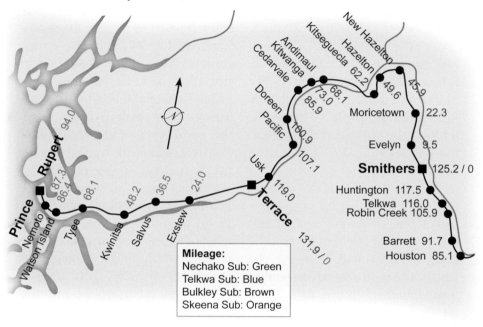

Mileage:
Nechako Sub: Green
Telkwa Sub: Blue
Bulkley Sub: Brown
Skeena Sub: Orange

west between mileages **3** and **4**, was renamed from Chicken Lake by the railway for use in its advertising. It was originally known to the First Nations people as Chicken Lake. In the background above the lake, you get some fine views of the Kathlyn Glacier atop Hudson Bay Mountain. Toboggan Creek is crossed at mileages **7.7** and **8.3**. The Toboggan Creek hatchery, on the north side of the tracks at mileage **9**, researches the management of the coho and steelhead stocks in the upper

Viaduct at mileage **13** and then enters a 400-foot (121-metre) tunnel. At mileage **19** the train crosses John Brown Creek and travels past the Wet'sewet'en First Nations reserve at Moricetown, mileage **22.3**.

Mileages 20–44: At mileage **22** look to the south for views of Brian Boru and Tiltu-sha peaks. Keep your camera ready for the spectacular view from the Boulder Creek Bridge at mileage **28.4**; the bridge curves to the north, offering a great opportunity to photograph your train. At mileage **31** you cross Porphyry Creek, with commanding views to the north of Mount Seaton and Blunt Mountain. The views continue at the Mud Creek trestle, with Hagwilget Peak to the south Look down to the river below to see glimpses of its white water at mileage **40.8**; you then immediately enter the longest *CN* tunnel that a

Rocher Deboule, the town was named for the abundance of hazelnuts in the area. Watch for totem poles in Hazelton, mileage **49.6**, a community that dates to 1866 when it was a Hudson Bay trading post; later it was a stop for the steamboats serving the isolated communities along the Skeena River. As the train crosses the Sealy Gulch Bridge at mileage **50**, look to the north to see the mountains of the Kispiox Mountain Range. Passing the impressive green rolling mountains, the train crosses the Skeena River at mileage **62.2**. The community of Kitseguecla can be seen on the north side of the river. (Try and get your fellow passengers to repeat

Lucas 79.0 · Topley 66.5 · Munsey 63.0 · Rose Lake 51.3 · Palling 45.4 · Burns Lake 35.0 · Tintagel 27.1 · Watson 17.8 · Freeport 15.0 · Endako 115.4 / 0 · Fraser Lake 107.7 · Fort Fraser 94.3 · Engen 82.6 · McCall 76.3 · Vanderhoof 69.4 · Cariboo 66.3 · Rose Lake 51.3 · Wedgwood 45.7 · Nichol 27.8 · Nechako 16.4 · Miworth 7.2 · Prince George 146.1 / 0

passenger train travels through, at 2,065 feet (629 metres). The train passes through two more tunnels at mileages **41.9** and **43.3**.

Mileages 44–84: Your train reaches New Hazelton at mileage **45.9**. Located at the base of

that name three times!) Kitwanga at mileage **73** has been inhabited by the Gitksan First Nations people for hundreds of years. Keep your camera pointed to the south to photograph one of the community's totem poles; the train then passes through the middle of the village's cemetery. Look to the south as the train crosses Highway 37 to catch a glimpse of the former railway station and the 1893 St. Paul's Anglican Church. The train passes through another tunnel at mileage **78**. A native smokehouse on the river bank is passed at mileage **83**.

Mileages 85–131: The venerable Mrs. Essex is now gone, but the Cedarvale general store and post office is still standing. It can be seen among the trees on the south side of the tracks at mileage **86.1**. Mrs. Essex, Canada's longest-serving post mistress, worked here for 73 years from 1923 to 1996. At mileage **90** you pass through another tunnel, and then cross Porcupine Creek at mileage **93**. There are good views to the north and south as you move along the river. Just a few buildings are left along a grassy trail in Doreen (mileage **100.9**), a town that has survived far better than Pacific at mileage **107.1**. A thriving community when steam locomotives served the region and prior to the move of the railway division point to Terrace, all that remains of Pacific is a stone fireplace and a few foundations. At mileage **119** watch carefully for the red and white poles used by the vehicle ferry in Usk. The ferry is propelled by the river's swift current and by large blades located underneath the vessel.

The tracks move away from the river to pass through a quartet of tunnels located at mileages **121.9**, **122.1**, **122.3**, and **122.8**. The bridge for the Kitimat Subdivision to the renowned aluminum refining centre crosses the river can be seen at mileage **130**. Terrace, home to 11,486 people in 2011, is reached at mileage **131.9**. Canada's most serious breach of military discipline occurred here in November 1944 when conscripted soldiers mutinied because they were ordered overseas against Mackenzie King's promises to the contrary.

Route Highlights
Terrace to Prince Rupert
Skeena Subdivision

Mileages 0–44: The last stretch through the Coastal Mountains offers some of the most spectacular sights of the entire trip. The river becomes wider as the train approaches the Pacific Ocean. In the summer months, it is quite common to see fishermen along the shore trying to catch a prize-winning salmon. The Kitsumkaylus River is crossed at mileage **3.1** and the Zimacord River at mileage **7.3**. At times the train moves away from the river, but you still get excellent views of the Kitimat Mountain Range to the south. Watch for bears along the shoreline; you may even catch a glimpse of the rare white Kermode

VIA's train at rest on the waterfront near the old passenger station in Prince Rupert BC after the spectacularly scenic trip to Jasper and back. *Michel Lortie photo*

bear. Also, watch the river for playful seals bobbing with the current and, above the train, for circling eagles. At mileage **34** the train crosses the Ex-Chom-Siks River. In July 1959 Heinz Wichman caught a record salmon on the Skeena, a 92-pound (4l.7-kg) Tyee. While crossing the Ka-Its-Siks River at mileage **39**, look up towards the cliff to see one of the many waterfalls. These cascading waterfalls are most common in the spring, when the snow from the mountains is melting. During the Second World War, this rail line was exceptionally busy, shipping supplies to Prince Rupert destined for Alaska and carrying troops headed overseas. At that time, it was feared that Japanese fishermen who knew the river well from pre-war days could give detailed information to the Japanese Navy; such information might then have been used to plan commando raids to blow up a railway bridge or tunnel. The Canadian Government and the *CNR* built Canada's No. 1

Armoured Train in Winnipeg to protect the vital rail link. It featured open gondola cars with a 75-mm gun on each end, 40-mm anti-aircraft guns, modified boxcars with 15-mm armour-plating, and a locomotive in the middle to move the train. Since it never saw combat, the train was relegated to training trips near the end of the war, with strict instructions to gunners NOT to damage private property.

Mileages 45–96: Mileage **48.2** was once the site of the Kwinitsa Station. In 1985 the station was barged down the Skeena River to Prince Rupert and preserved on the city's waterfront. The Ky-Ax River is crossed at mileage **60**. At mileage **67** look to the rocks on the north side of the tracks to see some recently uncovered First Nations pictographs. Next to the river you can see the large log pilings in the river; they are all that remain of a salmon cannery after the buildings were removed due to losses. At mileage **80** look to the west down the Skeena River for a fantastic view where the river empties into the Pacific Ocean. At mileage **81** you pass the North Pacific Fishing Village. This former cannery, built in 1889, was recognized as a National Historic Site in 1996. It features guided tours, a restaurant, and overnight accommodation. In the 1920s, Icelandic settlers from the Gimli, Manitoba, area settled the now-abandoned town of Osland, on Smith Island opposite mileage **83**. From mileage **84** to **87** Lelu and Ridley Islands can be seen in Chatham Sound. The train crosses a bridge over the Zanardi Rapids (located in the Wainwright Basin). At Nemoto, mile **87.3**, the train passes large coal and grain terminals and an intermodal shipping dock for trans-Pacific containers on Kaien Island. As the train skirts the Pacific Ocean, watch the shoreline along the tracks for the large concrete platform from which searchlights scanned the harbour during the Second World War. The newly combined BC Ferry and *VIA Rail* terminal is reached at mile **92.8** at the end of your journey.

Although he never lived to see the railway reach the port town he envisioned, a statue of Charles Melville Hays stands proudly beside the Prince Rupert City Hall. Whether you have come to visit for wildlife, history, or a fishing adventure, you will find no shortage of things to do. We highly recommend a visit to the Museum of Northern British Columbia, where you can learn more about the Haida First Nations people and their ancient culture. After your museum visit, stroll through Mariners' Memorial Park, dedicated to those who never returned to port. Further on, you come to Cow Bay, with its shops and cafés on Prince Rupert's waterfront. The city is known as the Halibut Capital of the World. The Fire Hall Museum, with its local law enforcement and fire fighter history, as well as a 1925 REO Speedwagon fire engine, is very interesting. To learn more about the rail trip you took to get here, and the area's rail heritage, do not miss the Kwinitsa Station Museum.

After your journey on the rails, we recommend the Pacific Inn, located at 909 Third Avenue West. Reservations can be made by calling them at: 888 663-1999. Web: *www.pacificinn.bc.ca*

For more information and to plan your visit in advance, we recommend you contact the Prince Rupert Visitor Info Centre at Tourism Prince Rupert, 260–110 lst Avenue West, Prince Rupert BC, V8J 1A8. Call: 800 667-1994. Web: *www.visitprincerupert.com* Email: *info@visitprincerupert.com*

THE EXCURSIONS

With Canada's rich history of rail travel, almost every corner of the country features an enjoyable rail excursion that can bring pleasure to young and old. These excursion trips are available across the country from the Atlantic to the Pacific and feature everything from an afternoon trip to a local flea market in Ontario to several-days touring in southern Alberta aboard a restored business car once used by Sir Winston Churchill!

Many of the excursions are operated by the volunteers of preservation groups who believe strongly in sharing their passion so that the next generation will experience the traditions of the past. The hard work of these organizations and their volunteers should not go unnoticed and unappreciated. The loving touches can be seen in everything they organize, from the period costumes they wear to the restoration of the equipment used. As well, tour companies operate rail excursions that feature outstanding scenery, and tell the stories of communities no longer served by regularly-scheduled passenger trains.

As schedules and frequencies are subject to change, we highly recommend that before you go, you research the location of the excursions, costs, and departure times. Don't hesitate to ask staff and volunteers about other displays that are associated with the excursions, or attractions and accommodations in the communities that they serve. The following selections do not encompass *every* excursion in Canada, many of which are operated at our country's railway museums. To learn more about each province's rail excursions we recommend you contact the provincial tourism organizations listed throughout this guide.

NEWFOUNDLAND

Before confederation with Canada in 1949, Newfoundland was a British colony. Its major passenger train was called the *Foreign Express* (it had steamship connections to the Canadian mainland), with later named trains such as the *Overland* and *Caribou*. While the former railway system no longer exists on the island province of Newfoundland, trains have lived on in stories and places where over 500 miles (more than 800 kilometres) of narrow gauge rail line crossed the province. The former route of the line is today a part of the Trans-Canada trail—which passes by the former railway buildings that live on to tell the story of the famed *Newfie Bullet*—as do one or two tall tales from the *"Trouters Special"*, or jokes about the line. For more information about all the province's rail heritage attractions, contact Newfoundland and Labrador Department of Tourism, Recreation and Culture, PO Box 8700, St. John's, NL. A1B 4J6. Call: 800 563-6353. Web: *www.newfoundlandlabrador.com* Email: *contactus@newfoundlandandlabrador.com*

Railway Coastal Museum
This museum is located at 495 Water Street, St. John's, in the restored Newfoundland Railway station that was built with local granite over 100 years ago. Many of the displays located inside are related to the history and operations of the *Newfoundland Railway*. One of the centerpiece displays provides a view of the different interiors of the passenger trains that served Newfoundland. The museum can be reached by calling: 866 600-7245. Web: *www.railwaycoastalmuseum.ca.* Email: *info@railwaycoastalmuseum.ca*

Port aux Basques Railway Heritage Centre
Owned and operated by the South West Coast Historical Society, the Port aux Basques Railway Heritage Centre is open mid-June to mid-September. Recapturing the importance of the railway in

Top: The magnificent Railway Coastal Museum building in St. John's was once the city's important railway station. *Kenneth Pieroway photo*
Bottom: Railway Society of Newfoundland members continue to care for Newfoundland Railway's steam locomotive 593 at Corner Brook. *Kenneth Pieroway photo*

Newfoundland's history, guided tours of a restored passenger train filled with artifacts from a century ago, gives visitors a glimpse of the legacy of the Newfoundland Railway. Open daily June through August 9 a.m. to 9 p.m. Call: 709 695-7560.

Railway Society of Newfoundland

Located in Corner Brook and open during the summer months, the famed *Newfie Bullet* train lives on in the form of a passenger train display led by former *Newfoundland Railway* 4-6-2 steam locomotive No. 193, later *CNR* 593, built in 1920 by Baldwin Locomotive Works. Also on display at the Riverside Drive location are additional pieces of rolling stock and the preserved Humbermouth station. They can be reached by calling 709 634-7089 or Tourism Cornerbrook: 709 637-1500. Web:*www.cornerbrook.com/tourism/one* Email: *tourism@cornerbrook.com*

NOVA SCOTIA

N ova Scotia had some of the first operating railway steam
locomotives in North America, so it should be no surprise
that the province has numerous heritage attractions and sites
related to the area's rail history. For the benefit of travellers to the
province, these attractions promote themselves as part of the Nova
Scotia Railway Heritage Society. This society supports everything from
preserved railway stations to working museums. It encourages the
preservation and interpretation of buildings, artifacts and information
related to the development and history of railways in Nova Scotia.
Their website is very comprehensive, providing a great way to choose
which places you will wish to visit. Start your journey to the province by
visiting their website *www.novascotiarailwayheritage.com.* For more
information on all the province's rail heritage attractions, contact Nova
Scotia Economic and Rural Development and Tourism, PO Box 456,
Halifax, NS, B3J 2R5. Phone: 800 565-0000. Web: *www.novasvotia.com*
Email: *explore@gov.ns.ca*

Train Station Inn

The Train Station Inn at Tatamagouche on Nova Scotia's Northumberland Strait shore served the
old Oxford short line through three counties. It is an internationally-renowned tourist attraction.
Train Station Inn photo

While *VIA Rail's Ocean* is the only passenger train travelling through the province connecting Halifax to Montreal, you can "board" another overnight "train" in Tatamagouche. Called the Train Station Inn, it had its humble beginnings in 1974 when 18 year old Jimmie LeFresne purchased the 1887-built *Intercolonial Railway* station in Tatamagouche, rescuing it from demolition. In 1987, restoration began, preparing the station for its next life as a bed and breakfast starting in 1989. The stationmaster's residence is on the second floor, with a café, museum and gift shop on the main floor. When the line that the station served fell into disuse, most of the rails were removed, but the tracks in front of the station were left in place, allowing the owners to acquire a growing collection of ex-*CN* cabooses and boxcars from across the country, all of which were transformed into hotel rooms. In recent years they have also added passenger cars including ex-*CNR* combination car No. 7209 called the *Cabot* which has been turned into a dining car. The *Alexandra*, a vice-regal railway car built in nearby Amherst in 1905, is also on display and serves as a lounge. Book your stay by calling 888 724-5233. Web: *www.trainstation.ca.* Email: *stationmaster@trainstation.ca*

Nova Scotia Attractions
Memory Lane Railway Museum
Located in Middleton, at 61 School Street, off Route 1, the museum features exhibits relevant to the *Dominion Atlantic Railway* and the *Halifax & South-western*. Both railways passed through this Annapolis Valley community. Call: 902 825-6062.
Web: *www.memorylanerailwaymuseum.org.*
Email: *info@memorylanerailwaymuseum.org*

Nova Scotia Museum of Industry
Just off the Trans-Canada Highway, exit 24, at Stellarton, this museum is home to the oldest surviving locomotive in Canada—Timothy Hackworth's *Samson* built in 1839. This provincial museum boasts the largest collection of locomotives east of Montreal. Open daily. Call: 902 755-5425. Web: *www.museum.gov.ns.ca* Email: *industry@gov.ns.ca*

Orangedale Railway Museum
The whistle blows, just as in the song, the Orangedale Whistle, at Orangedale, located 4 miles (6 kilometres) south of exit 4 on the Trans-Canada Highway on an active railway line between Sydney and Truro. The station was built for the *Intercolonial Railway* and is Nova Scotia's

oldest railway station. Numerous exhibits, small and large are to be found, including a snowplow and narrow gauge business car. Call: 902-756-3384.

Louisburg Station
Off Route 22, this is the home of the Sydney & Louisburg Historical Society. The collection documents a line that was once the busiest in North America, and one of the last to switch to diesel power in the 1960s. Key exhibits include the 1895 station, a registered Nova Scotia Heritage site which houses a tourist bureau and tells the story of railways, coal and ships in Louisburg. Call: 902 733-2720.

Musquodoboit Harbour Museum
This community museum on Route 7 is home to several items of rolling stock on the legendary "Dartmouth to Deans" line. The 1918 building includes an impressive collection of exhibits, a tourist bureau and there's an ice cream parlor on site! Open June through August. Call: 902 889-2689. Web: *www.novascotia.com*

Halifax & South-western Railway Museum
This Lunenburg museum houses artifacts from the *Canadian National, Central Nova Scotia,* and *Halifax & South-western* railways. An operating model railway depicts scenes from Nova Scotia's southern shore. 11188 Highway 3 (from Bridgewater to Lunenburg) near the Lunenburg town limits. Open daily May through October; weekends year round. Call: 902 634-3184. Web: *hswmuseum.ednet.ns.ca* Email: *hswmuseum@ns.aliantzinc.ca*

Liverpool Station
The *Hank Snow Country Music Centre* and the *Nova Scotia Country Music Hall of Fame* is on Route 3 in Liverpool. No Canadian recording artist sang more railroad songs than Hank Snow. The former *Canadian National/Halifax & South-western Railway* station houses memorabilia dedicated to the singing cowboy, and railway history. Open year round except weekends and holidays from mid-October through mid-May. Call: 902 354-4675. Web: *www.hanksnow.com* Email: *info@hanksnow.com*

PRINCE EDWARD ISLAND

Elmira's former *PEI Railway* station serves today as a museum. *Bill Linley photo*

The *Prince Edward Island Railway* was constructed in the 1870s as a 3'6" (1.07-metre) narrow gauge line, became dual-gauge after World War I, until it was gradually converted to standard-gauge in the 1920s. This permitted trains from the mainland to work on the island after traversing on the railway ferryboat. Legend has it that since the contractors who built the line were paid by the government by the mile, the route zigzagged through almost every small community of the day as the line meandered across the island province. In 1989, freight rail services came to an end across the province and the tracks were removed. Today some of the former rail routes can be enjoyed as part of the Confederation Trail. For more information on all the province's rail heritage attractions, contact Tourism Prince Edward Island at PO Box 2000, Charlottetown, PE, C1A 7N8. Call: 800 463-4734. Web: *www.tourismpei.com* Email: *tourismpei@gov.pe.ca*

Wearing its CN colour scheme from the 1960s, diesel locomotive 1762 stands all alone at Kensington PE station. *Bill Linley photo*

Kensington Station

Built in 1905 in a distinctive boulder design, by local contractor M.F. Schurman, the former *CNR* station in Kensington is a National Historic Site and today houses the Island Stone Pub. Nearby you can view preserved *CN* MLW diesel locomotive No. 1762 along the Confederation Trail. The pub may be reached at 902 836-3063.

Elmira Railway Museum

Helping to tell the history of the *Prince Edward Island Railway*, the Elmira Railway Museum is housed in the former Elmira *CNR* station on Route 16A in eastern PEI. Displays depict the story of railroading in the province and feature photos, maps and artifacts, along with a recreated station master office and ladies' waiting room. Ex Grand Trunk/CNR 1912 caboose 78431 and a miniature train ride should not be missed. The museum can be reached by calling: 902 357-7234. Web: *www.peimuseum.com* Email: *elmira@gov.pe.ca*

NEW BRUNSWICK

Wwhat a grand day it must have been on September 14th 1853 when Lady Head, wife of New Brunswick lieutenant-governor Sir Edmund Head turned the sod to start construction on the *European & North American Railway*. It eventually connected Saint John to Moncton and Pointe du Chêne. The ceremonial wheelbarrow that was used for the event was carved from black walnut and birdseye maple—to look like a lion. Since it still exists in excellent condition, it is doubtful it was actually used to build any part of the *E&NA*. For more information on all the province's rail heritage attractions, contact Tourism New Brunswick at PO Box 12345, Campbellton, NB, E3N 3T6. Call: 800 561-0123. Web: *www.tourismnewbrunswick.ca* or visit: *www.nbrailways.ca*

The New Brunswick Railway Museum
Located in Hillsborough in the heart of New Brunswick, on Route 114, 15 miles (25 kilometres) south of the city of Moncton, the museum features one of the best collections of railway equipment and artifacts in the province. Those who have travelled in the Maritimes by rail will enjoy the wall of images of New Brunswick railway stations past and present. The museum can be reached at: 506 734-3195. Web: *www.nbrm.ca* Email: *nbrailway@nb.aibn.com*

Shogomoc Railway
Located in the village of Bristol, three former CPR heavy- weight passenger cars are the centrepieces of the museum. Restauranteur Sara Caines offers fine dining in ex-CPR 1931-built sleeper "Grenfell" evenings except Sunday. To reserve call 506 392-6000 or Email: *info@ freshfinedining.com*. Also featured is the former Florenceville station that is a mirror-image of the Bristol station. Visitors are welcome to view the displays during the summer months. For more information, call 506 392-8226 or 392-6763. Web: *www.florencevillebristol.ca* Email: *tourism@florencevillebristol.ca*

Top: Former *Canadian Pacific Railway* station at McAdam, New Brunswick has been preserved for restoration. *Bill Linley photo*
Bottom: *L'Amiral (*"Prince of the Sea"*)* train awaits passengers at Gaspé's cruise and transportation terminal. *David Morris photo*

McAdam Station

Referred to as the most photographed building in the province, this grand station was built in three stages, starting in 1900. Constructed using local granite, the building is reminiscent of a Scottish castle. This large station features a waiting room and telegraph office. Unusually, the building features a lengthy lunch counter, hotel and dining room. The McAdam Historical Restoration Commission is continuing its efforts to restore and retain the building as a functioning facility that will provide an important reminder of McAdam's past. Tours are available in the summer months. Railway pie is available on selected Sunday afternoons! They can be reached by calling: 506 784-2293. Web: *www.mcadamnb.com* Email: *villageofmcadam@nb.aibn.co*

QUEBEC
L'AMIRAL ("PRINCE OF THE SEA")

L'Amiral on its inaugural trip between New Richmond and Bonaventure, is at Caplan, Quebec, running along the sandstone cliffs above the Baie de Chaleur. *Geoff Doane photo*

A new tour train is operating along the scenic Gaspé Coast overlooking the waters of the Gulf of St. Lawrence. Departures are scheduled from New Richmond to Bonaventure and from Gaspé to Coin du Banc. While you are in the tourist town of Bonaventure, tours may be arranged of the nearby Bioparc or the Acadian Museum. Similarly your tour to Percé could include a boat excursion around the world renowned bird sanctuary on Bonaventure Island and a view of Percé Rock, the island with the hole.

Ontario's former *GO Transit* commuter cars that more recently served in Montreal feature very large windows for your viewing pleasure. Food service is available and the train is licensed for your en route enjoyment.

Top: *L'Amiral* ("Prince of the Sea") train often hugs the craggy coast on its round trips from Gaspé. *David Morris photo*

Bottom: Water-level route of *Le Massif de Charlevoix* (see opposite page) skirts mountains, tidal flats, and St. Lawrence River. *Benjamin Gagnon photo*

The departure points are on Quebec Route 132 with New Richmond at mileage **68.9** of the Cascapedia subdivision and Gaspé at mileage **104.2** of the Chandler subdivision. A detailed description of your route is found in the *VIA* Montreal-Gaspé route beginning on page 35.

For further information contact the Gaspé Railway Society by calling 408 368-2372. Web: *www.trainamiral.com*
Email: *infoamiral@trainamiral.com*

LE MASSIF DE CHARLEVOIX

Like the scenery that the Charlevoix region is blessed with, this local excursion train is one part of a vision that includes the Massif Ski Resort, La Ferme Hotel in Baie Saint Paul and unique culinary experiences. Thinking big must come naturally to the group's driving force and chairman, Daniel Gauthier, who was co-founder of the renowned Cirque de Soleil. Perhaps this thinking big influenced the design of the passenger cars. These are former bilevel commuter cars from Chicago that have been rebuilt with the second floor removed to permit loft ceilings and larger windows, creating perhaps the most unique rail passenger cars operating in Canada.

Le Massif de Charlevoix train has left Quebec's Montmorency Falls, and is just east of the famed Ste. Anne de Beaupré shrine. *David Morris photo*

Travelling between Quebec City (Montmorency Falls), Baie Saint Paul and La Malbaie along the shoreline of the St. Lawrence River for the

Top: Quebec's picturesque villages provide serenely scenic views. *Benjamin Gagnon photo*
Bottom: Spectacular night view of Montmorency Falls from train. *Benjamin Gagnon photo*

majority of the journey, it is fitting that your adventure begins near the spectacular Montmorency Falls. Departures take place in the summer from mid-May to late October. The journeys include "Discovery of Baie Saint Paul" and "Escape to La Malbaie" (with recommended overnight stays in the region), as well as short supper cruises. There are also winter departures that take place between late December and April, all with gourmet meals included on the train. For more information, call toll-free: 877 536-2774. Web: *www.lemassif.com/train* Email: *infoletrain@lemassif.com*

ORFORD EXPRESS

ather Donald Thomson's vision, the *Orford Express* passenger train, travels through Quebec's Eastern Townships from early summer to the fall, providing a round- trip excursion from Sherbrooke, Quebec to Magog and Eastman. Built by the Canadian Pacific Railway, the line has more recently been operated by the Montreal, Maine & Atlantic Railway that moves freight between Montreal and the Unites States. On the *Orford Express*, you'll travel in style aboard restored rail diesel cars for an afternoon trip or enjoy a unique dining experience in a dome dining car powered by an equally unique MLW M-420TR locomotive, one of only two of its type. Trips are scheduled Wednesday through Sunday on a variety of routes from Sherbrooke or Magog. For more information, contact *Orford Express*, 806 Place de la Gare, Sherbrooke, QC, J1H 0E9. Call: 866 575-8081. Web: *www.orfordexpress.com* Email: *info@orfordexpress.com*

Orford Express provides delightful scenery as it travels through Quebec's Eastern Townships area. *David Morris photo*

Route Highlights
Sherbrooke-Magog-Eastman-Bromont
Sherbrooke Subdivision

Mileages 68-85: All trips begin at mileage **68.5** from the former *CPR* Sherbrooke station, built in 1910, the second station on site. It is located at the west end of Minot Street (Place de la Gare). Departing the station, Lac des Nations is seen to the north with the skyline of Sherbrooke. Then a long bridge crosses the lake, which soon turns into the Magog River. Deauville at mileage **77.5** provides a good view of Lac Magog. The fields to the north are part of the Le Cep d'Argent winery. You will pass under Highway 55 before entering the town of Magog. One itinerary ends at Merry Pointe Park where you will have ample time to stretch your legs, view 2,790-foot (850-metre) Mount Orford to the west and explore this popular tourist town before enjoying the train trip back to Sherbrooke. On trips continuing to Eastman or Bromont as you leave Magog, mileage **86.8**, you will see Lake Memphremagog which extends south into Vermont. Then you will skirt Orford Lake at mileage **93** and cross the viaduct at Eastman at mileage **96** where Lac d'Argent (Silver Lake) may be seen to the north. Foster is passed at mileage **105.6** where tracks formerly led north to Drummondville and south to Sutton. Bromont, formerly known as West Shefford, a popular ski-resort community, is reached at mileage **114.2**.

The 1849 replica steam locomotive John Molson in front of the Hayes Building on the grounds of Exporail (see opposite page). *Canadian Railway Museum*

EXPORAIL

You can ride the open observation car at Exporail, the Canadian Railway Museum, only 20 minutes by car or train from downtown Montreal. *Courtesy Stephen Cheasley*

L ocated just south of Montreal, Quebec, one of the largest railway museums in North America features over 140 pieces of railway equipment—including streetcars, locomotives, passenger and freight cars—as well as excellent displays focusing on the history of Canadian railways. A project of the Canadian Railroad Historical Association, the museum began life in the early1960s on a site that straddles the communities of Delson and St. Constant. Today the facility is recognized as one of the leading railway collections in the world and visitors should plan to spend the better part of a day to enjoy the entire museum and displays throughout the park.

During the summer months there is an option to travel to the museum by train on selected dates aboard the *"Museum Express"*. The journey begins in downtown Montreal just west of the former *CPR* Windsor Station (allow time for a visit) and the Bell Centre (home of the Montreal Canadiens hockey team) at Lucien-l'Allier station. You'll travel west

Panoramic view of the largest railway exhibit hall in Canada.

from downtown, passing historic Montreal West station, before crossing the St. Lawrence River on a long *CPR* bridge before arriving at Exporail. During summer months, the museum will operate equipment such as former Montreal streetcars, which you can ride, and a replica of an 1849 steam locomotive that operated in Canada, the *John Molson*. The stops around the museum site on the excursions provide the opportunity to view the main Angus display building, Barrington Station, the Hays Building and more.

Greeting visitors in the main building, the Angus Pavilion, is a replica of Canada's first steam locomotive, the *Dorchester*. You'll see *CPR* Royal Hudson No. 2850 that pulled the Royal Tour in 1939, and passenger-hauling diesel locomotive, *CNR* No. 6765, a Montreal Locomotive Works FPA-4. After viewing the underside of these large locomotives, you can explore the remainder of the displays, including forty items of rolling stock, as well as view the many ever-changing exhibits. Outside the Angus Pavilion, you will want to explore other railway equipment and display buildings throughout the site —from the 1882 Barrington Station to one of the passenger trains that operated in the last century on the Newfoundland narrow gauge system. There's even a smaller-scale minirail for the riding enjoyment of young and old. Visit Exporail year-round on weekends, daily in summer as well as Wednesday through Friday in the fall at 110 Sainte Pierre, Saint Constant, QC. Call: 450 632-2410. Web: *www.exporail.org* Email: *info@exporail.org*

ONTARIO
PORTAGE FLYER

Portage Flyer's historic open car awaits passengers and steam locomotive at Rotary Village Station in Huntsville. *D.R.Henderson photo*

The *Portage Flyer* captures the spirit of a bygone era of travel in the Muskokas. You can join them and step back in time to the days when this 42- inch (1.1 metre) gauge train was an essential link in reaching such famous destinations as the Wa Wa Hotel and the Bigwin Inn. From Muskoka Heritage Place's reconstruction of a typical 1920s station, your train departs for a 30-minute, 1.2-mile (2-kilometre) return trip along the Muskoka River. Your destination will be the Fairy Lake Station, originally a purser's cabin at Norway Point on the Lake of

To once again face forward for the next journey, fireman turns diminuitive *Portage Flyer* loco-motive on the aptly-named "Armstrong" turntable in front of the railway shops. *D.R. Henderson photo*

Bays. In mid-summer your train will likely be powered by 0-4-0T loco-motive No. 5 built in Montreal in 1926 for the Fundy Gypsum Company of Windsor, Nova Scotia. In 1948 it was acquired by the *Huntsville, Lake of Bays & Lake Simcoe Railway & Navigation Company*—commonly known as "the Portage Railway." Opened in 1902 between North Portage on the Fairy Lake appendage of the Muskoka River and South Portage, the line dropped 170 feet (51.8 metres) in 1⅛ miles (1.8 kilometres). South Portage provided access to the various resorts around the Lake of Bays aboard steamers such as the *Iroquois*. The railway closed in 1959 and the engine and the two former streetcars, used as coaches, were operated by Percy Broadbear in Pinafore Park at St. Thomas. In 1985 they came to Huntsville, two hours north of Toronto. Operations began in 2000 and the railway is now part of a museum and pioneer village located at 88 Brunel Road (County Road 2)—follow County Road 3 from Highway 11 in Huntsville, ON, P1H 1R1. The railway operates Tuesday through Saturday afternoons from mid-May to mid-October with a diesel or with the steamer during July and August. Call: 888 696-4255 or 705 789-7576. Web: *www.muskokaheritageplace.org* Email: *ron.gostlin@huntsville.ca*

YORK-DURHAM HERITAGE RAILWAY

York-Durham excursion train as it travels through the Oak Ridges.

Located about an hour northeast of Toronto, Ontario, the York-Durham Heritage Railway runs between Uxbridge and Stouffville. Connecting the two communities, the train travels through the Oak Ridges Moraine. It operates June through October, on weekends and holiday Mondays. Special trains and dining car trips are run periodically and you may arrange to ride in an ex-CPR caboose. For more information, contact York-Durham Heritage Railway, PO Box 462, Stouffville ON, L4A 7Z7. Call: 905 852-3696. Web: *www.ydhr.ca* Email: *ydhr@ydhr.ca*

Route Highlights
Uxbridge to Stouffville
Uxbridge Subdivision
York-Durham Railway

Mileages 28–40: Your journey begins at Uxbridge station, built in 1904 for the *Toronto & Nipissing Railway*. The station has a unique design known as a Witch's Hat. On your way out of Uxbridge, you see the H.H. Goode & Son Limited seed plant to the east as the train travels past residential back yards. Lookout Curve, at mileage **31**, is a great place to photograph your train. A large ornate farmhouse, typical of this area, can be seen on the east side of the tracks at mileage **32**. Big Garibaldi Hill, the highest point in Durham Region, can be seen to the east at mileage **34**. Also in this area the train passes a large pit to the west. Local pioneer Michael Chapman named his community's first tavern after his home in England—Goodwood House—which in turn provided the town at mileage **35.3** its name: Goodwood. The forests, rolling hills, and farms of the area can be seen on both sides between mileages **36** and **37**. At mileage **38** the train passes Toronto's Granite Club golf course. Just beyond, you will see *GO Transit*'s green and white bi-level passenger cars, which provide weekday commuter service to Toronto, next to their Lincolnville station At mileage **39** the Stouffville water tower comes into view —just before arriving at Stouffville's modern station at mileage **40.6**. Built in 1997, the station also houses the Whitchurch-Stouffville Chamber of Commerce and the Latcham Art Gallery.

SOUTH SIMCOE RAILWAY

Former CPR steam locomotive 136, with train, is ready at Tottenham.

Northwest of Toronto in the community of New Tecumseh (Tottenham), Ontario, the *South Simcoe Railway* is reminiscent of branchline railway operations up to the 1960s. The most commonly used locomotive to pull the train on this former *CNR* line is *Canadian Pacific Railway* 4-4-0 No. 136, built in 1883. This engine was featured in the Canadian Broadcast Corporation's mini-series "The National Dream" that was based on Pierre Berton's novel. There is a large yard full of historic railway equipment, some of which is on display to the public. Travelling through the scenic Beeton Creek Valley, the trains operate Sundays and holiday Mondays from May to October. Contact the South Simcoe Railway, PO Box 186, Tottenham, ON, L0G 1W0. Call: 905 936-5815. Web: *www.steamtrain.com* Email: *info@southsimcoerailway.ca*

Route Highlights
Tottenham to Beeton
South Simcoe Railway

South Simcoe Railway's No. 136 starred in the CBC's TV series "The National Dream", telling of the early history of the Canadian Pacific Railway. *Marilynn Linley photo*

Mileages 54–55: Departing the South Simcoe yard at mileage **54.9**, for the 50-minute roundtrip, the train passes the railway's collection of historic equipment.

Mileages 55–59: Curving to the northeast, the train crosses a high fill offering great views to both sides. At mileage **57**, Beeton Creek can be seen to the east.

The *South Simcoe Railway* passes underneath the *Canadian Pacific Railway*. Watch for modern diesel locomotives and long freight trains on the mainline, "Yesterday meets today." Then Beeton Creek is crossed before reaching the station sign at Nowhere, mileage **58.4**. Beeton and the end of the line are reached at mileage **59.1**. The train then makes its way back to Tottenham.

CREDIT VALLEY EXPLORER

Crossing the river at Forks of the Credit aboard *Credit Valley Explorer*. *Ron Bouwhuis photo*

The *Credit Valley Railway* completed a line from Toronto to Orangeville, Ontario, in 1879. Five years later the company came under control of the *Canadian Pacific Railway*. The line was purchased from *CPR* by the Town of Orangeville in 2000 and is today operated as the *Orangeville-Brampton Railway* to maintain a connection with the *CPR* at Streetsville.

Now, you may enjoy a 46-mile (74-kilometre), three-hour, return trip from Orangeville through the Credit River Valley and Hills of Headwaters, one of southern Ontario's most scenic areas. Brunch and scenic tour trains operate on selected dates throughout the year, with a variety of meal and beverage options offered. A Twilight Dinner Train runs on selected Saturdays from May to September, followed by fall colour excursions in autumn and Snow Trains in February.

First line, ex-*CN* coaches from their *Super Continental* of 1955 ensure large picture windows, climate control and a smooth ride. The fleet also includes an ex-*Wabash* stainless steel dome car; as well you will see a rare ex-*Boston & Maine*, Budd RDC-9 formerly used in commuter service around Boston. Locomotive No. 4009, another *CNR* veteran, was built in nearby London in 1959 as No. 4331. Write: Credit Valley Explorer Tour Train, Box 351, Orangeville, ON, L9W 2Z7.
Call 888-346-0046.
Web: *www.creditvalleyexplorer.com.*
Email: *info@creditvalleyexplorer.ca*

Route Highlights
Orangeville to Snelgrove
Owen Sound Subdivision

Mileages 34.6–12.2: Your train departs from the station at 49 Townline Road, west on Highway 9 from the junction with Highway 10, at mileage **34.6**, on the site of the CPR's Orangeville station. The station was built in 2007 and is styled with a distinctive witch's hat tower reminiscent of the original. Near Melville, mileage **31.8**, you will twice cross the Credit River. You pass Alton at mileage **29.7** and soon thereafter begin a descent along the west side of the Credit River. Amidst rolling hills and valleys, at mileage **24.0**, you will cross the curved trestle bridge over the Credit River at Forks of the Credit. As you approach Inglewood, mileage **19.8**, your train continues to descend the Niagara Escarpment that runs across Ontario from Niagara Falls to Tobermory. At Inglewood your train may pause while you explore this quaint rural community. Don't miss the general store. Cheltenham, mileage **17.1** is passed en route to your turnaround point near mileage **12.2** in Snelgrove on the north side of Brampton.

WATERLOO CENTRAL RAILWAY

Waterloo Central Railway carries many passengers who shop at the famous Farmer's Market in St. Jacobs.

For years, trains took farmers' produce from the country farm to markets in the towns and now you can take the train to the farmers' market! A trip on the Waterloo Spur features six miles of both urban and country scenic views, beginning from Mileage **2** at the Waterloo Station, pausing at the St. Jacobs Farmers' Market at mileage **5.8**, and concluding 45 minutes later at the Village of St Jacobs, mileage **7.7**. Once a year, you might get some sticky fingers if you take part in the special trips to Elmira, Ontario (mileage **11.8**) for the Maple Syrup Festival. Once on board, ask if your trip will feature a crossing of the Conestogo River so you can keep your camera ready for a beautiful shot.

There are also excursions including those celebrating Easter and Halloween; in December, Santa has been seen on the train. The busy

St. Thomas Psychiatric Hospital at mileage **18** was not opened until after its Second World War incarnation as a Royal Air Force Training Centre. Passing the backyards of homes in St. Thomas, the train reaches mileage **16.9**, where you see Parkside High School to the east.

Top: General Electric locomotive "Stanley" hauls passengers in distinctive open-air cars.
Bottom: On today's first trip, a caboose has been added to handle extra passengers.
Both photos by Warren Mayhew

MANITOBA
PRAIRIE DOG CENTRAL

The *Prairie Dog Central*. *Murray Hammond photo*

The *Prairie Dog Central* in Manitoba gives passengers a glimpse of what it was like to cross the prairies by rail at the turn of the century. The train is pulled by either a vintage GP9 diesel locomotive or by 4-4-0 steam locomotive No. 3. The latter, Canada's oldest operating locomotive, originally built for the Canadian Pacific Railway in 1882,then worked for Winnipeg Hydro between Lac du Bonnet, Pointe du Bois, and Slave Falls for the City Hydro Tramway. Passengers travel in grand style in restored wooden coaches which feature fully-restored interiors. The train operates weekends and holidays from mid-May to the end of September with Halloween Expresses later in October. Ride in a caboose, and or be an engineer for a day! For more information, contact the Vintage Locomotive Society,

PO Box 33021, RPO Polo Park, Winnipeg, MB, R3G 3N4. Call: 866 751-2348. Web: *www.pdcrailway.com*

Route Highlights
Inkster Junction to Warren
Oak Point Subdivision

Mileages 9–27.5: Departing for a three-hour return trip from the Inkster Junction station (built in 1910 and once situated in St. James at mileage **7.6**), the train passes the large building where the locomotive and train are stored and serviced. At Lilyfield (mileage **11.0** of this former *CNR* line), you see a large modern throughput grain elevator to the west. The rich soil of the Red River Valley makes for some of the best farming in Canada. Between mileages **13** and **16** the train passes fields of wheat, barley, and sometimes sunflowers. Grosse Isle is reached at mileage **20.2**. The concrete foundation of a water tower and a simple class 1 station are located along the tracks. The land in the centre of the wye here (used to turn trains) is a Provincial Heritage Site—it is an example of natural prairie that has never been cultivated. At mileage **21** a Hutterite Colony can be seen to the west, and to the east an old wooden boxcar lives on as a shed in a farmer's yard. You reach Warren at mileage **26.6**. The train proceeds to another wye at mileage **27.5** where the locomotive and combination coach will be turned for the trip home. While here, passengers can stretch their legs, see the locomotive up close, and visit the country market.

PRAIRIE DOG CENTRAL

SASKATCHEWAN
SOUTHERN PRAIRIE RAILWAY

When people talk about the scenery of Saskatchewan, they often refer to the flatlands' never-ending horizon, but the *Southern Prairie Railway* excursions actually travel to Horizon! Saskatchewan's only rail passenger excursion railway is based in Ogema, mileage **51.4** of *Canadian Pacific Railway*`s former Assiniboine Subdivision, which is now owned by *Red Coat Road & Rail Limited* and operated by *Great Western Rail*. When on the train you will want to keep a watchful eye on the passing prairie vistas for the area's abundant wildlife, as past trips have been known to see deer, fox, coyote, a very large variety of birds, and maybe even some cows.

Trips begin and end at the Ogema train station, which was relocated from Simpson, Saskatchewan to replace the original station of the same design. Journeys operate primarily on the weekends. They include the Farmer's Market train to Pangman, mileage **37.2**, on Saturday mornings, and trips to Horizon, mileage **66.8**, for viewing of their heritage grain elevator. Special trips scheduled throughout the summer include the Pitchfork Fondue and Star Gazer trips to Horizon. The operation features an ex-Maine Central 44-ton General Electric locomotive and an ex-*Lackawanna* coach. You will also want to make time to visit Ogema's Deep South Pioneer Museum heritage village that has about thirty buildings. To plan your visit, you can reach the Southern Prairie Railway, call: 855 459-1200. Web: *www.southernprairierailway.com* Email: *ceo@southernprairierailway.com*

Left: Passengers at Southern Prairie Railway's Ogema Station can also visit the nearby heritage village at Ogema's Pioneer Museum.

ALBERTA
ALBERTA PRAIRIE STEAM

Arriving at Big Valley, Alberta. *Bill Linley photo*

Formed in 1990, *Alberta Prairie Steam Tours* has worked hard to develop a major tourist attraction with economic benefits to the area of east central Alberta. The company offers a range of day trips aboard steam- and diesel-locomotive-powered vintage trains. As well, most include a full-course, buffet-style meal at the destination.

Trips are scheduled on select weekdays and weekends mid-May through mid-October and several weekends during the winter. For more information, contact Alberta Prairie Steam Tours Ltd, PO Box 1600, Stettler, AB. T0C 2L0. Call: 800 282-3994. Web *www.absteamtrain.com* Email: *info@absteamtrain.com*

Hundreds of huge grain elevators and no-longer-used cabooses were familiar trackside sights all across Canada's prairies. You can still see them at Alberta Prairie Steam. *Bill Linley photo*

Route Highlights
Big Valley to Stettler
Stettler Subdivision

Mileages 50–72: All excursions originate from and return to the Stettler station at mileage **50.9**. The only problem with some of these trips is that you are bound to get held up by a gang of masked ruffians on horseback, who force the train to stop and then proceed to "rob" the passengers. Rumour has it that the bandits are really good guys who donate the money they "steal" to charities, a la Robin Hood. Along the route in Warden (mileage **55.9**) you'll see railway yards and maintenance-of-way buildings. The train arrives at the historic *Canadian Northern* station in Big Valley at mileage **72.1**. Visitors will have a chance to explore the community of Big Valley and the Roundhouse Interpretive Centre, which offers a self-guided tour of these once-busy railway shops. Also at Big Valley is the newly-established "Canadian Railway Hall of Fame," honouring people, communities, and technology that have made a significant contribution to the Canadian railway industry.

FORT EDMONTON PARK

T he City of Edmonton operates an excellent attraction called Fort Edmonton Park which interprets the rich history of the community. The *Edmonton, Yukon & Pacific Railway* is a major component of the Park and offers rides in open-sided coaches pulled by a Prairie (2-6-2) type steam locomotive built by Baldwin in Philadelphia in 1919 for a lumber company in Louisiana.

City-operated Fort Edmonton Park admission includes your ride in steam-hauled open-sided cars. *Bill Linley photo*

The steam train operates from Victoria Day through Labour Day on a frequent, forty-minute ride through the park. The ride is included in your admission to the Park and one may alight at the 1846 Hudson' Bay Fort to visit the many historic buildings in the nearby town-site. While

Top: Passengers enjoying their steam-hauled excursion in Fort Edmonton Park.
Both photos Bill Linley
Bottom: Edmonton Radial Railway car 42 built in St. Louis in 1912 heads south on 1920 Street.

visiting, you should also enjoy a ride on one of the numerous vintage streetcars operated by the Edmonton Radial Railway Society. Fort Edmonton is located along the south bank of the North Saskatchewan River, on Fox Drive just east of Route 2, the Whitemud Drive near Fox Drive NW. Call: 780 442-5311 On the web: *www.fortedmontonpark.ca* Email: *info@fortedmontonpark.ca*

ALBERTA RAILWAY MUSEUM

Vintage CNR diesel locomotive 9000 heads up holiday-weekend trains throughout Edmonton's summer season. *Alberta Railway Museum photo*

Edmonton is home to the third largest railway museum in Canada, the Alberta Railway Museum. There are over 75 cars and locomotives on the site. Ex *Canadian Northern* Ten-Wheeler type steam engine 1392 built in Montreal in 1913 hauls a passenger train on Holiday weekends from Victoria Day through Labour Day. Hourly trips are offered from 11 a.m. to 4 p.m. The same schedule applies on other summer weekends using "speeders"—self powered railway inspection cars which offer a unique perspective of the passing scene. The museum specializes in the *Canadian National* and *Northern Alberta* railways as well as work train equipment. *Canadian National* 9000, their first production model diesel cab unit is featured. The museum is located in the northern part of the city at 24215–34th St NW, Edmonton, AB, T5Y 6B4 Call: 780 472-6229. On the web: *www.albertarailwaymuseum.com* Email: *albertarailwaymuseum@gmail.com*

BRITISH COLUMBIA
ROCKY MOUNTAINEER

Canada's magnificent mountains backdrop the *Rocky Mountaineer* at Banff, Alberta. *John Leeming photo*

Before the last spike on the *Canadian Pacific Railway* could be put in place at Craigellachie, British Columbia, there was a country to cross. The first Canadian prime minister, Sir John A. MacDonald, met with a group of prominent Montreal businessmen including the president of the Bank of Montreal, George Stephen; the Chief Commissioner of the Hudson Bay Company, Donald Smith; Richard B. Angus; and financier and railway promoter James J. Hill. These men, together with others, formed the Canadian Pacific syndicate and began the task of constructing a line across Canada to the Pacific Ocean.

The new company quickly acquired the *Brockville & Ottawa Railway* in Ontario. Government financing built a line in Manitoba from Emerson, at the Canada-US border, north to Selkirk and east to Cross Lake. In British Columbia, the company employed experienced surveyor Major Albert Bowman Rogers to look for a southern route through the mountains for the proposed line. The demanding task of supervising and building the line across the Canadian landscape fell to William Cornelius Van Horne, who arrived in Winnipeg on New Year's Eve 1881, and began his duties as the General Manager of the *Canadian Pacific Railway* the following day. Under his guidance, construction teams worked east and west from Winnipeg, as well as west from Ontario and east from the Pacific, under the supervision of railway contractor Andrew Onderdonk. By 1883 the rail line had reached Calgary, but funds were soon used up because of the expensive construction in both the Rocky Mountains and the rugged Canadian Shield. The government told the company to expect no more funding, jeopardizing the future of the railway.

Salvation came from an unexpected source in 1885, when the Metis people, led by charismatic leader Louis Riel, started the second Northwest Rebellion in Saskatchewan. Van Horne turned the railway's darkest hour into one of its finest moments by promising the government that the railway could move troops and supplies in five days to the troubled area to overcome the rebellion. Although troops still had to march through sections of northern Ontario where the rail line was not yet completed, they made it in five days and suppressed the rebellion.

A grateful government pledged its renewed support for completion of the line. Thus, on November 7th 1885, with little fanfare and before a collection of railway employees, *CPR* President Donald Smith drove home the last spike on the railway. General Manger William Cornelius Van Horne proclaimed simply: "All I can say is that the work has been well done in every way". Soon after the line was opened through the mountains, tourists came to view the fantastic rugged scenery that challenged the railway. Today the scenery is best experienced from the Great Canadian Rail Tour Company's *Rocky Mountaineer*, which travels between Vancouver, Banff, and Calgary, as well as Vancouver to Jasper, on all-daylight two-day-long excursions. An overnight stop in Kamloops, where travellers stay in comfortable accommodations, is included in the ticket price. The trains run from April to October, with special trips in the winter months. Other routes link North Vancouver, Whistler and Jasper as well as Seattle to Vancouver. For more information, contact Rocky Mountaineer Rail Tours, Suite 101–369 Terminal Avenue, Vancouver, BC, V6A 4C4. Call: 877 460-3200. Web: *www.rockymountaineer.com*

Our journey, "*First Passage to the West*", begins in the city of Calgary. For overnight accommodation we recommend the classic hotel built by Canadian Pacific Railway, The Fairmont Palliser. Call toll free: 866 540-

4477. Web: *www.fairmont.com/palliser* Email: *palliserhotel@fairmont. com*. Visitors to this city of 1,214,839 persons in 2011 will want to visit attractions such as the Eau Claire Market and the large Heritage Park, featuring heritage buildings from around Alberta, a working steam train, and an operating trolley car. For more information on these attractions and the world famous Calgary Stampede, we recommend you contact Tourism Calgary located at Suite 200, 238 11th Avenue SE, Calgary, AB, T2G 0X8. Call: 800 661-1678. Web: *www.visitor.calgary.com*

Route Highlights
Calgary to Field
CP Laggan Subdivision

Mileages 0–136: Calgary station is located in a modern mall near the Calgary Tower and the Fairmont Palliser Hotel. As the train departs the downtown area, you can see large glass and concrete skyscrapers to the north of the tracks. Then the Bow River comes into the view to the north, as the train moves through the Lawrey Gardens Natural Area. Between mileages **5** and **6** watch to the south to see the high ski jumps built for the 1988 Olympic Winter Games. At mileages **7.7** and **7.8** the twin bridges, each 216 feet (65.8 metres) in length, enable the train to cross the Bow River (with help from a small island). To the south at mileage **11** the train passes the Bearspaw Dam, built in 1954 to reduce flooding; the reservoir is also a source of Calgary's drinking water.

The earliest of Alberta's ranches were located near Cochrane (mileages **22–23**). The train crosses the Bow River at mileage **25** over a 403-foot (125-metre) long bridge. Ghost Reservoir, another source of Calgary's drinking water, can be seen to the north at Radnor, mileage **33.4**. Good views continue as the train travels past the foothills towards the mountains. The train crosses the Kananaskis River at mileage **51.8**, before crossing the Bow River again at mileage **53**. The entrance to the Rocky Mountains is at mileage **55**; to the north at Exshaw, mileage **56.1** are large limestone quarries from which Lafarge Canada produces over a million tonnes of cement every year. As you approach Canmore (mileage **68.7**), watch to the south for the Three Sisters Mountain. At mileage **72** the train passes the eastern border of Banff National Park. Mount Rundle's steep cliffs are seen clearly to the south at mileage **73**. Banff station is reached at mileage **81.9**. This resort community, Canada's first National Park, is named after Banffshire, Scotland, the birthplace of two major financiers of the *CPR*, George Stephen and Donald Smith.

Formed around the hot springs on Sulpher Mountain, it was promoted as a tourist destination by *CPR* president W.C. Van Horne who said, "Since we can't export the scenery, we'll have to import the tourists". A landmark is the Banff Springs Hotel, which opened in 1888. Another east-west transportation route, the Trans- Canada Highway, can be seen above at mileage **85**. Keep your camera aimed first to the south to photograph the Massive Mountain Range at mileage **92**, then to the north for Castle Mountain at mileage **99**. Morant's Curve (mileage **113**) is a well-known photographer's spot. With the Bow River on the west side of the tracks and Mount Temple, Saddle Peak, Fairview Peak, and Mount St. Piran to the distance, this was a favourite venue of *CPR*'s official photographer Nicholas Morant. The tracks divide between mileages **116.2** and **123**. This separation, completed in 1981, reduced the grade for westbound trains to one percent and permitted significantly increased train speeds and freight capacity. At mileage

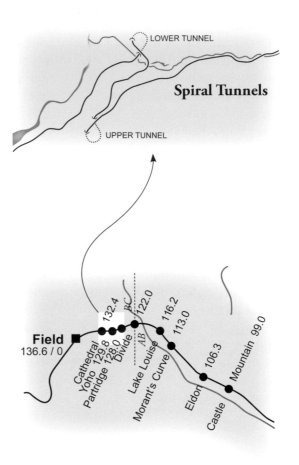

Spiral Tunnels

LOWER TUNNEL

UPPER TUNNEL

Field
136.6 / 0

116.6 the train passes the historic log station in Lake Louise, now a restaurant where you can dine inside the building; in former *CPR* dining car *Delamere*; or in business car *Killarney*.

Watch for the sign and small cairn at mileage **122** (south side) that marks the Continental Divide. This is the highest point on the line and is the watershed where all water flowing to the east heads

ROCKY MOUNTAINEER

toward the Arctic Ocean and to the west, the Pacific. It is also the boundary between the provinces of Alberta and British Columbia (as well as between Banff National Park in Alberta and Yoho National Park in BC). The train is now in the Kicking Horse Pass, named for the incident in which noted explorer James Hector was rendered unconscious for a few days when his horse lost its balance and kicked its rider while crossing the river. The source of the Kicking Horse River, the blue waters of Lake Wapta, can be seen on the north side of the tracks. This location was once known as Hector. It was the eastern side of what was known as the "Big

brakes as the train moved down the hill. This steep grade was reduced with the opening of the world-famous Spiral Tunnels, for which construction began in 1907. This reduced the grade to a more manageable 2.2 percent. Partridge, (mileage **128.0**), is named after locomotive engineer Seth Partridge. At this spot, on August 9th 1925, after hearing a rumbling sound from the mountains above, he stopped his train and scrambled down the mountainside to warn the occupants of the Yoho Station who escaped only moments before a landslide buried the area. The train remained on the tracks, having stopped a short distance

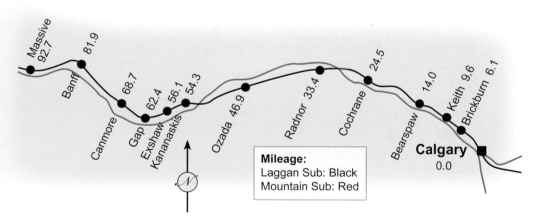

Massive 92.7
Banff 81.9
Canmore 68.7
Gap 62.4
Exshaw 56.1
Kananaskis 54.3
Ozada 46.9
Radnor 33.4
Cochrane 24.5
Bearspaw 14.0
Keith 9.6
Brickburn 6.1
Calgary 0.0

N

Mileage:
Laggan Sub: Black
Mountain Sub: Red

Hill," so named because, when the railway was opened in 1886, the eight miles between here and Field featured a treacherous 4.5 percent grade. Imagine brakemen in the late 1800s, situated on the top of boxcars, controlling hand

from the path of the slide. Keep watching to the north to see the Lower Spiral Tunnel and the Observation Point near the Trans-Canada Highway, before you enter Cathedral Mountain and Upper Spiral Tunnel at mileage **128.8**. Here the train curves 250 degrees in the 3,254-foot (992-metre) long tunnel, emerging 55 feet (17 metres) below the point where it entered. You pass the site of the former Yoho station at mileage **129.8** before entering the Lower Spiral Tunnel and Mount Ogden at mileage **131.1**. The train curves 226 degrees in the 2,920-foot (890-metre) long tunnel, emerging 50 feet (15.2 metres) below where it entered before crossing the Kicking Horse River at mileage **131.7**. A 178-foot (54.5-metre) long tunnel, built as part of the

black water tank, and stops at the International-style station built in 1953 at mileage **136.6**. In the days of steam, locomotives were added at Field to the trains for additional pulling power to help deal with the steep grades that you have just descended. The community was named for American financier Cyrus Field, following his visit to the area during the railway's construction. Field is also the dividing point between the Mountain

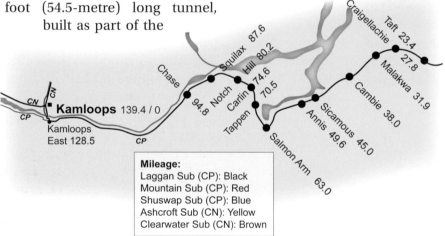

Mileage:
Laggan Sub (CP): Black
Mountain Sub (CP): Red
Shuswap Sub (CP): Blue
Ashcroft Sub (CN): Yellow
Clearwater Sub (CN): Brown

same Spiral Tunnels system, is passed at mileage **133.1** near the 492-foot (150-metre) long snowshed, the tracks rejoin the route built in 1884 and enter the 131-foot (40-metre) long Mount Stephen Tunnel, named for the *CPR*'s first president, George Stephen. Arriving in the community of Field, the train curves around the former section foreman's house, close to the large

and Pacific Time zones, so move your travel clocks and watches one hour back if travelling west or one hour forward if travelling east.

Route Highlights
Field to Revelstoke
CP Mountain Subdivision

Mileages 0–125: The wide Kicking Horse River is clearly seen to the north; the route crosses the Kicking Horse a total of seven times, with one of these made at mileage **9.2** on a 157-

er's rapids before you enter another tunnel at mileage **30**. At mileage **31** there are two crossings of

Fraine
Griffith 68.3
Stoney Creek 71.7
77.7

MacDonald
Glacier

Illecillewaet

Albert

Canyon 105.8

Revelstoke

Three Valley 15.5
Clanwilliam 8.9
125.7 / 0

98.1

85.5
84.9
Wakely 75.0
Bear Creek 79.3

Redgrave 57.3
Beavermouth 62.0

Golden 35.0

Glenogle 28.1
Palliser 22.4
Leanchoil 16.9

Field

Ottertail 8.2
136.6 / 0

foot (48-metre) long bridge. Chancellor Peak Campground sits on an island in the middle of the Kicking Horse River and can be seen to the south at mileage **14**. At mileage **19** the train passes the western border of Yoho National Park. A mile later, it enters Kicking Horse Canyon. At mileage **21.3** the train comes to the 309-foot (94.4-metre) long Palliser Tunnel. After you exit the tunnel, look to the river to see the starting point for white water rafting tours. The river is crossed again at mileage **24.5** on a 235-foot (71.9-metre) long bridge. To the south, between mileages **27** and **29**, there are great views of the riv-

the Kicking Horse River—the lower one is the route of your train and the upper one (supported by steel stilts/beams). is that of the Trans-Canada Highway, 495 feet (150 metres) above the valley floor The train passes through Holt's Tunnel, named after a railway contractor, at mileage **33**. At Golden (mileage **35.0**), passengers once transferred from the train to sternwheelers that travelled south on the Columbia River, a practice that ended when the Kootenay Central Railway was completed in 1907.

West of Golden, the *Rocky Mountaineer* travels through the Columbia River Valley; good views are offered on both sides at mileage **52.5** where the train crosses the Columbia River. The abandoned tunnel at mileage **57** was part of a

Glacier, British Columbia, is one of many spectacular scenic destinations aboard the *Rocky Mountaineer*. John Leeming photo

1974 route change, when the headwaters of the Mica Dam flooded the original route between here and mileage **66**. At Fraine, mileage **68.3**, the MacDonald Track opened in 1988 diverges to the south on a lower gradient assult of the Selkirk Mountains to pass through the 9.1-mile (14.7-kilometre) MacDonald tunnel, the longest in the Americas. This line rejoins your route at MacDonald, mileage **84.9**. At mileage **70** the train passes the eastern boundary of Glacier National Park, before crossing Mountain Creek at mileage **70.8** on a 600-foot (213.3-metre) span and Surprise Creek at mileage **74.4**. One of the most stunning views from any railway in Canada is at mileage **76.2**—the Stoney Creek Bridge. Keep your camera ready at mileage **77.7** for the view from the 484-foot (147-metre) long steel arch bridge across Stoney Creek, 325 feet (99 metres) below. Between mileages **80** and **85** the train travels through Mount MacDonald by way of the 5-mile (8-kilometre) Connaught Tunnel. Opened in 1916 by the Governor General of Canada, the Duke of Connaught, the tunnel originally featured two tracks. In 1959, the roadbed was lowered and single-tracked to make room for taller freight trains. Watch to the south at mileage **85.5** to see the log station at Glacier, built by the CPR in 1916. Since heavy snowfall is common in winter months in the Selkirk Mountains, the train passes through numerous snowsheds and avalanche detection zones. You will cross the Illecillewaet River numerous times before the passing the western boundary of Glacier National Park at mileage **95**. The Illecillewaet River is crossed again on a 223-foot (68-metre) long bridge at mileage **112.3**. At mileage **124**, the train approaches Revelstoke, named for Lord Revelstoke who

ROCKY MOUNTAINEER

represented the English bank that loaned money to the CPR during a financial crisis when the line was being built. The train arrives at the modern station at mileage **125.7**.

Route Highlights
Revelstoke to Kamloops
CP Shuswap Subdivision

Mileages 0–128: Departing Revelstoke, watch to the east for the Revelstoke Railway Museum building housing *CPR* 5468, a Mikado (2-8-2) class steam locomotive once used on this line, business car No. 4, and a locomotive simulator. The fourth railway bridge at this location spans the Columbia River, 1,122 feet (341 metres) long, offering good views to both sides. Upon reaching the west side of the river, the train travels towards Eagle Pass, named after a story told about explorer Walter Moberly, who reportedly fired a shot toward an eagle's nest and then, to find a suitable passage, followed the direction that the startled birds flew. Whether the story is true or not, the train enters the Eagle Pass at mileage **9** through the three Clanwilliam tunnels built in 1907. Watch to the south between mileages **12** and **14** for the green waters of Three Valley Lake; the red-roofed building is the 200-room Three Valley Gap Chateau and Ghost Town. The track parallels and then crosses Eagle River at mileage **18.5**. To the south, near mileage **20**, you see the popular tourist attraction known as the Enchanted Forest. Also to the south, you can catch a glimpse of Kay Falls at mileage **22**. The train crosses Crazy Creek at mileage **24.4** on a 101-foot (31-metre) long bridge and the Eagle River at mileage **25.6** on a 105-foot 32-metre long bridge. Named after a Scottish clansmen's rally cry, Craigellachie (mileage **27.8**) was also the cry exclaimed when financing for the completion of the *Canadian Pacific Railway* was secured. Here on November 7th 1885, at 9:22 a.m. in the company of executives (and 17-year old Edward Mallandine—the only non-railway employee or journalist present), Donald Smith drove home the last spike. In the park on the north side of the tracks is a cairn that was built in 1927 (with a 100th Anniversary addition at its base) to mark the spot, with *CP* caboose 437336 and the Last Spike Gift Shoppe. The train continues to play tag with the Eagle River, crossing it numerous times at mileages **31.1**, **32.6**, **36.9**, **40.2**, and **43.5**. Then, at mileage **44.1**, the train crosses the 580-foot (177-metre) long Sicamous Narrows Bridge; the bridge can swing to allow boat traffic to pass between Mara Lake to the south and Shuswap Lake to the north. Also to the north, watch for Sicamous Beach Park and the arched pedestrian bridge above the mouth of the Eagle River. Sicamous (mileage **45**) once was a significant railway stop, featuring the three-storey Sicamous station and hotel on the north side of the tracks, overlooking the lake. It provided convenient facilities where passengers could dine during the station stop. It served as a summer resort until 1956 and was torn down in 1964. You can see why Shuswap Lake is known as the houseboat capital of Canada as the train skirts the lake for the next 25 miles. Photo opportunities continue along the lakeside, but disappear briefly because of tunnels at mileages **47** and **51**. The route then begins its large half-circle trip around the end of the lake before Salmon Arm comes into view at mileage **60**. To the north, at mileage **62**, is the Salmon Arm Nature Bay, home to over 250 species of birds and the largest nesting grounds of the western grebe. The train passes the downtown area of Salmon Arm at mileage **63**. After moving through a ranching area, at Tappen (mileage **70.5**) the train begins its climb up Notch Hill, so named for the ridge that separates the Shuswap Lake region and the South Thompson Valley. Although it may not look like it, the considerable grade here is steep enough to have caused the *CP* to create a second route for its westbound trains. The large horseshoe curve between mileages **76** and **78** is the only one of its type in Can-

ada and offers nice views to the south; this new eleven-mile route was completed in 1979. Watch for the pioneer church at Notch Hill, mileage **80.2**. At mileage **85** the train is over 492 feet (150 metres) above Shuswap Lake; at mileage **87** Little Shuswap Lake comes into view to the east. Look into the forest along the tracks for bears at Squilax (mileage **87.6**) which was named after a First Nations word meaning "black bear." The train then skirts the shoreline of Little Shuswap Lake between mileages **90** and **92** before reaching the community of Chase (mileage **94.8**), named for American gold-seeker-turned-settler Whitfield Chase. The South Thompson River is seen to the north at mileage **96** where the lush landscape changes to an arid area of ranchland and rolling hills and the lakes empty into the river. Watch on both sides of the tracks for the unique pillar rock formations called Hoodoos. Near mileage **114** is the site where "Gentleman Bandit" Bill Miner staged his second train robbery. The American stagecoach thief successfully perpetrated British Columbia's first train robbery in 1904 near Mission, BC, getting away with over $7,000. After living in Princeton for a few years he travelled to the Kamloops area to do some prospecting—or, at least that's what the locals were told. Along with accomplices Shorty Dunn and Louis Colquhoun, their real goal was to rob the *CPR*'s westbound *Imperial Limited*. One night in March 1906, they boarded the engine at Ducks and ordered the crew to uncouple the first car and move ahead a couple of miles. Unfortunately for the robbers, the car removed was the baggage car, not the express car. They escaped into the night with $15 and a bottle of liver pills, but were caught a few days later by the Royal Canadian Mounted Police. At mileage **127** the train enters the city of Kamloops at Kamloops East, and transfers to the *Canadian National*'s Okanagan Connecting Track. Stopping alongside Lorne Street, passengers on the *Rocky Mountaineer* will transfer to buses that will take them to their evening accommodation.

Route Highlights
Kamloops to Ashcroft Sub,
CN Okanagan Connecting Track

Travelling on the *Rocky Mountaineer*, you pass the former *CNR* downtown Kamloops station at mileage **2.8** on the 3.5-mile (5.6-kilometre) Okanagan Spur and cross the South Thompson River. The route of the Kamloops Heritage Railway begins at the station. Look to the west when on the bridge to see the North Thompson River and South Thompson River. Once across, your train travels through the Kamloops First Nations Reserve before curving to the northeast and joining the *CN* Ashcroft Subdivision. The highlights of the journey continue on page 138 with the details of the route of the *Canadian*.

Rocky Mountaineer passes through Glacier, British Columbia on a sunny day in May.
John Leeming photo

KAMLOOPS HERITAGE RAILWAY

Excursionists enjoy the scene as CNR Consolidation 2141 heads towards Kamloops Junction.
Bob Webster photo.

The "Spirit of Kamloops" utilizes restored *Canadian National* locomotive 2141 to take visitors from the downtown Kamloops, British Columbia, historic *CNR* station for a trip reminiscent of the days when steam locomotives served this British Columbia interior community. The excursion begins with boarding the train's heritage or open-air coach. Steamer 2141 built by the Canadian Locomotive Company of Kingston, Ontario in 1912 for the *Canadian Northern*, is the star attraction. After departing the station, the train's route will travel across the South Thompson River on a 1927 steel bridge with great views of the river on both sides, arriving at the edge of the Kamloops *CN* rail yard before heading back to the station. For more information contact: Station Ticket Office and Gift Store, 3–510 Lorne Street, (Station Plaza), Kamloops, BC, V2C 1W3. Call: 250 374-2141. Web: *www.kamrail.com* Email: *info@kamrail.com*

CANADIAN MUSEUM OF RAIL TRAVEL

A complete seven-car Trans-Canada Limited train has been restored and preserved for visitors.
All photos courtesy Canadian Museum of Rail Travel

A bygone era of rail travel can still be experienced in Cranbrook, British Columbia, which is located, fittingly enough, at 57 Van Horne Drive (Highway 3/95). Here visitors can tour preserved Canadian passenger trains that operated from 1887 to 1955. These include a complete seven-car set of the 1929 *Trans-Canada Limited* and the 1907 *Soo-Spokane Train Deluxe*. The tour's detailed commentary describes the restoration of the cars and how they operated. Displays also include the former CPR Elko Station and the restored, enclosed water tower from Cranbrook. Visitors also can view the Royal Alexandra Hall, which was rescued from Winnipeg's former *CPR* hotel of the same name, where it was then known as the "Grand Café." It has now been resurrected and restored in Cranbrook as the museum centrepiece, detailing for future generations the superb architecture of Canada's great railway hotels. The museum is open daily year-round, except Sundays and Mondays during the period mid-

October through mid-May. For more information, call: 250 489-3918. Web: *www.trainsdeluxe.com* Email: *mail@trainsdeluxe.com*

Top: Deluxe interiors of century-old passenger cars provide a glimpse into the luxurious travel possibilities a century ago.
Bottom: The elegant hall from CPR's Royal Alexandra Hotel in Winnipeg has been preserved and reconstructed at the Canadian Museum of Rail Travel.

KETTLE VALLEY STEAM

A great deal of the area's history was influenced by the *Canadian Pacific* Railway's Kettle Valley Subdivision. Today, the heritage of this railway that served the southern portion of the British Columbia interior lives on in Summerland. Excursions are operated Saturdays through Mondays and often more frequently from May through September. More information is available by contacting the Kettle Valley Steam Railway, PO Box 1288, Summerland, BC, V0H 1Z0. Call: 877 494-8424. Web: *www.kettlevalleyrail.org*

Route Highlights
Prairie Valley to Canyon View
Princeton Subdivision

Mileages 13–7.5: The train departs from the Prairie Valley station, featuring the Trout Creek Trading Company and the Rail's End concession. Because water availability was always a great concern to the early farmers and ranchers in the semi-arid climate of the Okanagan, the Prairie Valley Reservoir, at mileage **12.5**, was put into place by 1903. The large concrete flume follows the railway right-of-way, transporting water from Trout Creek to the reservoir. The Summerland Rodeo Grounds are just beyond the flume. The line runs along the north side of Conkle Mountain, skirting the southern perimeter of Prairie Valley. At mileage **11.5**, those who have keen eyesight might be able to spot the roadbed and the Little Tunnel of the Kettle Valley Railway across the lake. The line goes through a number of rock cuts as it enters Prairie Valley. At mileage **11** the train passes over Fyffe Road. At mileage **10.5**, as the train travels a horseshoe curve at Little Conkle Mountain, the view stretches north to Garnett Valley, another picturesque pastoral valley with more pastures than orchards. The Summerland town centre can also be seen from here. The station known as West Summerland, built in 1916, was originally located at mileage **9.7**, but was removed in

1964 when *CPR* passenger service ceased on the KVR; all that remains from the original building is the concrete water tower base. At mileage **8** you can see the Scherzinger Vineyards and Winery to the south. Keep your camera ready to photograph the Trout Creek Canyon to the north, where Trout Creek cuts a deep path on its way to Okanagan Lake. A siding was built here by the KVR Society to allow the locomotive to switch to the other end of the train and pull the coaches back up to Prairie Valley. At this point, the steam locomotive also fills up with water for the return trip. Passengers may detrain here briefly and view the Trout Creek Bridge, built in 1913 to enable the Kettle Valley Railway to proceed on to Summerland.

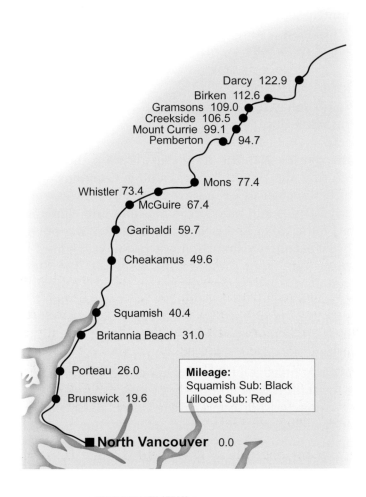

Darcy 122.9
Birken 112.6
Gramsons 109.0
Creekside 106.5
Mount Currie 99.1
Pemberton 94.7

Mons 77.4
Whistler 73.4
McGuire 67.4
Garibaldi 59.7
Cheakamus 49.6
Squamish 40.4
Britannia Beach 31.0
Porteau 26.0

Mileage:
Squamish Sub: Black
Lillooet Sub: Red

Brunswick 19.6

■**North Vancouver** 0.0

WHISTLER SEA TO SKY CLIMB
RAINFOREST TO GOLD RUSH

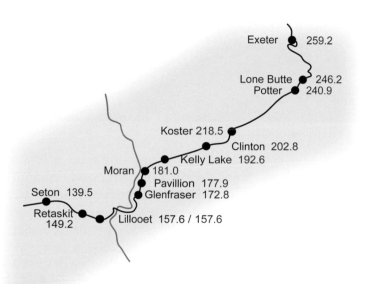

Exeter 259.2

Lone Butte 246.2
Potter 240.9

Koster 218.5

Clinton 202.8

Kelly Lake 192.6

Moran 181.0

Pavillion 177.9

Glenfraser 172.8

Seton 139.5

Retaskit
149.2

Lillooet 157.6 / 157.6

The idea was simple enough—build a railway linking Vancouver and the lower mainland of British Columbia to Prince George, connecting there with the east-west *Grand Trunk Pacific* (later *Canadian National*) line, thus opening up the virtually untouched interior of the province with all its resources. To attract wealthy British investors, the line was named the *Pacific Great Eastern*, after England's *Great Eastern Railway*. Over the years, the railway also acquired some cute nicknames, including "Past God's Endurance" or "Please Go Easy" (probably in reference to the incredibly difficult terrain through which the line had to be built).

Operations began in 1912, but the difficult construction and trying

Whistler Sea to Sky Climb train seen along Howe Sound. *Rocky Mountaineer*

to run over such severe terrain took its toll; the railway was bankrupt in 1918. The provincial government took over the project, extending the line from Squamish to Quesnel, while operating the railway on a shoestring budget. Into the 1940s, the railway continued to be a political hot potato, providing fodder for editorial writers and cartoonists alike. They began referring to the PGE as the "Province's Greatest Expense." All this changed with the economic boom after the Second World War. In 1952, the line was further extended to Prince George. Beginning in 1972, the railway operated freight and passenger services for thirty years under the name "BC Rail", including the well-known ex-CPR Royal Hudson No. 2860 summer

daytrip excursion service between North Vancouver and Squamish. In 2004 *BC Rail's* operations were leased to *Canadian National* amidst much political intrigue. Royal Hudson 2860 is now part of the heritage collection at the West Coast Railway Heritage Park in Squamish. The WCRA organizes excursions pulled by steam or diesel locomotives on portions of the former *BC Rail* line. They can be reached on the web at *www. wcra.org*

Today Rocky Mountaineer Vacations operates the *"Whistler Sea to Sky Climb"* service between North Vancouver and the resort municipality of Whistler, BC on a daily summer schedule. Another weekly service runs between Whistler and Jasper, Alberta with an overnight stop in Quesnel, BC on the company's *"Rainforest to Gold Rush"* route. For information, contact Rocky Mountaineer Rail Tours at 877 460-3200. Web: *www.rockymountaineer.com*

Route Highlights
North Vancouver to Lillooet
Squamish Subdivision

Mileages 0–40: Your journey begins in North Vancouver. At mileage **2.5** the train passes under the mile-long Lions Gate Bridge, completed in 1938 at a cost of $5 million by the Guinness family, known world-wide for their brewed beverages. The train then crosses over the Capilano River. On the west side of the river, impressive views of Vancouver's Stanley Park and the Burrard Inlet are offered as the train passes through Ambleside Park. At mileages **4–5**, John Lawson Park, with its popular seaside walkway, is seen along the south side of the tracks.

Beginning in 1914, the railway offered passenger services between North Vancouver and Horseshoe Bay. They used a self-propelled car, affectionately known as a "Doodlebug", one of which may be seen at the museum in Squamish. Passengers could go no further because there wasn't any connecting track to Squamish. Poor economics forced service

cancellations in 1928. With no traffic, the weeds began to grow between the ties. When railway surveyors returned in 1955 to re-open the long-dormant right of way, they found that the residents along the tracks had planted gardens and built houses almost hanging over the line. The route gives you an excellent opportunity to view some of the opulent homes in Vancouver's suburbs opened by the Guiness family and still known as the British Properties. At mileage **10**, Nelson Creek is crossed on a curving trestle. At mileage **10.9** the train enters the Horseshoe Bay Tunnel. Opened in 1973, it is the longest tunnel on the route at 4,568 feet (1,392 metres). On the north side of the tunnel, look to the west to see the BC Ferries Terminal. Keep your camera ready for the view as the train winds its way along Howe Sound. At mileage **26** the train passes Porteau Cove Provincial Park. The Pacific Ocean provides the water trap that surrounds the 14th-hole green of the Furry Creek Golf Club. The train passes through more tunnels at mileages **28.7** and **29.7**. At mileage **31.0** (on the opposite side of the Sea to Sky Highway) is the former Britannia Mine. The site is now the BC Museum of Mining where you can learn more about mining in British Columbia generally, and about the Britannia Mine, which was once the largest producer of copper in the British

Empire. It was not possible to take the train to Squamish, 2011 population 17,158, (mileage **40.4**) until 1956. Prior to that time, the only public transit between Squamish and Vancouver was provided by steamship. For this reason, the railway's large shops (still seen today) were located at the original "end of the line" in Squamish. The buildings are now used as indoor stages for movie shoots and some form part of the West Coast Railway Heritage Park's operations. During your stay in the Lower Mainland, a visit to this excellent railway museum, about an hour's drive north of Vancouver, is highly recommended.

Mileages 41–80: At mileage **41.6** the train crosses the Squamish River. The Cheekye River Bridge at mileage **47** offers great views to the west. As the train snakes through Cheakamus Canyon, it passes through tunnels at mileages **53.5**, **55.7** and **55.9**. Before the Cheakamus River is crossed at mileage **56**, look to the east to see the top of the Brandywine Falls. Whistler station is located at mileage **73.4**. Whistler is the boarding point for Rocky Mountaineer's *Rainforest to Gold Rush* route. Some of the area's world-famous ski-hills can be seen to the east at mileage **76**. Also to the east beyond Mons siding at mileage **77.4** is Green Lake, with its large cottages, between mileages **78** and **80**.

Mileages 81–157: The train crosses the Soo River at mileage **86** and the Rutherford River at mileage **89** before entering the Green River Gorge at mileage **91**. Watch to the east at mileage **92** for Nairn Falls. Pemberton is reached at mileage **94.7**; the lush Pemberton Valley can be seen while crossing the Lillooet River. At mileage **99.1** the train passes by the Mount Currie First Nation Reserve. The Birkenhead River is crossed at mileage **103.** At mileage **109.0** you reach Gramsons (No. 10 Downing Street), named for a World War I veteran who settled here. Birkengates Lake is passed to the east between mileages **113–114**. The train hugs the west shore of Anderson Lake between mileages **123–138**, passing through a tunnel at mileage **125**. The numerous station shelters along the way provide evidence that this area is only serviced by rail, not by highways. (Indeed, a special service is run from Seton, mileage **139.5** by the Seton Lake Indian Band to carry school children to their classes in Lillooet. Individual passengers are welcome and reservations can be made by calling 250 259-8300.) The original glacial lake here was divided into two separate bodies of water by a mountain slide. Seton Lake is passed between mileages **141–155**. The large pipes running along the side of the mountain at mileage **141** carry water from the Carpenter Lake Reservoir (7 miles/11.3 kilometre away) to the Bridge River Hydro complex alongside the tracks here. The curve at mileage **154** provides a good spot to photograph your train.

Route Highlights
Lillooet to Williams Lake
Lillooet Subdivision

Mileages 157–192: Lillooet, 2011 population 2,321, was mileage **0** of the Cariboo Trail, which was built in 1861–62 to assist the wave of gold seekers headed to Barkerville in the province's interior. In 1862 Bactrian camels were purchased from the U.S. Army Camel Corps to ferry freight along the Trail. The train crosses the Fraser River at mileage **160**. First Nations fishing camps may be seen along the river. At mileage **162**, look west to see where the clear water from the Bridge River empties into the muddy Fraser River. (Between late June and early September the water can appear to be black, because it is filled with migrating salmon.) The train now begins climbing on a thirty-mile ascent, the longest and most severe in North America, up the Fraser Canyon to the Cariboo Plateau. At mileage **168** you enter a tunnel that interrupts the view. At Pavilion, between mileages **176** and **178**, the train rounds a horseshoe curve, a

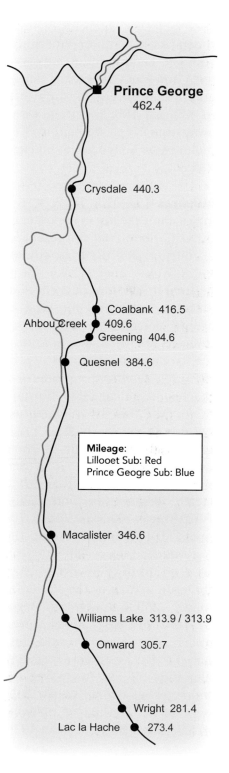

Prince George
462.4

Crysdale 440.3

Coalbank 416.5
Ahbou Creek 409.6
Greening 404.6

Quesnel 384.6

Mileage:
Lillooet Sub: Red
Prince Geogre Sub: Blue

Macalister 346.6

Williams Lake 313.9 / 313.9

Onward 305.7

Wright 281.4
Lac la Hache 273.4

good place to watch for bighorn sheep. As it continues to climb, you get commanding views of the Camelsfoot Mountain Range and Mount Brew to the west. At mileage **188**, the train turns away from the canyon and passes picturesque Kelly Lake at mileage **192.6**.

Mileages 194–313: Many of the area's names relate to the mileage of the Cariboo Trail. For example, at mileage **206**, the train crosses the Fiftyone Creek canyon (on a high curving trestle), later crossing Sixtyone Creek and the view of Mount Bowman to the west at mileage **214**. This area is known for its guest ranches and one of the original ones, the Flying U, is reached at mileage **236**. Summit at mileage **244** is aptly named because it is the highest point on the line. Lone Butte, mileage **246.2**, still retains its enclosed water tower from the days when steam locomotives worked the *PGE*. Exeter/100 Mile House, 100 miles (161 kilometre) along the Caribou Tail from Lillooet, can be seen from miles away before the train arrives at the station at mileage **259.2**. Between mileages **275–282** the line passes seven miles of the eleven-mile-long Lac La Hache. After travelling alongside the San Jose River, the train reaches Williams Lake, 2011 population 10,832, at mileage **313.9**. The station, built in 1920,

features the Station House Gallery.

Route Highlights
Williams Lake to Prince George
Prince George Subdivision

Mileages 313–384: The train winds along the Williams Lake River, and offers one of the best views of the gorge at mileage **319**. At mileage **324**, the Fraser River again comes into view. At mileage **329**, with its very appropriate name, the Deep Creek Bridge, at 312 feet (95 metres), is in fact the highest bridge on the line. Then, Soda Creek is crossed at mileage **335**. From mileage **340** you pass some interesting rock formations and emerge to an outstanding view from a rock cut at mileage **343**. Good views over this arid ranching region continue until mileage **384.6**, when the train arrives in Quesnel, 2011 population 10,007. The name derives from Jules Maurice Quesnel, who accompanied Simon Fraser on his journey to the Pacific Ocean in 1808. The museum here, which can be seen to the west, details the history of this community that was formed during the gold rush era.

Mileages 385–462: The train once again moves away from the Fraser River, with the train reaching the Cottonwood River at mileage **398**. This wide river was the hard-to-traverse expanse that stopped the

Top: Hugging the shore just north of Darcy, BC, this beautiful, isolated and rugged railway route along Anderson and Seton lakes heads toward Lillooet, BC. *Doug Lawson photo*
Bottom: Just north of Clinton, BC in the historic Cariboo Region, an impressive trestle over a mere trickle of water known as Fiftyone Creek. *Doug Lawson photo*

railway from connecting with Prince George for thirty years. To cross it, the railway built a bridge that is 1,023 feet (312 metres) long and 235 feet (71 metres) above the river below. Keep your camera ready as good views are offered from both sides. At mileage **409.6**, the Ahbau Creek is crossed on a 920-foot (280-metre) long bridge. The clearing along the tracks just north of the bridge marks the site where the inaugural train to Prince George stopped to perform a "silver spike ceremony" on October 31st 1952. At mileage **426**, the train crosses the Canyon Creek Bridge above the junction of Canyon and Hixon Creeks. The Fraser River can again be seen to the west for the next few miles. The Pacific Great Eastern was also affectionately known as "Prince George Eventually" because it took more than forty years after the railway was incorporated for it to arrive at Prince George mileage **462.4**. Your journey to Jasper continues on *CN* rails along *VIA*'s Jasper–Prince George–Prince Rupert route described on page 158.

COASTAL PASSAGE

R ocky Mountaineer operates the *Coastal Passage* route from Seattle, Washington to Vancouver. From Seattle the route provides many vistas of Puget Sound as it runs on tracks of the *Burlington Northern Santa Fe* on its way north. This route is also used by *Amtrak* providing twice-daily scheduled service from Seattle and intermediate communities to Vancouver. The map of *The Canadian* route on page 138 also shows details for this excursion.

The line was built by the *Great Northern Railway* owned by railway magnate James J. Hill. It was completed in 1908. For more information on the *Coastal Passage*, contact Rocky Mountaineer Rail Tours, Suite 101–369 Terminal Avenue Vancouver, BC, V6A 4C4. Call: 877 460-3200. Web: *www.rockymountaineer.com*

Route Highlights
White Rock–Fraser River Junction
New Westminster (BNSF) Subdivision

The Canadian-American border is crossed just south of White Rock, BC at mileage **119.6** of the *BNSF*'s New Westminster Subdivision. Ocean views continue on the Canadian side of the border as you pass White Rock. Watch for wildlife as you run alongside Mud Bay after you cross the Nikomekl River. At mileage **127.6** the train crosses the Mud Bay swingbridge. Colebrook is reached at mileage **130.8** and marks the junction with *BC Rail*'s Port Subdivision which provides access to the vast ship-to- shore facilities at Roberts Banks, some 16 miles (25.7 kilometre) to the west. First opened in 1970, the Roberts Bank Superport generates huge volumes of coal and container traffic for *BNSF*, *CN* and *CP*. The Deltaport container terminal is the largest in Canada with a capacity of 1.8 million TEUs. Beyond Colebrook, the line turns inland, skirting the city of Surrey. At Townsend, mileage **136.9**, the 4.1-mile (6.6-kilometre) Tilbury Spur heads west to Tilbury Island in the Fraser

Top: Rocky Mountaineer's Coastal Passage train, on its run from Seattle WA to Vancouver BC, is photographed on pile trestle near Colebrook BC. *Clayton Jones photo*
Bottom: Mileage **147.5**, at dusk, near Cariboo Road in Burnaby on CN's New Westminster Sub, northbound for Vancouver. *Andy Cassidy photo*

River. Anacis Island is seen in the Fraser to the west as your train turns northeast following the river towards a crossing at Port Mann. At Fraser River Junction, mileage **141.3**, operating control is assumed by *CN* for the remaining 13 miles (21 kilometres) in to Vancouver. The remainder of this route is described in the description of the route of *VIA*'s *Canadian* on page 144.

ALBERNI PACIFIC RAILWAY

Although most of the logging camps on Vancouver Island are long gone, their history lives on, and is best experienced during the summer months. Passengers on the *Alberni Pacific Railway* ride behind Baldwin locomotive 2-8-2T No. 7, which began its career on Vancouver Island in 1929. Your route begins at Port Alberni's former *E&N* station and takes you to the McLean Mill National Historic Site. The train runs Thursday through Sunday in July and August with special excursions run in May, June and September. Watch for a Santa Train, too. For more information, contact the Alberni Valley Heritage Network, 3100 Kingsway, Port Alberni, BC, V9Y 3B1. Call: 250 723-2118. Web: *www.alberniheritage.com* Email: *info@alberniheritage.com*

Route Highlights
Port Alberni to Maclean Mill
Port Alberni Subdivision

Mileages 38–33: The train departs from the Port Alberni station at mileage **37.9**. Built by the *Esquimalt & Nanaimo Railway* in 1912, the station is located at the entrance to the Alberni Harbour Quay. Moving along the Port Alberni industrial waterfront at a leisurely pace, at mileage **37.4** the train crosses the first of two wooden trestles, forty feet (twelve metres) above Rogers Creek and the second eighty feet (24 metres) above Kitsucksis Creek at mileage **37.0**. The train moves through the lush forested Beaver Creek area before arriving at the McLean Mill National Historic site at mileage **33.0**. Over thirty restored buildings and structures are located here depicting a typical logging camp circa 1965 where mill employees lived and worked. Visitors can view the milling process with the 1926 steam sawmill as the centrepiece of activity, accompanied by a fleet of restored logging trucks.

ALASKA–BRITISH COLUMBIA
GOLD RUSH ROUTE

White Pass & Yukon Route train crosses "new" bridge, with original Cut-off Gulch Bridge, abandoned in 1969, prominent in left foreground. *Eric Johnson photo*

The Gold Rush Route follows the trail taken by the gold seekers of 1898 who left Skagway, Alaska some 1,000 miles north of Seattle to reach the goldfields of the Klondike. Three prospectors, George Washington Carmack, Skookum Jim and Dawson Charlie had discovered gold in Bonanza Creek near the future site of Dawson City in the Yukon Territory on August 17th 1896. This set off a stampede of legendary proportions that saw about 100,000 people, mostly men, pursue their dream of instant riches. While very few, perhaps one tenth of one percent, were lastingly successful, many legacies were created including the *White Pass & Yukon Route* railway (WP&YR).

Chartered in 1898, the railway was the dream of Skagway pioneer William Moore, and within 26 months the railway reached 110 miles from the Lynn Canal on the Pacific up and over the White Pass in the St. Elias Mountains to Lake Bennett and Carcross. Turning north towards the Yukon River and its junction with the Pelly River at Fort Selkirk, the railway reached Whitehorse where riverboats connected with the goldfields, 500 miles downstream at Dawson.

From 1900 through 1982 the railway served the mines and carried freight and passengers destined for Whitehorse and beyond. The railway was built to a three-foot (9.14-metre) gauge which was very unusual in Canada but relatively common in the mining areas of Colorado and Utah in the late 1800s. Nonetheless its presence was particularly welcome during World War II when it helped greatly in warding off invasion and in the construction of the Alaska Highway. In 1956 the *WP&Y* was a pioneer in containerization transferring freight from truck to train to ship. In June 1982, the *WP&YR*'s largest customer, Cyprus Anvil Mining, operator of the world's largest open pit lead-zinc operation at Faro, Yukon closed as commodity prices plunged. The railway languished until 1988 when it was resurrected as a tourist operation extending from Skagway to Summit BC. Although 37,000 passengers were carried that first year, this is a far cry from the almost 400,000 carried annually in recent times. Operations were extended to Bennett BC in 1989 and to Carcross in 2000 to mark the centennial of the railway's completion.

Along the way, the railway climbs almost 3,000 feet (914.4 metres) in the first 20 miles (32 kilometres) as it winds its way up the mountain-side, sometimes on the steepest mainline ascent in North America at 3.9 feet per hundred feet travelled—a 3.9% grade. Elsewhere, a grade one third as steep is considered significant. The route is now an Inter-national Historic Engineering Landmark along with such marvels as the Quebec Bridge and the Eiffel Tower in Paris.

For most of the last century, *WP&YR* headquarters were in Vancouver BC, then later, Whitehorse, Yukon. On becoming a non-freight, tourist-only carrier in the 1980s, the railway operations headquarters were relocated from Canada to Skagway, Alaska. However, the *WP&YR* continues to be wholly-owned by a Canadian corporation, ClubLink Enterprises Limited (formerly Tri-White Corporation), based in Toronto, Ontario.

Several travel options are available by advance reservation between early May and late September. Those arriving in Skagway by cruise ship are encouraged to book onboard to avoid disappointment. The more popular among the available options are the return trip excursions to White Pass Summit or Bennett and the steam-powered excursion to Fraser Meadows. Also popular are longer, combined bus and rail tours to Carcross and Whitehorse. Rail enthusiasts should note that the Carcross to Whitehorse tracks are out of service and will want to plan accordingly. Full details are available from the *White Pass & Yukon Route* at Box 435, Skagway, AK, 99840 or call 800 343-7373. On the web: *www.wpyr.com* Email: *info@wpyr.com*

Route highlights
Skagway to White Pass
American Division

Mileages 0.6–20.4: Your train departs from Skagway on the Lynn Canal and starting point for the Chilkoot and White Pass Trails followed by gold-seekers from 1897 through to the opening of the railway to Bennett in July 1899. While in Skagway, plan to visit the Trail of '98 Museum. Skagway is a native term for "end of the saltwater". The main shops of the railway may be seen to the west at mileage **2.3**. At mileage **2.5** look east to see a graveyard that is home to Soapy Smith who died in a shootout along with "good guy" Frank Reid, leader of a citizens' group determined to put an end to Soapy's career. Having gained experience in the silver rushes to Leadville and Central City, Colorado, Soapy came to Skagway in early 1897 to lead a gang of gamblers and bootleggers whose activities seriously obstructed construction of the railway.

At Rocky Point mileage **6.9**, look back for a grand view of Skagway and the Lynn Canal. Look ahead to see the Trail of '98– 300 feet (91.4 metres) below in the gorge of the Skagway River. Near mileage **8**, Hanging Rock protrudes above the track followed by a sign "On to Alaska with Buchanan" painted by a Cleveland boys club in the 1930s. It commemorates George Buchanan, a coal dealer from Detroit who sponsored young males to outdoor-oriented adventure trips for fifteen years beginning in 1923. Near mileage **12** to the west, 22 cataracts are visible in the Bridal Veil Falls gorge.

At mileage **9**, Pitchfork Falls is crossed on a bridge as it plummets 1,000 feet (304.8 metres) down the mountainside. Beyond mileage **13** look up to the west to see what appears to be a tiny set of rails entering the 250-

Steaming southbound from Bennett BC towards Skagway Alaska. *John Hyde photo, courtesy WP&YR*

foot (76.2-metre) Tunnel Mountain. That's where your train is headed. Your train's speed will not exceed 20 mph (32 kph) or 3 (1.9) minutes per mile (kilometre). Speeds are reduced by 10% on the downward trip. The Skagway River is crossed at mileage **14.2** and your train begins to ascend the 3.9% grade. At mileage **15.9** a bridge spans Glacier Gulch and the train approaches Inspiration Point, mileage **16.2**, where a panoramic view of the glaciers, mountains and sea may be enjoyed. At mileage **19**, you will see Dead Horse Gulch Viaduct which replaced a switchback where trains reversed to gain altitude that was similarly replaced by a bridge and tunnel in 1969. At mileage **20.4** the border with Canada is reached at the summit of White Pass named in 1887 for Canadian minister of the interior Thomas White. Travellers on the summit excursion will return to Skagway from White Pass.

Route highlights
Bennett to Carcross and Whitehorse
Canadian Division

Mileages 20.4–41.0: An ice-scarred plateau is crossed for 13 miles (20.9 kilometres) after the border in an area that is protected by snowsheds from the fierce winter winds. At mileage **24**, the train is 2,940 feet above Skagway and at the highest point on the *WP&YR*. Meadows in an area that spawns the Yukon River is passed at mileage **25.4** at the summit of mile long Fraser Hill. Fraser at mileage **27.7** is the turning point for the steam-powered excursions using Mikado 193 (Baldwin 1947) or Consolidation 69 (Baldwin 1908). Fraser is also home to a unique, enclosed station combined with a water tank and maintenance shed. At mileage **37** watch to the west for beaver lodges on Beaver Lake as you descend Bennett Hill. Lake Lindeman to the west at mileage **40** was the start of navigation on the Yukon River. Bennett on Lake Bennett is reached at mileage **40.6**, and is named for the controversial publisher of the sensational *New York Herald*, Gordon Bennett. It was here in the spring of 1898 that upwards of 10,000 miners left on 7,000 homemade boats for the goldfields. Another 20,000 followed that summer. Your visit will be less hectic as you may enjoy a hot and hearty meal in the restored 1910 station. Northbound Train 1 to Carcross meets Southbound Train 2 at Bennett and your trip may continue by train or bus.

Mileages 41–67.5: The blue-green waters of glacially-fed Lake Bennett to the west beyond mileage **41** reflect the Bennett Range of the Coast Mountains. At mileage **43.5**, the railway's sharpest curve, Guard Rail Curve, slows trains to just ten mph (sixteen kph) from a maximum permitted train speed of 25 mph (40 kph). A sign on Pennington Island at mileage **52.5** marks the British Columbia/Yukon border. At Watson, mileage **59.4** look west up the west arm of Lake Bennett which divides the Bennett range to the south from the Boundary range to the north. Carcross at mileage **67.5** lies at the foot of Caribou Mountain and is approached on a wooden swing bridge that once allowed sternwheelers to access the lake. The *Duchess*, a steam engine that carried its water in a saddle tank atop the boiler has been preserved in Carcross since 1931. Built by Baldwin in Philadelphia in 1878, it hauled coal on Vancouver Island until moved north in 1900. Until replaced in 1920, it operated on the 2.5-mile (4-kilometre) *Taku Tramway*. The tramway, accessed by a sternwheeler, the *S.S. Tutshi* from Carcross via the Tagish lake system, linked Taku Arm to a steamer connection on Atlin Lake where the *WP&YR* owned the Atlin Inn resort. The Inn at Atlin BC closed in 1936. Carcross is also the eternal resting place of the three prospectors who touched off the Klondike Gold Rush and created the need for the *White Pass & Yukon Route* railway.

Southbound excursion *White Pass & Yukon Route* train 22 on Bridge 15C. *Eric Johnson photo*

INDEX

VIA's Canadian 96-147